Cost-Benefit Analysis

COST-BENEFIT ANALYSIS

READINGS

Edited by Michael Mulreany

IPA
INSTITUTE OF PUBLIC
ADMINISTRATION

First published 2002
Institute of Public Administration
57–61 Lansdowne Road
Dublin 4
Ireland

ISBN   1 902448 72 3

British Library Cataloguing in Publication Data
A catalogue record for this book is available from the British Library

The articles in this book were first published in the 1980s and 1990s. The earlier articles refer to punts and the later articles to euro.

Cover design by M. and J. Graphics Ltd.
Typeset in 10/12.5 Times Roman by Computertype Ltd., Dublin
Printed by Digital Print Dynamics

Contents

Contributors

Seán Barrett is Senior Lecturer in economics at Trinity College Dublin and a fellow of the college

John Blackwell was an economist at the OECD at the time of his death in 1993

Philip Byrne is Senior Specialist, Local Authorities Unit, Institute of Public Administration

J. Peter Clinch is Director of Graduate Studies, Department of Environmental Studies, University College Dublin

Frank J. Convery is Heritage Trust Professor of Environmental Studies, Department of Environmental Studies, University College Dublin

John Devlin is Senior Advisor at the Department of the Environment and Local Government

Bernard Feeney is Managing Director, Goodbody Economic Consultants

Patrick Honohan is Professor at the Economic and Social Research Institute and works with the Development Research Group of the World Bank

Owen P. Keegan is Director of Traffic and Assistant City Manager, Dublin City Council

Fergal Lynch is a Principal Officer in the Department of Health and Children

David Mooney is Managing Director of Global Capital Markets and Risk Management, Bank of America, New York

Michael Mulreany is Senior Lecturer in Economics, Institute of Public Administration

Introduction

Expenditure on current account by central government in Ireland in 2000 was roughly one fifth of GNP. In 2000 also, local authority current expenditure was roughly three per cent of GNP. In addition the Public Capital Programme was roughly seven per cent of GNP and approximately one quarter of fixed investment in Ireland.

The case for economic appraisal is made simply by rehearsing these figures. These are significant expenditures and decisions about their scale and allocation should be well-informed, objective and governed by accepted efficiency criteria. Decision-makers should be in a position to clearly and consistently appraise whether or not to undertake a given project or programme. Similarly, they should be able to choose between alternative projects or programmes.

Decisions on public expenditure span a diverse range from education, health and social welfare to transport, environment and agriculture and from the criminal justice system, defence and marine emergency to sports, language and culture. The diversity does not end there: decisions abound within any of the above areas. Take public spending on health as an example: How should expenditure be allocated between accident and emergency services, maternity services, hip replacements, speech therapy and so forth? How do we know that this money is spent efficiently and effectively?

Cost-benefit analysis is the principal methodology used to evaluate public expenditure decisions. In common with other forms of evaluation it attempts to reduce and control the number of variables and thereby enable decision-takers to make rational choices. In cost-benefit analysis this entails placing diverse costs and benefits on a common monetary scale and choosing projects and programmes so as to confer the greatest net benefit on society. Cost-benefit analysis can be applied to decisions on capital expenditure such as transport or on current expenditure such as education. Indeed it can be applied to public policy decisions such as whether to regulate, tax or subsidise.

Of course, an evaluator may approach a project or programme with an objective other than maximising the net benefit to society, and the type of appraisal will vary accordingly. Technical appraisal assesses the construction process and subsequent operations of a project. Institutional appraisal assesses managerial and human resource issues. Commercial appraisal assesses procurement of inputs and marketing of outputs. Social appraisal assesses social objectives such as income distribution and health outcomes. Financial appraisal assesses financial viability by asking whether an enterprise can raise funds, meet financial obligations and produce a reasonable return on the capital employed.

Financial appraisal has much in common with economic appraisal. A full financial appraisal would identify alternative projects or programmes, estimate costs and revenues over time, state the costs and revenues in current money terms, calculate expected profits from each project or programme and choose the most profitable option.

Economic analysis follows much the same course. However, financial analysis adopts the perspective of the enterprise. The economic analysis of projects or programmes also involves a financial analysis but in addition adopts the perspective of society. In so doing, economic appraisal will, for example, look at positive and negative externalities, that is outputs for which no market exists. Positive externalities include such unmarketed outputs as the sense of personal safety and the sense of aesthetic appeal. Negative externalities include such unmarketed outputs as marine and aerial pollution, congestion, noise and disturbance.

A further example of the difference in approach is that financial appraisal adopts market prices as a basis for valuations. By contrast, economic appraisal asks whether markets are competitive because uncompetitive markets cause distortions to prices which in turn affect economic analysis. Where uncompetitive markets exist economic appraisal may use 'shadow prices', that is estimates of the prices that would be set by competitive markets.

It is not surprising therefore that cost-benefit analysis gives rise to substantial theoretical and practical challenges. The theoretical challenges were recognised at least as early as Dupuit's (1952) seminal paper 'On Management of the Utility of Public Works' first published in 1844 and republished in 1952. The practical challenges have been in clear focus at least since the 1950s when cost-benefit analysis began to be widely used, initially in the United States and particularly for water and transport projects.

This book examines theoretical and practical issues in cost-benefit analysis. It assembles key articles and reports on cost-benefit analysis published in Ireland in the period from 1984 to 1999. In that period the Irish economy has been transformed. Some of the chapters from earlier in the period were written against a background of labour surplus whereas the contemporary preoccupation is with labour shortage. Reassuringly, the principles of cost-benefit analysis are applied regardless of the vagaries of the economic cycle.

The opening chapters look at theoretical issues and historical framework. Chapters 4–7 look at elements of economic appraisal. The succeeding chapters look at applied aspects of cost-benefit analysis in such areas as industrial policy, health care, the environment and, particularly, transport. Internationally, transport has been a 'locus classicus' of cost-benefit analysis. This has also been the case in Ireland and the published literature on cost-benefit analysis has accordingly been strong on transport appraisals. The final chapter of the book deals with general problems in appraising public projects, what Mishan (1982) calls 'traps for the unwary'.

The theoretical issues, the elements of appraisal and the applied aspects of cost-benefit analysis are not strictly segregated: two or more of these themes may occur in a chapter. This is natural because economic appraisal is an amalgam of these components.

The chapters have been chosen to convey an understanding of the methodology and usefulness of cost-benefit analysis. They should also convey an insight into its limitations: cost-benefit analysis can only be as robust as the assumptions and valuations on which it rests. The process of economic appraisal is well served by users, whether students or professionals, who are prepared and equipped to question the precision or, indeed, the objectivity of analysis. Equally the pursuit of efficiency and effectiveness in public expenditure is well served, even when project goals are poorly stated and values are unclear, by rigorous application of cost-benefit analysis.

The book is accessible to anyone with a basic knowledge of economics. It should be useful not only to students of economics and public management, lecturers and economists but to public servants, engineers, healthcare professionals, environmentalists and so forth.

Finally some words of thanks: I am grateful to the authors and organisations who have agreed to have their work republished. My particular thanks are due to Kathryn Finney, Carmel Murphy, Patricia Ryan, Emma Bollard and Eleanor Ashe who have worked on successive versions of the text.

REFERENCES

Dupuit, J. (1952), *On the Measurement of the Utility of Public Works*, London: International Economic Papers, vol 2, pp 83-110

Mishan, E.J. (1982), *Cost-Benefit Analysis: An Informal Introduction*, London: George Allen and Unwin

1

Cost-Benefit Analysis*

MICHAEL MULREANY

Introduction

Cost-benefit analysis is the most important technique for project appraisal in the public sector. In classical microeconomic theory the market system leads to maximum efficiency: producers minimise costs, society maximises output, consumers maximise satisfaction and any redistribution of output could not increase one person's satisfaction without reducing that of another.

Would that things were so perfect. In practice, there are many market failures (e.g. see Stiglitz 1988). One such failure is due to externalities or spillover effects, i.e. certain 'goods' and 'bads' which are not allocated by the market system. For example, 'bads' such as environmental pollution or traffic congestion are not generally taken into account in the production of or the demand for market products.

Welfare economics goes beyond the market system to consider the effects of externalities and more generally to analyse how successfully society is achieving certain objectives which may not be attainable by the free play of market forces.

The main technique for using welfare economics in practice is cost-benefit analysis. In essence, cost-benefit analysis attempts to evaluate what the market system omits; its perspective is that of society. Cost-benefit analysis attempts to evaluate on a common monetary scale the costs and benefits of all the marketed and unmarketed consequences of projects and to estimate the net social benefits.

Cost-benefit analysis allows quantified social costs and benefits to be incorporated into the appraisal of investments. Of course the appraisal and subsequent investment decisions will be based on a combination of the social along with the underlying market-valued costs and benefits.

Generally, cost-benefit analysis is conducted 'ex-ante' – it appraises projects before they are undertaken. The appraisal can be used to answer such questions as, should a project be undertaken? And, if so in what form and at

1

what scale? The basic rationale behind cost-benefit analysis is the pursuit of economic efficiency. Once a government has decided on the sectoral distribution of public money then cost-benefit analysis can indicate how best it can be allocated among the various investment opportunities in any sector.

The procedure of cost-benefit analysis

The theory of cost-benefit analysis has its roots in nineteenth century welfare economics. The practice has developed mostly in the twentieth century and particularly in the areas of transport and water related projects. The scope of cost-benefit analysis has been extended to include areas as diverse as training programmes and health care and medical procedures.

In Ireland, cost-benefit analysis has developed from the late 1960s especially in the area of transport and also in areas such as drainage (see Blackwell 1991). The high levels of investment in physical infrastructure in the late 1980s and 1990s combined with public concern over safety and environmental damage has led to a fresh momentum to cost-benefit analysis studies and to some renewal of interest in methodological issues (e.g. Honohan 1998, Gray 1995).

The procedure followed in cost-benefit analysis consists of several steps. Exactly how the steps are identified will inevitably give rise to some dispute. Here we will adopt the approach outlined by the Department of Finance as stated in the Public Capital Programme 1984 (Department of Finance 1983).

According to this outline, economic and/or financial appraisals should contain the following elements:

- A clearly defined set of objectives for the project

- A statement of alternatives that would meet the objectives

- A statement of the constraints (*viz.* technological, physical, financial and statutory) that impinge on the project, together with a listing of those alternatives that do not fall within the constraints

- In respect of each chosen alternative:
  - A list of the benefits and costs expected over the economic life of the project and underlying assumptions
  - A quantification of the benefits and costs in cash flows or economic flows as appropriate
  - A statement of projected cash flows or a cost/benefit balance sheet, as appropriate
  - A calculation of the decision criteria (net present value, cost/benefit ratio, internal rate of return, maximum effectiveness at least cost) and a test for sensitivity to changes in key variables

- Identification, and whenever possible quantification, of the distributional effects of the costs and the benefits
- An assessment of the pay-back period (where appropriate)
- A recommendation as to the preferred alternative.

This is a reasonably succinct outline of the steps, from defining objectives to making a decision or recommendation. The Department of Finance (1994) and the Community Support Framework Evaluation Unit (1999) have produced more detailed guidelines for the appraisal of capital expenditure proposals in the public sector. We will refer to these as we proceed.

Defining objectives

The importance of setting and specifying objectives is crucial. Here we will add some points of direct relevance to project and programme appraisal.

Objectives should be made as explicit, precise and amenable to measurement as possible. For example, in a flood control project an objective stated in the form 'to reduce flood damage by €A in area B by year C' is vastly preferable to the form 'to reduce flood damage'. Similarly for a literacy programme an objective in the form 'to increase reading scores' is much weaker than in the form 'to increase reading scores by X among group Y by year Z.' Such a formulation allows the possibility of identifying alternative ways to meet the objective and facilitates assessment of the costs and benefits of each alternative. It also clarifies for whom the benefit is intended which in turn enables consideration of potential 'gainers' and 'losers'.

The definition of objectives is closely bound-up with the definition of the project itself, i.e. with the specification of the boundaries of the project and the resources to be allocated. For example, the definition of a project to upgrade a stretch of rail should clarify what is included and excluded. Are train stations and adjoining car parks to be included or excluded?

Finally, in this brief discussion of objectives we might consider the fact that some projects and programmes have multiple objectives. Where this is the case, in order to have effective resource allocation and appraisal, the objectives should be both explicit and prioritised.

Identifying alternatives

Properly specified objectives may facilitate the identification of alternatives but care is still needed. The alternatives either of doing nothing or of minimal intervention are often overlooked, yet these are often feasible alternatives.

The inclusion of the 'do-nothing' option requires care in drawing inferences. For example, if the option of an urban road building programme can be shown to be preferable to doing nothing then the reflex inference may be to go ahead and put the programme in place. However, all we know is that the programme is better than nothing; perhaps it would be better to choose just part of the programme or a different alternative such as improved public transport.

The Department of Finance (1994) cautions against any presumption that public sector responses are the only available ones and indicates that alternatives involving or relying on the private sector should also be considered. The Department suggests that, where appropriate, different scales of the same response should be included as separate alternatives. It also suggests that any conflict that may occur between certain alternatives and existing policies be referred to decision-makers who might then wish to review the policies.

A standard caveat in the analysis of alternatives is to be vigilant for the manipulation of options intended to present a particular one in a favourable light. The one-time US Secretary of State, Henry Kissinger, put the point as follows: 'I have seen it happen ... that when one asks for choices one is always given three: two absurd ones and the preferred one.' One would expect higher standards from Irish public servants.

Constraints

Constraints take several forms and it is important to identify which are relevant in any particular appraisal.

Budgetary constraints are familiar. Constraints on expenditure may take the form either of set amounts to be fully spent, or sums to be spent with discretion up to a maximum, or a requirement that a certain percentage of expenditure be self-financed. The form of the constraint will influence the appraisal; for example, where there is discretion to spend up to a maximum, considerations of opportunity cost are particularly relevant.

There is a natural tendency to think of budgetary constraints as targets for restraints on expenditure, but targets may also apply to revenue. Such is the case, for example, where enterprises are given targets for profit.

Environmental constraints may take the form of natural terrain or of geological deposits which must be protected. Input, or physical constraints, may take the form of unavailability of supply, inelasticity of supply or technological incompatibility of inputs. Input constraints may apply to raw materials, labour, skills, information technology and so forth. Technical constraints arise where there is a technically limited number of ways in which to produce a good or deliver a service.

Legal constraints are common. They may limit the activities of organisations, types of land-use, rights of access, pricing options and so forth. Administrative constraints may also exist as when there are staff, skills or information technology shortages which limit what can be processed through the administrative system.

This is quite a formidable list and not an exhaustive one. There may be policy constraints requiring consistency with existing decisions on policy or investment. Or there may be distributional constraints intended to favour certain regions or income groups; this is an issue to which we will return later in the chapter. At this juncture, however, we have established the variety of the constraints and their importance for project appraisal.

Identifying costs and benefits

The relevant costs and benefits of projects may be direct, indirect, tangible or intangible or some combination of these. For a road project, for example, identification would include a listing of the resources used such as concrete, tarmac and labour and the benefits such as time saved, reduction in traffic fatalities and so forth. We would also list effects on property prices, local businesses, quality of the landscape and so forth.

Additionality, deadweight and displacement

Important concepts to bear in mind when identifying and listing costs and benefits are additionality, deadweight and displacement. Additionality and deadweight are closely related and refer to the net impacts of programmes and projects. Deadweight occurs when part of a public expenditure programme confers benefits on recipients other than those intended. For example, in the case of a publicly funded programme to promote business start-ups, some participants may in any event have started their own businesses. For these, the programme is not strictly needed and they represent deadweight. Viewed in another way, in terms of additionality, the benefit should be measured net of any start-ups that would have occurred in the absence of the programme.

Displacement occurs when the creation of a positive project or programme output leads to a loss of output elsewhere. For example, a grant-aided leisure facility may displace a commercially funded one or graduates from a job training programme may displace people from employment.

Categorising costs and benefits

Musgrave and Musgrave (1984) provide a useful categorisation of costs and benefits as exemplified in Table 1.1. The categorisation is rehearsed here to highlight some key distinctions between types of costs and benefits.

Table 1.1 Types of costs and benefits

Irrigation Project			
		Benefits	Costs
Real			
• *Direct*	tangible	Increased farm output	Cost of pipes
	intangible	Beautification of area	Loss of wilderness
• *Indirect*	tangible	Reduced soil erosion	Diversion of water
	intangible	Preservation of rural society	Destruction of wildlife
Pecuniary		Relative improvement in farm equipment industry	

The main distinctions to be drawn are:

Real and pecuniary

Real benefits are those derived by the final consumer. They add to the welfare of society and can be set against the real cost of resources used. Pecuniary costs and benefits derive from changes in relative prices in secondary markets. For example, the improvement of a road may lead to increased earnings for roadside restaurants. However, these earnings are not a net gain to society; rather they are gains to particular businesses which, at least in part, are likely to be offset by reduced food purchases and restaurant earnings elsewhere. Generally, therefore, pecuniary costs and benefits are not included in the economic evaluation of costs and benefits.

Direct and indirect

Real costs and benefits can be sub-classified as direct (primary) or indirect (secondary) in relation to the main objectives of projects or programmes. For example, an education programme may be directly aimed at increasing the earning power of a certain cohort of school-leavers but may have the secondary effect of reducing delinquency.

Tangible and intangible

Tangible costs and benefits are those which can be valued by the market; intangible costs and benefits are those which cannot. In the example in Table 1.1 the tangible cost of water pipes is set alongside the intangible cost of loss of wilderness and the tangible benefit of increased farm output alongside the intangible benefit of beautification of the area. Intangible costs and benefits give rise to measurement difficulties to which we will return.

The foregoing are the more obvious distinctions. Others include the distinction between final and intermediate, i.e. between the provision of goods directly to consumers and the provision of goods as inputs to the production of other goods; and between inside and outside, i.e. between costs and benefits which occur within the area where the project or programme is undertaken and those which occur outside the area.

An important question to emerge from this categorisation and discussion of costs and benefits is, how far should the analysis go in pursuing costs and benefits? Analysis itself imposes costs and it would be unwise to incur such costs in pursuit of minor impacts of projects or programmes which are being evaluated.

Transfer payments

In identifying costs and benefits two pitfalls in particular must be avoided. Firstly, transfer payments should be excluded. Taxation provides some good examples. A private enterprise, in assessing a project, will view tax as an expense and look for net profits on the bottom line. From society's point of view, however, taxation transfers part of the project's benefit from the enterprise to other members of society. In cost-benefit analysis as a general rule, it is gross, not net, profit which is relevant. An exception to this arises with foreign direct investment: for outward investment the taxation of profit paid abroad must be deducted because this part of the benefit accrues abroad. For inward investment the taxation of profits is reckonable as a benefit but the part of the profit remitted to the parent company cannot be included as a benefit.

Another example of transfer payment arises when a project affects indirect tax revenues and unemployment benefit. If, for instance, a project, by affecting employment levels or consumption, leads to additional payments of unemployment benefits and reductions in indirect tax revenues there is no effect on real resources. However, there are redistributions of money through the exchequer. These redistributions are more properly the subject of exchequer cash flow analysis than cost-benefit analysis.

Double-counting

The second major pitfall in identifying costs and benefits is double-counting. In our discussion above of the distinction between real and pecuniary benefits we considered the case of improvements to a road which confer benefits on roadside restaurants. This scenario could easily be extended to benefits to garages on the road, effects on adjoining land and so forth. As a general rule, these types of benefit are not additional and are not included in cost-benefit analysis. This is partly because of offsetting reductions in profitability for garages and restaurants on other roads. Even if this were not the case, however, the increased profitability is due to more journeys being taken than before the road improvement rather than extra satisfaction gained by consumers from using the restaurants and garages.

Another example is where a new rail line, or the upgrading of an existing rail line, leads to an increase in the prices of houses conveniently located to the line. Increases in house prices are due to the additional benefits of quicker and easier access to jobs, shopping or entertainment venues. These benefits are estimated in cost-benefit analysis. To count the rise in house prices as well would be double-counting; the rise in house prices being the capitalised value of the stream of future benefits of quick and easy access.

In essence, in cost-benefit analysis every attempt is made to eliminate transfer and distributional items from the appraisal and to count the additional output arising from any given investment as opposed to the increase in value of existing assets.

Valuing costs and benefits

When costs and benefits have been identified the next step in cost-benefit analysis is valuation in common units by use of prices. If market prices exist which accurately reflect the cost and benefits to society then the process of measuring values is relatively straightforward.

Market prices and social values

But market prices may sometimes embody distortions which make them poor indicators of social costs and benefits. Or, as is often the case with public sector output, goods and services may be untraded and no market price may exist. We will examine both of these scenarios.

The classic reason, why market prices may not reflect social costs and benefits occurs in imperfect competition where prices are higher and output is lower than in competitive conditions. Imperfect competition entails production where the consumer's willingness to pay does not equal the cost of an extra unit of output; consumers willing to pay more than the cost of the extra unit of output are not supplied and hence market prices are poor indicators from a social point of view.

Taxes on expenditure are included in market prices and are another reason for divergence between market prices and social costs and benefits. Government intervention to support prices, as when the prices of certain agricultural products are artificially raised, will also create a divergence. So will tariffs, import controls and subsidies.

A divergence between private and social cost may occur where there is unemployment. An extreme case is where a project hires workers who have been unemployed and drawing unemployment benefit hitherto and who could be expected to remain unemployed in the absence of the project. The unemployment benefit is a transfer payment which we have established should be ignored for the purpose of analysis. In this extreme case there is no output foregone by society due to employing workers on the project. The workers are drawn from among the unemployed and not from other projects so the opportunity cost is zero. Prest and Turvey (1965) in their still authoritative review of cost-benefit analysis stated, 'when there is an excess of supply at the current market price of any input, that price overstates the social cost of using that input.' In the example just considered the market price, namely the wage paid to workers on the project, overstates its social opportunity cost.

At the heart of the analysis of costs in cost-benefit analysis is the attempt to measure the use of a real resource while excluding transfer payments. Opportunity cost gives the real cost of resource withdrawal from other uses and is therefore central to cost-benefit analysis.

On the benefits side, evaluation in monetary terms assumes that the value of a project to an individual is equal to his or her willingness-to-pay for it and that the social value of the project is the aggregation of individual values.

The concept of willingness-to-pay raises issues of consumer surplus namely the difference between what a consumer actually pays for a good or service and what he or she would have been willing to pay. If I pay a €1 toll to cross a bridge but would have been willing to pay €3 then my consumer surplus is €2. Consumer surplus is used as a measure of welfare changes. A measure of the gross benefit of a project is got by adding the consumer surplus to the market price where the latter is either a good reflection of social value or adjusted to be a good reflection, as we will see below.

The absence of market prices

The first of the two scenarios introduced in this section was where market prices gave a misleading measure of social opportunity cost. The second, to which we now turn, is where market prices may not exist at all.

Market prices do not exist where there are public goods, externalities and intangibles. Public goods such as defence are not marketed; they are supplied collectively and the willingness-to-pay of individuals cannot be ascertained. Similarly there are difficulties in arriving at values for the elimination of negative externalities such as noise or for the appraisal of intangibles such as scenic value, the value of life, historic value, prestige, the value of loss of wilderness, the value of a sense of security and so forth.

In the absence of market prices, information on value can be obtained by questionnaires and by a range of relatively recently developed methodologies such as contingent valuation. Of course, using questionnaires to ascertain the public's willingness-to-pay for the benefit of a project runs the gauntlet of people misrepresenting their preferences in order to influence the result of the analysis.

Value of time

A common way to value untraded goods is by analysing markets in which close substitutes are sold. Time savings are the largest benefits of most transportation projects. Time savings can be valued at the cost of employing users of the completed projects – their wages plus the overheads borne by employers including pension and national insurance contributions. Assumptions play a vital role in such valuations. In this case the key assumptions are that the value of a person's output is at least equal to the cost of employing him or her and that a saving in time will allow production to increase by a corresponding amount. In practice, there are real difficulties in valuing time; different people have different abilities to vary the time they work and hence to use time saved in travel. Different destinations are more conducive to work. Hence, for example, time saved in getting from an office to an airport is not the same as in getting from an airport to an office.

Leisure time is valued more cheaply than work time but it gives rise to even greater difficulties of estimation. Leisure time is valued by analysing how much people are willing to pay for time savings when alternative means of transport are available – one slower and cheaper and the other faster and more expensive. The alternative means of transport include walking, cycling, car, bus, train and so forth.

A common problem which arises with savings of both working and leisure time is that the time savings in individual journeys may range from seconds to a few minutes. When a large number of individual journeys are aggregated the time savings look very significant. For most people, however, the saving of a minute or two does not significantly add to work output or enjoyment of leisure. The aggregate figure, therefore, may give an excessive valuation.

Value of life

The most controversial aspect of cost-benefit analysis is the attempt to value human life. Distasteful as this may seem it is inseparable from the analysis of many projects, especially transport and healthcare projects. A moralist might well condemn such valuation; an economist, obliged to give advice on expenditure decisions which affect road safety or the treatment of disease, must grapple with it.

Zerbe and Dively (1994) provide a review of the methods of life valuation and the issues that arise, in which they comment that:

> the value placed on a human life depends on the purpose of the evaluation. In war the value placed on the lives of enemy soldiers is usually negative. The value generals place on the lives of their own men seems to be the opportunity cost of other uses of their lives to win the war. In some cases, lives may be valued *ex post* (after the fact) for the purpose of compensation. In other cases, lives may be valued *ex ante* (before the fact) for the purpose of preventing death and injury. Lives may be seen in the abstract where the names of the individuals are not known, such as when investments are made in highway guard rails as a way to save lives. Alternatively, lives may be seen in the particular where the names of the individuals are known .... These contrasts illustrate that valuing lives does not lend itself to a simple and direct approach that applies in all circumstances.

The most common approach to life valuation is that used by the courts to decide on awards for wrongful injury or death. Based on foregone earnings, it estimates the value of a life as the lifetime contribution to national output expressed in present values. This method assumes that people's earnings are a good reflection of what they add to a society's production. This assumption is untenable in some cases.

A more significant criticism is that this method does not distinguish between lifetime production and the value of life. Bearing this distinction in mind is an antidote to indirect inferences from this method that, for example, a well-paid person's life is more valuable than a poorly-paid person's or that one's life has no value after retirement.

The approach to valuation of life preferred by economists is to estimate the willingness-to-pay for additional safety or the willingness-to-accept payment for bearing additional risk to life. The foregone earnings approach only roughly conforms to this view because a person's earnings may greatly differ from the amount he or she would pay for additional safety, or accept, to bear additional risk.

An alternative method which does recognise risk is based on wage premiums. This method estimates the value of life by analysing how much extra income is needed to compensate people for an increase in risk to life. Some occupations are riskier than others and people working in these occupations earn a risk premium. Risk premiums can also be discerned in consumer choices whether it be the choice to smoke or not, drive a fast car or consume foods about which there are health scares.

There are difficulties also with this method. People may be either poorly informed about the risks they face or may pay little heed to the information they have. A person's wealth also has a big influence: a poorer person will in general be more likely than a rich person to accept a wage premium for accepting greater risk.

A final method of valuing life is the most recent. It uses questionnaire studies to gain information about behaviour under risk. This is called the contingent valuation approach. It is to be expected that there will be difficulties in estimating a value for human life. These difficulties can be extended to the need to allow for the quality of life, not just the number of lives. Whatever the difficulties, the valuation of life must proceed if projects which entail risks to life are to be evaluated.

Shadow prices

In this section we have discussed two broad scenarios that arise in the valuation of costs and benefits; one is where market prices provide a poor guide to social values and the other is where market prices do not exist. In both cases it may be necessary to construct artificial prices known as shadow prices (sometimes the term 'surrogate price' is used where market prices do not exist). For example, the wage rate may be taken as the shadow price of travel time. We have already seen that in conditions of high unemployment the market price, or wage, of employing people on a project may overstate the social opportunity cost. In such cases it can be argued that the market wage be replaced by a lower shadow price.

The construction of a 'shadow price' is complex not least because it is difficult to trace the full consequences of a project. The Department of Finance (1994) sensibly states that:

> ... market prices are generally reliable and, normally, verifiable. They generally provide the appropriate basis for valuing a project's costs and benefits; they should be used, unless there are clear and convincing reasons that they are inappropriate and also that it is possible to derive shadow prices using a sound means of calculation.
>
> If shadow prices are used, market prices, if available, should be applied also. If the analysis on both bases leads to differing conclusions, reliance should be placed on results using shadow prices only where it can be clearly justified.

Of course, where market prices do not exist the estimation of a shadow or surrogate price may be unavoidable. It may, for example, be possible to estimate a surrogate price for the benefit derived by an area from the provision of extra policing by analysing the increase in house values as a result of an increase in the sense of security.

Present values

When the costs and benefits relevant to a project have been expressed in monetary terms they must be converted into present values. Money has a time value: costs and benefit accruing in various future years are different when viewed from the present. A hundred euro which accrues next year is not the same as a hundred euro today. By stating costs and benefits in present value terms we can meaningfully compare them.

An obvious reason to prefer a given sum of money immediately is the desire to spend rather than defer consumption. But a person may also prefer the money immediately in order to accumulate interest: if the interest rate is 5 per cent then the €100 will grow to €105 in a year. By compounding interest (i.e. by multiplying by $(1 + i)n$ where i is the rate of interest and n the number of years) we can trace the value of money into the future. In ten years time €100 invested at five per cent will be worth €162.89 and in 50 years it will grow to €1,146.74. This is due to the effects of interest rates and not inflation: even if inflation is zero the growth in investment will occur.

Adopting a different perspective we can ask what is the present value of €105 due in one year's time. If the interest rate, or in this context the discount rate, is five per cent then the answer obviously is €100. In general terms the present value V of a given amount S accruing n years from now can be stated as

$$V = \frac{(S_n)}{(1 + i)^n}$$

or

$$V = Sn \left[1/(1 + i)^n \right]$$

The expression $[1/(1 + i)^n]$ is known as the discount factor. Discount factors will have values between 0 and 1. The further into the future a cost or benefit accrues, the lower the discount factor. Also, the higher the discount rate the lower the discount factor. Appendix I shows discount factors for different values of n and i.

Using the discount table in Appendix I we see that, at a five per cent discount rate, €100 receivable in 10 years' time is worth €61.39 now and, if receivable in 25 years time, it is worth €29.53. Put another way, a person who today invests two sums, one of €61.39 and the other of €29.53, will receive sums of €100 in 10 years and again in 25 years' time.

In general, a project with benefits occurring early and with deferred costs is preferable to one with early costs and deferred benefits. With capital projects, however, the returns tend to accrue over a period of time and the costs, although they also occur over time, tend mostly to occur in the early years.

The social discount rate

The discounting process outlined above is equally applicable to commercial and non-commercial, or social, cost-benefit analysis. However, things are not that simple. We need to ask what rate should be chosen with which to discount future costs and benefits and whether the same rate can be used for commercial and non-commercial projects.

For long-term projects the choice of discount rate may be critical: a project which is attractive at a five per cent rate may be dismissed at a ten per cent rate. In general, as the rate of discount increases, projects with early net benefits will appear more favourable than projects whose net benefits occur further into the future.

However, at any given time there exist many different rates of interest. For example, different rates apply depending on the duration of a loan, the purpose for which it is required, the security offered and the track-record of the borrower. These factors affect the cost of capital which along with other considerations, such as the risk-profile of investment, contribute to the choice of discount rate for commercial projects.

Much greater care is needed in selecting discount rates for non-commercial, or social, cost-benefit analysis. Market interest rates are not appropriate for several reasons. People tend to be short-sighted about future costs and benefits which affect them and tend to prefer current consumption. This preference not only affects the efficiency of private investment but also may affect the wider society. By reflecting private rather than social rates of time preference the market interest rate takes inadequate account of future generations. We can expect the market rate to be above the social rate of time preference. Therefore, discounting by the market rate will attach a lower than appropriate value to future benefits to society.

From the point of view of social cost-benefit analysis, market rates are also suspect because built into them tends to be a premium to cover risk. Investment in the public sector is generally less risky than in the private sector; the public sector is, for example, in a better position to spread risks (Brown and Jackson 1990). This is another reason why the market rate may exceed the social discount rate.

The use of different discount rates for public and private sector projects may give rise to its own problems. Care must be exercised that the use of different rates does not favour poorer quality public sector projects at the expense of better private sector ones.

If circumstances merit the use of a social discount rate the question which arises is: which rate? In theory, probably the best rate to use is the opportunity cost of capital. Funds used in public projects are obtained either from the private sector, via tax or borrowing, or within the public sector by diverting funds from other projects. In each case the funds have alternative returns which could be earned. However, rates of return vary from one type of investment to the next and in practice it is difficult to get a weighted average of all the rates of return for all the displaced uses of the funds.

An alternative approach attempts to construct a social rate of time preference to reflect society's evaluation of the relative merits of present rather than future returns. This approach takes the perspective of society as a whole in valuing future returns. The previous approach takes the perspective of a given point in time and values the resources transferred from other uses. Both approaches are likely to create practical difficulties of estimation.

The solution most easily applied to these problems is to use the yield on long-term government bonds. A government borrowing rate of this type gives a reasonable proxy for the risk-free (i.e. free of the risk of default) rate of interest appropriate to public sector investments.

The Department of Finance (1994) has recommended that the same basic discount rate, usually called the test discount rate, should be used in all cost-benefit and cost-effectiveness analyses of public sector projects. The test discount rate recommended was five per cent in real terms. This means that, before discounting, all nominal flows of costs and benefits should be deflated by the expected level of price inflation.

Decision criteria

Assuming that we can identify and quantify all the costs and benefits relevant to a number of projects, what criterion should we use to choose between them?

Undiscounted measures

Undiscounted measures do not take account of the time value of money. Consequently, although they give some guidance in choosing between projects they cannot be relied upon. The measures are: payback period; proceeds per unit of outlay; average income on book value of investment.

Payback period

This is the period from the beginning of the project to the point where net value of production equals the amount of the capital investment. This is an uncomplicated indicator of how long it takes to recover an initial investment and has some appeal when projects have a high degree of risk. Lucey, McCabe and McHugh (1995) found that, consistent with evidence from the UK, payback is the most popular method of investment appraisal among Irish firms.

There are some obvious drawbacks of this measure for the ranking of projects. Firstly, it does not take account of earnings after the payback date. Consider two projects both of which require a capital investment of €1 million. If project A earns €2 million in the first year and project B earns €1 million then project A will be preferred. However, this would be a wrong choice if in subsequent years project A earns €1 million and project B earns €2 million per annum.

The second weakness is the neglect of the timing of proceeds. We know that money has a time value and that the earlier benefits are received the more valuable they are. The payback period measure does not take account of this.

Proceeds per unit of outlay

This method ranks investments by dividing the total net value of production by the total investment. Once again, this approach neglects timing by failing to distinguish between money today and money in the future.

A variation of this method is the average annual proceeds per unit of outlay. This begins by dividing the total net value of production by the expected life of the project in years, thereby yielding an average of the annual proceeds which is then divided by the original investment.

This refinement fails to solve the problem of timing. It does not consider the span of time over which benefits accrue. Hence it will not distinguish between projects which earn money early from those that earn it later.

Average income on book value of investment

The book value of an investment is the value after subtracting depreciation. This measure states the ratio of average income to the book value. Although this is a useful measure of the performance of a firm it is inadequate as an investment criterion because, yet again, it fails to take account of the timing of the stream of benefits.

Discounted measures

These methods allow for the time value for money. A brief outline of the main methods follows.

Net present value

This criterion is based simply on whether the sum of discounted gains exceeds the sum of discounted losses. The costs and benefits are estimated for each year of a project's life, the costs are subtracted from the benefits and the net benefits are expressed at their present value.

Thus the discounting process is applied just once to the net benefit stream. Alternatively, but more onerously, both the cost and benefit streams can be separately discounted and then the costs subtracted from the benefits. Either way the use of the NPV criterion requires a decision about the appropriate rate of discount.

At the chosen rate of discount if the net present value (NPV) is positive then a project should be accepted. If the NPV is zero then the decision-maker is indifferent about the project and if the NPV is negative then the present value of the benefit stream will be insufficient to recover the investment and the project will be rejected.

Projects with positive NPVs enable efficient allocation of resources and represent an improvement to the welfare of society.

When choosing between mutually exclusive projects, i.e. when the acceptance of one excludes the acceptance of any others, NPV is the preferred criterion. The projects are ranked according to the NPVs and the project with the highest positive NPV is chosen.

The NPV criterion is less successful in ranking alternative independent projects, i.e. projects which are not mutually exclusive. The decision criterion is to accept all independent projects with positive NPVs. However, this creates difficulties in providing a ranking for order of implementation. For example, a small but highly attractive project may have a lower NPV than a large, but only moderately attractive, one. The NPV criterion does not register such differences and will accept both projects as long as each has a positive NPV and there are sufficient funds with which to proceed.

Notwithstanding this difficulty, the NPV criterion is satisfactory from the point of view of efficient resource allocation and the welfare of society and because it is free from problems associated with alternative discounted measures to which we now turn.

Internal rate of return

The internal rate of return (IRR) is the maximum rate of interest that a project can afford to pay for the resources used which allows the project to cover its investment and operating expenses and still break even. The IRR is the discount rate which will make the NPV of a project equal zero. An IRR of 15 per cent means that at a discount rate of 15 per cent the project just breaks even; in other words it could earn back all the capital and operating costs incurred and pay 15 per cent for the use of the money in the meantime.

The IRR approach is based on a cut-off rate, or target rate of return, which is a pre-determined rate which usually approximates the opportunity cost of the funds to be invested. For independent (i.e. not mutually exclusive) projects the IRR approach will accept all projects with an IRR greater than the cut-off rate.

There are however several difficulties with the IRR approach. There are difficulties in using the IRR to rank projects, either independent projects subject to capital rationing (i.e. where there is an expenditure constraint) or mutually exclusive projects. The IRR compares the return on a project to the opportunity cost of funds; it does not compare performance across several projects. It is possible for two projects to have the same IRR and therefore the same ranking but because the incidence of their costs and benefits are timed differently, they may have different rankings when net benefits are discounted to present value using a common rate such as a social discount rate or a market rate.

The IRR has other, sometimes exaggerated, difficulties. Some projects can generate multiple IRRs and create obvious difficulties about which one to use.

In general, the NPV criterion has several advantages over the IRR criterion. In practice the IRR continues to be used partly because it can be calculated without the need to select a discount rate in advance, which, as we have seen, creates its own difficulties.

Cost-benefit ratio

This is the ratio of discounted benefits to discounted costs. Using this approach independent projects will be accepted if the ratio exceeds one.

This method is relatively simple to apply but ranking of projects, whether independent projects subject to an expenditure constraint or mutually exclusive projects, can lead to wrong choices. For example, project A may have a slightly higher benefit-cost ratio than project B but project A may be small-scale and project B may be large-scale with greater capacity to generate future benefits.

In the final analysis each of the foregoing discounted measures is useful. However, the drawbacks associated with the IRR and benefit-cost ratio approaches favour the NPV criterion as the most reliable.

Uncertainty and risk

Up to now we have assumed that measured costs and benefits are known with certainty. Where this is so, the NPV criterion can show the relative efficiency of projects. But for cost-benefit analysis conducted 'ex ante', costs and benefits are estimates which are subject to change. For example, a cost-benefit analysis of a transport project is based on estimates of future physical flows, such as traffic, and relative values, such as fuel prices.

There are many ways to allow for uncertainty; some relatively uncomplicated and others highly sophisticated. For example, a relatively uncomplicated way to deal with uncertainty about the life of equipment, perhaps because of technological change, is to reduce the estimated life of the project.

Another easy-to-apply approach is to increase the discount rate. This will most heavily reduce the present value of projects where significant benefits accrue more remotely into the future. This approach is not always appropriate. Stiglitz (1988) argued that the most common mistake in dealing with uncertainty is the inappropriate use of higher discount rates. If, for example, a project has uncertain costs which will occur at the end of its life then discounting at a higher rate will reduce the present value of costs and make the project more attractive. To guard against this possibility the flow of net benefits could first be adjusted for risk by use of a risk premium and then present values could be calculated by using the regular discount rates.

A more sophisticated approach is to take each uncertain variable and assess the probability, say high, medium and low, of a number of values occurring. Each stated value could then be assigned a probability weighting based on the likelihood that it will occur. An NPV could then be calculated for every combination of stated value and each NPV could be ascribed a probability measure leading to a probability distribution of NPVs. For example, for a given project there may be a 65 per cent chance that the NPV lies in the range €5 million and €10 million, a 20 per cent chance that it lies between €10 million and €15 million and so forth.

Whatever its sophistication this approach bears an important *caveat*: it depends on the informed judgement of analysts in assigning probabilities.

Finally we will consider what in practice is the most useful method for dealing with risk and uncertainty, namely sensitivity analysis. This involves recalculating the NPV in line with changes to the values of important parameters or assumptions.

These parameters include the discount rate, the physical quantities of inputs and outputs, the shadow prices of inputs and outputs and the project life span. In particular the NPV will often critically depend on the discount rate chosen.

Sensitivity analysis allows the analyst to discover to which parameters or assumptions the NPV is most sensitive. When these have been found then the analyst can attempt to refine estimates of the parameters and, once the project is started, project managers can attempt to monitor or guide carefully these parameters.

Sensitivity analysis is an effective means of dealing with uncertainty. But sensitivity analysis is just part of the decision process. In assessing each uncertain outcome the decision maker must be conscious of his or her attitude to risk. For example, people may be risk-averse or risk-loving.

Distributional issues

Cost-benefit analysis attempts to select projects and policies which are efficient in their use of resources. It assumes implicitly that the existing distribution of income is an acceptable one. We have seen earlier in this chapter that values in cost-benefit analysis are partly measured by willingness-to-pay. This in turn depends on ability-to-pay which of course is based on the distribution of income.

The calculation of NPVs makes no allowance for the distribution among people of costs and benefits. If one person is made better-off by €200 and another is disadvantaged by €100 then this is regarded as a net gain for society because in principle it would be possible for those who gain to compensate those who lose and still be better-off than heretofore. This is a potential compensation criterion which we will discuss later in the chapter.

However, there are cases where redistribution is an explicit objective of public expenditure. Even when there are no explicit objectives the effects of public projects may be so large as to affect distribution in a way that cannot be ignored.

One way to take account of distributional issues is to attach weights to the benefits and costs accruing to different people. The relevant population could be divided into different income groups and if, for example, the government felt that benefits accruing to low-income groups were of greater value than similar benefits accruing to high-income groups then additional weights could be assigned so as to amplify the benefits accruing to the low-income groups.

In practice, there are many problems with the use of distributional weights and they are seldom used. The problematic questions include: how are groups to be defined? how is the impact on the groups to be evaluated? and, of course, what weights should be used?

An alternative to the use of distributional weights is to compare measures of inequality both without, and then, with the project. Discussion of inequality measures is beyond the scope of this chapter but a discussion of these measures in the context of cost-benefit analysis can be found in Stiglitz (1988).

Deciding between alternatives

An efficient allocation of resources requires that investment should continue until its marginal benefit equals (or, less precisely, approximates) its marginal cost.

This is illustrated in Table 1.2 which is adapted from Eckstein (1967). It shows flood damage prior to government intervention and then for four progressively bigger flood protection projects which are, of course, mutually exclusive.

Project A appears attractive: it has a benefit-cost ratio of €6 million to €3 million, i.e. 2:1, the best for any of the projects, and a net benefit of €3 million. However, project B is an improvement on project A because for an additional

€7 million there is additional benefit of €10 million; the net benefit of project B is €6 million. Project C represents yet a further improvement because for a marginal cost of €8 million there is a marginal benefit of €9 million; the net benefit of project C is €7 million. With project C we have the nearest approximation of marginal costs and marginal benefits. Project C represents the most efficient allocation of resources: moving beyond it to project D would entail a marginal cost of €12 million but a marginal benefit of only €7 million and a net benefit of just €2 million.

Table 1.2: Flood control projects

Project	Annual cost	Average annual damage	Benefit (reduction in damage)	Net benefit	Marginal cost	Marginal benefit
Before project	0	38	0	0	0	0
Project A	3	32	6	3	3	6
Project B	10	22	16	6	7	10
Project C	18	13	25	7	8	9
Project D	30	6	32	2	12	7

The logic of equating marginal cost and marginal benefit is familiar from the microeconomic theory of the firm. It provides a guideline for decision-making in cost-benefit analysis. In practice, where there are large indivisible projects, fine marginal adjustments are not possible. The underlying logic, however, remains, namely to maximise the net benefit.

A second example which is adapted from Musgrave and Musgrave (1984) is illustrated in Table 1.3 which presents information about seven alternative independent road projects. Decision-makers must choose which projects to pursue within a budget of €700 million.

In deciding which projects to pursue within the budget of €700 million we can turn to several decision rules.

Firstly, we could rank projects by their benefit-cost ratio and use this ordering to choose projects within the budget constraint. From Table 1.4 we see that using this approach, projects D, A, E and C would be chosen at a cost of €630 million. Project B, which is next in the ranking, cannot be included because at an additional cost of €145 million it would breach the budget constraint. Applying the benefit-cost ratio approach, therefore, will provide gross benefits of €1,049 million and net benefits of €419 at a cost of €630 million, leaving €70 million unspent.

Table 1.3: Project selection under fixed budget

		€million			
Project	Costs	Benefits	Net benefits	Benefit-cost ratio	Benefit-cost ranking
A	200	400	200	2.0	2
B	145	175	30	1.2	5
C	80	104	24	1.3	4
D	50	125	75	2.5	1
E	300	420	120	1.4	3
F	305	330	25	1.1	6
G	125	100	−25	0.8	7

Secondly, we could apply the rule of maximising net benefit. By trial and error we can find that projects D, A, E and B maximise net benefit. With this approach gross benefits are €1,120 million, net benefits are €425 million, the cost is €695 million and €5 million is unspent.

Thirdly, we might adopt a decision rule to minimise the amount left unspent. This approach would select projects A, B, D and F thereby yielding gross benefits of €1,030 million and net benefits of €330 million at a cost of €700 million with nothing left unspent.

The costs and benefits associated with each of the decision rules are set out in Table 1.4.

Table 1.4 Decision rules – costs and benefits

		€ million			
Decision rule	Projects selected	Benefits	Costs	Net benefits	Amount unspent
Benefit-cost ratio	D, A, E, C	1,049	630	419	70
Maximum net benefit	D, A, E, B	1,120	695	425	5
Minimum left unspent	D, A, B, F	1,030	700	330	0

Table1.4 clearly shows that the approach of minimising the amount left unspent can be dismissed: it spends more and buys fewer net benefits than the other approaches. The benefit-cost ratio approach is attractive because it chooses projects which yield the highest return per euro spent.

However, as we would expect, the best decision is to maximise net benefits. This approach costs €65 million more than the benefit-cost ratio approach but buys €71 million more benefits thereby yielding €6 million more net benefits.

Cost-effectiveness analysis

A full cost-benefit analysis is a painstaking activity. In particular, there are difficulties in estimating benefits. This is due both to problems in assigning money values to certain benefits and to the tendency for benefits to accrue further into the future than costs.

Cost-benefit analysis enables comparison of alternative projects or programmes even when they are not aimed at common objectives. Hence cost-benefit analysis estimates for education, healthcare, housing and transport projects might be compared. Such comparisons are fraught with difficulties and doubts about whether like is being compared with like.

Cost-effectiveness analysis is an alternative to, indeed some would say a type of, cost-benefit analysis. Unlike cost-benefit analysis it does not entail the conversion of costs and benefits to a common money measure. Instead cost-effectiveness analysis assesses the effectiveness of projects and programmes in relation to the monetary value of costs.

Cost-effectiveness analysis is used where benefits are hard to value in money terms or when the total expenditure available to a project is fixed or when the output from alternative projects is expected to be similar.

If an objective is clear, for example to increase reading scores (or convert smokers to non-smokers or reduce road fatalities etc) by amount x in group y by time z, then cost-effectiveness analysis allows projects to be compared and ordered.

Cost-effectiveness analysis can also be used to compare the costs of achieving different degrees of an objective. For example, if the objective is to reduce a certain type of mortality then the additional costs of successive reductions in that type of mortality due to different policy interventions can be estimated. This might help identify reasonably large reductions in mortality for relatively small additional costs.

If there are multiple benefits or outputs then some element of subjective preference by decision-makers is necessary. This might take the form of placing the benefits on a scale from say 1 to 10. The ratio of scaled outputs or benefits to costs could then be compared.

Cost-effectiveness analysis is, in effect, a variation of cost-benefit analysis which is based on the same principles and uses the same methods. In cost-effectiveness analysis the NPV approach is applied to the stream of costs, both the capital and the recurring costs.

Cost-effectiveness analysis has weaknesses. Although it can help clarify the most effective way to achieve an objective within an expenditure limit, it cannot assist in selecting the optimal expenditure level for a project. It can compare the relative costs of different options for achieving an objective but is not, in itself, sufficient for deciding whether or not to proceed with a project.

Cost-effectiveness analysis tends to compare a more narrow range of variables than cost-benefit analysis and is not as useful as cost-benefit analysis in comparing marginal costs and marginal benefits.

Private and public sector cost-benefit analysis

Private enterprises continually assess new investment opportunities. In so doing they will consider their objectives, identify alternative means of achieving the objectives, assign money values to inputs and outputs, assess the costs and benefits and estimate profitability.

Social cost-benefit analysis tries to apply in the public sector the type of decision that would be made if private sector markets worked properly. Cost-benefit analysis in the public sector differs from the private sector in certain key respects. It takes account of externalities such as effects on the environment and generally adopts a wider perspective than private sector appraisal. Public sector projects may also differ in having concerns about and objectives in the area of income distribution.

Social cost-benefit analysis may adjust market prices where they exist or substitute proxy prices where no market prices exist. It does so with a view to promoting efficient allocation of resources for society. Thus social cost-benefit analysis may attempt to value untraded and indeed intangible goods such as time saved, lives saved, peace and quiet and so forth.

Social cost-benefit analysis may also differ from private sector appraisal in the choice of discount rate. The rate of discount for cost-benefit analysis in the public sector may be lower than the rate applied in private appraisals either because government wishes to place a higher value on future benefits than would be the case with commercial rates or simply because government may borrow more cheaply than private enterprises.

There is no scope here to enter a discussion of private sector investment and its analysis. Interested readers may wish to pursue treatments such as those by NESC (1998) and Lucey, McCabe and McHugh (1995).

Criticisms and drawbacks of cost-benefit analysis

Cost-benefit analysis is an application of welfare economics. It is predicated on the belief that society's welfare is promoted through people's estimation of what things are worth to them. Values are established by people's willingness-to-pay for things they want or their willingness to accept payment to put up with things they do not want.

There are two broad purposes for which cost-benefit analysis is used. Firstly, in the case of public sector investment, it is used to identify the most efficient project or programme from among possible alternatives. In Ireland, cost-benefit analysis usually takes this form. Secondly, it is used to evaluate government intervention in the private sector such as road safety programmes, environmental regulations, the deregulation of commercial services and so forth.

Cost-benefit analysis is subject to criticism at the technical and procedural level and at a more conceptual level.

We have considered drawbacks of a technical nature throughout this chapter. They arise all along the line: there are problems of estimation surrounding future output and prices, shadow prices, surrogate prices, consumer surplus, willingness-to-pay, risk and uncertainty opportunity costs and so forth. There are hazards in the choice of discount rate and investment criterion (NPV, IRR, cost-benefit ratio) for public sector projects and of the weights to be applied for distributional purposes. There is a need for vigilance about double-counting and consciousness about the inherent errors and incompleteness in much economic data.

There are also inherent difficulties in economic analysis: unlike laboratory conditions, economic projects do not always afford the opportunity to examine outcomes both with and without an intervention.

In a similar vein, there are problems of the scope of analysis. For example, should an analysis of urban railways include the car parking facilities? Alternatively, if an analysis of the costs and benefits of by-passing a town estimates a certain level of net benefit, is this a meaningful number if a consequence of the bypass is partly to move a traffic bottleneck on to the next town?

There are also wider issues to consider. The use of different discount rates in public and private sectors has an associated danger that some public sector projects may displace other more worthy private sector projects. Alternatively the use of cost-benefit analysis to select one project, say a town by-pass on a busy inter-city route, in preference to another, say a town by-pass between two moderately busy regional centres, may be based on the higher value of time saved on the former. However, by proceeding with the former the decision-makers may be compounding regional inequity.

In making comparisons it is also worth bearing in mind that it is more convincing to compare like with like. Hence it is more acceptable to compare one option for road-building with another rather than to compare the building of a hospital with a school.

Drawbacks of a technical nature are well known to economists. Indeed, economists are accustomed to identifying and dealing with these drawbacks. Economic analysts are often first to highlight drawbacks but usually within the context that the analysis will proceed and drawbacks will be dealt with as best possible. Whether or not cost-benefit analysis should be used at all is a separate issue which arises at a more conceptual level.

Criticisms, at a conceptual level, of cost-benefit analysis take several forms. There are criticisms of the assumptions on which it is based. For example, there are reservations about whether people's willingness-to-pay should be the appropriate standard for policy decisions. There are criticisms also of the potential compensation criterion, i.e. that a project is worthwhile if the gainers could compensate the losers and still be better-off. This, the Kaldor-Hicks criterion is derived from the Pareto criterion which holds that the best policy or course of action is that which benefits some people without causing losses to anyone. The Kaldor-Hicks potential compensation criterion causes difficulties by not being concerned about who gains and who loses nor about whether the compensation is actually paid. A project might pass the cost-benefit test if it conferred €1,000 on the well-to-do in society and imposed €900 costs on the low-paid. But this is an extreme scenario.

There are also objections based on whether certain policy problems can be meaningfully reduced to costs and benefits. For example, policies which involve life or the environment may be seen by some as too important to be formulated by market-type rules for efficiency and effectiveness. There may be reservations that placing a price on life will diminish its value in people's minds. These are understandable reservations; yet when policies which save lives are being analysed costs and benefits are stubbornly relevant.

There are also a host of criticisms based on the objectivity, or the perceived lack of objectivity, of cost-benefit analysis and on the use of subjective judgements. There are questions about whether analysts, with their positivist training and professional socialisation, can be objective in identifying project goals, costs and benefits and there are reservations about whether analysts, particularly if retained by commercial enterprises, can be objective in conducting cost-benefit analysis and interpreting results.

Another source of criticism is based on what some believe to be the inappropriate extension of economic reasoning to the social or political domain where there may be lack of data, sudden changes in policy or project content, multiple objectives and so forth.

The foregoing criticisms are clearly important. They indicate the limits and weaknesses of economic evaluation. In the final analysis, however, they are not sufficient to make cost-benefit analysis redundant. Used with care and acknowledging its inherent limits and imprecision, cost-benefit analysis does provide a relatively coherent and disciplined approach to decision-making in practice. It is certainly preferable to arbitrary decision-making and to decision-making based on assumptions and values which are not open to scrutiny.

Conclusion

In this chapter we have reviewed the main issues that arise in cost-benefit analysis. Much greater depth can be found in a range of texts including Brent (1996), Layard and Glaister (1994), Mishan (1982), Ray (1984), Squire and van der Tak (1975), Walshe and Daffern (1990) and Zerbe and Dively (1994). There are also many case studies of cost-benefit analysis in practice such as the classic study in the UK of the Victoria underground railway line (Foster and Beesley 1963) and the analysis of the Naas bypass in Ireland (Barrett and Mooney 1984).

Cost-benefit analysis is an important aspect of evaluation. It is the most developed and soundly based means of evaluating the efficiency of public sector programmes. It helps discipline decision-making in the public sector when market forces do not exist to penalise poor decisions and reward good ones.

It has been said that everything is economics but economics isn't everything. Similarly, cost-benefit analysis isn't everything in public sector decision-making. Projects which would be selected by cost-benefit analysis may not be politically acceptable. This is as we would expect in democratic society. Cost-benefit analysis is, however, available to decision-makers requiring a rational, coherent and comprehensive means of evaluating public projects and programmes.

*

This article was first published in Mulreany, M., (ed.), *Economic & Financial Evaluation: Measurement, Meaning and Management,* Dublin: Institute of Public Administration, 1999

NOTES

1. The Community Support Framework Evaluation Unit (1999) in their proposed working rules for cost benefit analysis state that shadow prices should be used when market prices do not reflect opportunity costs due to some clearly identified market failure. Hence, for example, labour costs should be included at market prices unless there is a clearly identified case for an alternative approach. Even then, according to the proposed working rules, the shadow wage used should not be less than 80 per cent of the market wage and there should be a sensitivity analysis based on a shadow wage of 100 per cent.

REFERENCES

Barrett, S.D. and D. Mooney (1984). 'The Naas Motorway Bypass – A Cost-Benefit Analysis,' *Quarterly Economic Commentary*, January, 1984, pp 21-34

Blackwell, J. (1991). 'Efficiency and Effectiveness in Public Investment Appraisal,' in T.P. Hardiman and M. Mulreany (eds) *Efficiency and Effectiveness in the Public Domain*, Dublin: Institute of Public Administration

Brent, R.J., (1996). *Applied Cost-Benefit Analysis*, Cheltenham: Edward Elgar

Brown, C.V. and P.M. Jackson (1990). *Public Sector Economics*, Fourth edition, Oxford: Basil Blackwell

Community Support Framework Evaluation Unit (1999). *Proposed Working Rules for Cost-Benefit Analysis*, Dublin: CSF Evaluation Unit

Department of Finance (1983). *Public Capital Programme 1984*, Dublin: Stationery Office Department of Finance (1994). *Guidelines for the Appraisals and Management of Capital*
Expenditure Proposals in the Public Sector, Dublin: Department of Finance
Eckstein, O. (1967). *Public Finance, Second Edition*, Englewood Cliffs: Prentice-Hall
Foster, C.D. and M.E. Beesley (1963). 'Estimating the Social Benefit of Constructing an Underground Railway in London,' *Journal of the Royal Statistical Society*, vol 126, pp 46-58
Gray, A.W. (1995). *EU Structural Funds and other Public Sector Investments: A Guide to Evaluation Methods*, Dublin: Gill and Macmillan
Honohan, P. (1998). *Key Issues of Cost-Benefit Methodology for Irish Industrial Policy*, Dublin: Economic and Social Research Institute
Layard, G. and S. Glaister (1994). *Cost-Benefit Analysis, Second Edition*, Cambridge: Cambridge University Press
Mishan, E. J. (1982). *Cost-Benefit Analysis: An Informal Introduction*, Third Edition, London: George Allan and Unwin
Musgrave R. A. and P.B. Musgrave (1984). *Public Finance in Theory and Practice*, Maidenhead: McGraw-Hill
Prest, A.R. and R. Turvey (1965). 'Cost-Benefit Analysis: A Survey', *Economic Journal*, vol 75, pp 685-705
Lucey, B.M., P. McCabe and G. McHugh (1995). 'An Analysis of the Investment Appraisal Practices of Irish Companies, *IBAR*, vol 16, 1995, pp 101-114
NESC (1998). *Private Sector Investment in Ireland*, Dublin: National Economic and Social Council
Ray, A. (1984). *Cost-Benefit Analysis: Issues and Methodologies*, Baltimore: The Johns Hopkins University Press
Squire, L. and H. van der Tak (1975). *Economic Analysis of Projects*, Baltimore: The Johns Hopkins University Press
Stiglitz, J.E. (1988). *Economics of the Public Sector*, Second Edition, New York: Norton
Walshe, G. and P. Daffern (1990). *Managing Cost-Benefit Analysis*, London: Macmillan
Zerbe, R.O. and D.O. Dively (1994). *Benefit-Cost Analysis: In Theory and Practice*, New York: Harper-Collins

2

Efficiency and Effectiveness in Public Investment Appraisal*

JOHN BLACKWELL

This chapter deals with efficiency and effectiveness in capital project appraisal and is particularly concerned with public projects. We commence with an outline of some of the key principles underlying the evaluation of capital projects. Then some of the main features of the published studies featuring capital appraisal in Ireland are assessed. The main problems that have arisen in these studies are outlined and their implications for future work are indicated.

The justification for attention to this topic hardly needs pleading. Despite real reductions in recent years, the Public Capital Programme in Ireland remains a substantial proportion (currently a third) of total gross fixed investment and of gross national product. Moreover, monetary and exchange rate policy changes, and the limits that apply to the use of fiscal policy in an interdependent Europe, have made clear the limitations that now attach to the use of discretionary fiscal policy in Ireland. This highlights the need – always present, but hitherto often unappreciated – to focus clearly on efficiency in the use of resources in economic policy-making in Ireland.

Private and public evaluation

At the outset, some points of principle can be made about the difference between private and public evaluations of capital projects. There is a long history of project appraisal applied to public projects, with a good deal of work done on water resources and transport projects in the United States from the 1940s onwards. The methods used had an influence on capital project appraisal in Europe, and especially on the appraisal of transport projects. It is a sobering thought that the first paper on the appraisal of transport projects was published by an engineer, Dupuit, in the nineteenth century and languished for many decades before the principles outlined were used in assessments of capital projects. The high-water mark of the programme budgeting approach to the evaluation of public expenditure was reached in the United States in the 1960s. This had an influence on the approach used in Ireland in the 1960s and 1970s. In 1970, a comprehensive budgeting system was adopted in the civil service, with the aims of clarifying the objectives of public expenditure and analysing alternative ways of achieving these objectives. For a time, Public Capital Programme projects were evaluated. In recent years, a thoroughgoing approach of formal investment appraisal has not been used for the Public Capital Programme. However, a welcome advance was made through the publication by the Department of Finance of *Comprehensive Public Expenditure Programmes* (an outline of programmes, their main components, their objectives and the public expenditure associated with them but not, unfortunately, the tax losses or so-called 'tax expenditures'). Other recent developments are noted below.

Private firms continually assess whether proposed investments are likely to be worthwhile, although it seems that in the private sector in Ireland there has been little use of formal methods of assessment. This reflects the size distribution of Irish industry, which contains a large proportion of relatively small firms, with limited resources to devote to formal assessment. It also reflects the fact that the large-scale capital projects in areas such as fertilisers, gas, and steel have tended to fall within the ambit of state-sponsored bodies.

The standard techniques of capital investment appraisal are well established. They involve an assessment of the consequences of the project over a defined life, taking account of the outputs which in turn involves assumptions both about the price at which the output is sold and about foreign exchange rates in the case of exports. Account has also to be taken of the costs of the project, including the labour costs for different skills, and the costs of various materials used in the process of production. The additional benefits – in this case the gross revenue in euro – are compared with the additional costs. Among the various alternatives, the firm should choose the one with the highest net benefit or profits. In assessing net benefits or profits account must be taken on the costs side, of opportunity costs, i.e. the return on investment that the firm could have obtained elsewhere.

While this procedure wins a good deal of acceptance, it is less clear that this framework is seen as one that can be used to compare various different methods of achieving outcomes. In the case where a firm wishes to increase its capacity, there can be a number of different ways, in principle, that are open to it. For instance, different types of technology can be used, different combinations of capital and labour resources can be deployed and different combinations of output can be produced.

Moreover, this seemingly straightforward account has to be qualified. A feature of capital projects is that the returns to the investment accrue over a period of time. Indeed, the costs will also occur over a period, although much of the capital expenditure is likely to be bunched towards the early years of the planning period. This raises two questions: over what period are the returns and the costs to be projected? And how are the returns and the costs that accrue in different years to be compared with one another? Some projects such as electricity generation and forestry can show a marked stream of returns only over many decades. A firm cannot be expected to put the same value on a pound received today as on a pound received in ten years' time.

This difficulty can be handled by using the property that a euro today is worth more than a euro received in a number of years' time (since today's euro can be invested at the going rate of interest to reap a return per annum). Hence, the income streams occurring in various years can be discounted, using a discount factor which is smaller, the further into the future is the income stream. The classic case of the problems that arise in relation to the time horizon is the case of forestry, where the major part of returns can take 35-40 years to accrue. If the rate of interest is 5 per cent (relatively low by comparison with the rate actually used in many instances in recent years), then a euro received forty years from now is worth only 14.2 cent today. If a discount rate of 10 per cent is used, the euro received forty years from now is worth only 2.2 cent today!

While precise evidence on the use of evaluation in the private sector in Ireland is lacking, it does seem that in many instances, 'rules of thumb' such as a 'payback' rule (which focuses on the period of years over which the initial investment is recovered) are used, rather than the idealised procedure outlined above. Alternatively, quite short time periods are used, within which the flows of revenue and outgoings are compared. This may be defended as a way of handling increased uncertainty about such matters as product prices (due to exchange rate fluctuations between Ireland and non-EMS trading partners) and interest rates (given the marked rise in real interest rates that has occurred in recent years). While uncertainty is considered below, at this stage it can be argued that uncertainty can best be handled within the above framework by putting limits, and possibly probabilities, on the various possible outcomes.

Where lie the differences between this type of private investment appraisal and cost-benefit analysis as used by government? There are three main differences. Firstly, the firm will be interested only in the returns and costs that pertain to itself. By contrast, government may be concerned with the benefits and costs that apply to a much wider group, such as all consumers, and all producers. For instance, there could be adverse consequences for the environment as a result of a project, consequences which can affect a wide group of consumers and producers.

Secondly, the firm will use market prices to value both costs and returns. In the case of government appraisal, market prices might not be used for a number of reasons. It may be that there is no market for the product in question. For instance, clean air may be 'produced', but the question is what price to put on this. Even more difficult issues can arise. The classic one, associated in particular with transport projects, concerns the value to be put on the avoidance of accidents and the saving of life itself. Another reason why market prices may not be a guide arises where the prices that *are* in the market do not represent the true cost of benefits to society. A related question that often arises here, and is very relevant to the Irish case, is what wage rate to use on the cost side of a project (where labour costs consist of employment times the wage) if there is a high rate of unemployment. This is discussed below.

Thirdly, the discount factor used can differ between private and public evaluations. The government may feel that is has to take the welfare of future generations into account, by using a rate of discount that would be lower than that used by a private firm. While there is not the opportunity here to consider the complex and much debated issue of the appropriate discount factor for public projects, it can be noted that, in practice in many instances, the government will use a discount rate lower than that used by private firms. This is because a favoured approach is to use as a guide the rate at which borrowing can be undertaken. The rate at which government can borrow will always tend to be below that applying to even the most solid of private firms.

The method of cost-benefit analysis, as outlined above, concentrated on economic efficiency as the key criterion in the evaluation of alternative policies. Implicitly, the aim is to maximise economic efficiency, or to achieve objectives with the least commitment of resources. Reflecting this is the criterion that the project with the highest net benefit (excess of benefits over resource costs) should be chosen.

However, public projects could also have objectives in the sphere of income distribution. Even if there are no specific objectives about income distribution, most projects will provide gains or costs to some groups more than to others. One instance of a proposal that brought out income distribution effects in the starkest terms was that for an oil refinery in Dublin Bay in the 1970s. Among the losers would be the residents of Dublin Bay, the income of whom tends to be above average, and who would lose amenity benefits. However, the amenity benefits of the bay would also be lost by a much larger group of people with a variety of incomes. This shows the difficulties in practice that can apply in allowing for income distribution effects.

If no allowance is made for income distribution, the implicit assumption is that a pound of benefit or cost is the same, no matter who benefits or loses.

In principle, distributional weights could be attached to the estimates of benefits and costs. That is, the population could be divided into income groups with particular weights given to net benefits that accrue to each group. If the aim is to redistribute income towards group A, then this group's net benefit would attract a higher weighting. While this is the principle, there are few instances in the literature on cost-benefit analysis where distributional weights have been used. This reflects, in part at least, the difficulties in arriving at a set of distributional weights. One can say that the weighting is up to the decision-maker rather than the analyst, but this does little to diminish the difficulties of arriving at a set of weights. The weights could come from an analysis of past behaviour: by examining the actual choices made, it might be possible to obtain at least a range of weights. In summary, the advantage of using weights is that it makes explicit the value judgements that otherwise might remain hidden, and helps to ensure consistency between different investment decisions. The argument against the use of weights is that in most cases it asks too much of the administrative and political system of decision-making. In no cases, in fact, have distributional weights been used in Ireland.

There are alternative methods of allowing for income distribution. In line with the requirement that project evaluation needs to use the 'with-without' criterion (or a comparison of outcomes in the presence of the project with outcomes without the project) there could be a report on the distribution of income with and without the project. However, in the Irish case the statistics on income distribution are so inadequate that this approach could hardly be used.

Less ambitiously, there could be a report on how the project affects particular groups in the population. This could have the merit of at least making clear the 'trade-offs' that can be involved in the selection of projects. For instance, one proposal could benefit a group that is felt to be particularly deserving, but at the cost of an efficiency loss, by comparison with an alternative proposal. This method of allowing for income distribution effects has rarely if ever been used in Ireland. It might be argued that neglect in this area does not matter, on the grounds that the government could always redistribute income directly, if it wanted to, by means such as taxes and transfers. This is hardly defensible, especially when it is recognised that the battery of 'direct' methods of income redistribution involve economic costs to society. Moreover, some forms of investment are particularly associated with objectives to redistribute income. Health care and education are two instances of this. If income distribution is left out of account in these areas, an important dimension is missing. In fact these are areas where little has been published in Ireland by way of formal evaluation. This is no small matter, since 'social infrastructure' currently makes up approximately one fifth of the Public Capital Programme in Ireland. On balance, there is a strong case that the impacts of projects on the distribution of income should be assessed and shown, without using distributional weights. In this way, the trade-offs involved can be made clear. Also in this way, proposals can be ranked in order from the point of view of their impacts on income distribution.

Cost-benefit analysis and cost-effectiveness

In some cases, instead of using full-blown cost-benefit analysis to analyse projects, governments may use cost-effectiveness analysis, that is an analysis of the extent to which a programme attains its objectives. This method tends to be used in those cases where the assessment of benefits gives rise to particular difficulties: for instance where the saving of life is involved. Suppose that there are a number of public health programmes that are expected to result in a reduction in mortality. The costs associated with achieving the objective of reducing mortality under each of the programmes can be estimated. The programme with the least cost can be identified. In one sense, this is a more limited exercise than that of the full cost-benefit analysis. Instead of putting a money value on benefits along many different dimensions, one benefit is focused on. Moreover, a money value is not put on this particular benefit.

In general, it has to be recognised that the benefit side tends to give rise to most of the problems in public project appraisal, for at least two reasons. Firstly, the benefits tend to accrue further ahead than the bulk of the costs – giving rise to greater difficulties of projection over future years than typically rise in the case of costs. Secondly, as indicated above, the placing of a money value on some benefits has often been an especially difficult task. Hence, there are instances where cost-effectiveness analysis can well be justified.

There is also the potentially useful device of mapping out the incremental costs and incremental benefits associated with a project. Put in cost-effectiveness terms, staying with the public health example, the incremental costs associated with incremental reductions in mortality under various methods can be estimated. This is potentially useful, since one suspects that there are cases where along some range of activity, there could be large marginal returns for relatively small incremental outlays. Such cases could be emphasised as a priority for investment. An example of the possibility of such areas of high incremental return is the case of investment in environment improvement. Starting from a relatively polluted position it is quite likely that large incremental reductions in pollution could be achieved in the early stages of programmes.

Cost-effectiveness analysis is easiest to use in cases where it is possible to concentrate on one objective. If there are a number of different objectives, one is again confronted with many of the problems that arise on the benefit side in cost-benefit analysis and in particular the difficulty of how different types of benefits are to be weighed up. In cost-benefit analysis, the measuring rod is the money price that people would be prepared to pay to obtain benefits. By contrast, in cost-effectiveness analysis this measuring rod is not used.

Problems of allowing for a multiplicity of objectives have been notable in the sphere of health care – a sphere of inquiry where there has been a dearth of published studies of an evaluative nature in Ireland. On the output side in health care, there can be a number of different objectives. In the specific instance of care of the elderly, the objectives can include the maintenance of health and independence, social integration, and relief of the burden carried by family and friends in providing long-term care to elderly people (Wright, 1978, p. 47). Despite the difficulties posed by allowing for multiple outcomes in health care, 'modified' cost-effectiveness analysis has been used when comparing alternative ways of caring for people. One study (Wallston *et al.*, cited in Goddard 198, pp 25-26) uses interview data in order to ascertain weights to be applied to the outcomes on different dimensions, thereby leading to a single measure of outcome.

Evaluation of social policies

Relatively little published work is available in Ireland on the evaluation of social policies. One possible area, mentioned above, involves the care of the elderly and a particular method deserves mention, even though we do not have the opportunity to go into it in detail here. I refer to the 'production of welfare' approach. In one particular case, it has been used in assessing work on costs of residential care of the elderly (Knapp, 1981). This approach distinguishes between the final outputs of a project and the intermediate outputs. The final outputs consist of the impact on people: in the specific case of residential care for the elderly, they would consist of changes in individual well-being. The final outputs measure the degree to which objectives such as reduction in loneliness, and the provision of shelter and nutrition, are met. By contrast, intermediate outputs measure the services themselves, such as, in this example, the number of places provided in residential homes and the services provided within the homes. Much of the official discussion of care will refer to intermediate outputs, but a good deal of importance attaches to the final outputs which are often not estimated or considered. Indeed the ultimate objectives relate to the final outputs rather than to the intermediate ones.

In this approach, there are two types of input. Firstly, there are economic resources that are typically counted in evaluations of expenditure, that is the labour contributions and the capital equipment. Secondly, there are the non-resource inputs which would include the social and caring environment within the home in this example, and the characteristics of residents themselves. These are usually not considered in evaluation studies. Whether or not the provision of resource inputs has beneficial effects on final outputs can depend on the extent to which the non-resource inputs are working in the same direction. While there has been little or no application of this methodology in published studies in Ireland, it has been used in a number of evaluations in the

United Kingdom, including studies on long-term care of the elderly (Challis and Davies, 1986).

Public investment appraisal in Ireland

While this chapter concentrates on the evaluations done over the past two decades, assessments of the Public Capital Programme were also carried out, as indicated above, in the late 1960s and early 1970s. Published work includes studies by Bristow and Fell (1971) on Bord na Móna, by O'Donoghue (1968-69) on Aer Lingus, and by Mulvey (1970-71) on Irish Shipping. One inherent difficulty that arises in studies such as these is that they were concerned with relatively global operations of a firm or sector. That immediately leads to problems since the method of cost-benefit is more appropriate to a limited project where one does not have to take account of wider effects on the economic system. If one tries to apply the 'with-without' criterion to an economic sector, there are difficulties with working out the main inter-connections between that sector and the economy and society at large.

Since the 1970s, project work has continued within the Department of Finance (especially in the analysis section), in the Institute of Public Admin-istration and in individual state-sponsored bodies, although much of this work has not been disseminated. The lack of dissemination of evaluations is unfortunate, since that means that one of the main ways in which progress is possible – through debate and constructive criticism about alternative approaches – has to a degree been blocked. It also means that any 'outside' view on the state of evaluation will be based on only a part of the total pool of evaluations undertaken.

Much of the published work has been in the sphere of transport and in areas such as drainage – very much reflecting the classic origins of cost-benefit analysis. One example, worth noting for its level of detail and its concern with enumerating a wide range of effects, is by Farrell and Howard (1975). Another notable publication in the same area is a cost-benefit analysis of the River Maigue drainage scheme (OPW, 1978). The 1975 study was concerned with the arterial drainage system. The benefits comprised the increases in land-holders' incomes and the savings in terms of discontinued maintenance of earlier schemes; the costs comprised capital and maintenance costs, the investment by landholders, and the loss of income due to factors such as the widening of channels. The study compares a full scheduled scheme with an abridged scheme. However, three aspects of this study can be questioned. Firstly, benefits and costs are grouped into primary and secondary impacts. Ideally, all the impacts should be grouped together. Secondly, employment and training are treated as benefits while the opportunity cost of labour (discussed below) is treated as a cost. Labour costs should be entered on the cost side of the calculation, and should include any adjustment for opportunity costs, as discussed below. The inclusion of training raises at the very least the possibility of double counting. If output and hence income effects are calculated, this should embody the imparting of skills which are a part of the execution of the project. Thirdly, while some effort was made to consider a range of alternative investments, the range considered seems to have been a limited one.

In the mid-1970s cost-benefit was applied to the road programme (Barrett, pp 175-76). This study estimated the net benefits from investment in the programme. As tends to be the case in the evaluation of transport investment, the value of time savings accounted for most of the benefits. We have noted above that difficulties can arise when a global programme is assessed. In this particular case, the problem concerned the inter-dependency in the road network. One aspect of this is that if one segment of a road is improved, there can follow congestion elsewhere in an urban area. Another aspect is that a move to a higher level of service on the road system as a whole is not a marginal change, but has wide effect such as changes in aggregate demand and in costs throughout the economy. The study engaged in some testing of the sensitivity of outcomes to different values of time, but there was room for more sensitivity tests of this nature, for example to different values for accident costs, different rates of growth in car numbers and in traffic volumes, and different growth rates in the value of time savings over time.

A more recent study, the case of the Naas motorway by pass (Barrett and Mooney, 1984) had the advantage of dealing with a more delimited road investment. While it was estimated that there would be savings in accident and fuel costs, the bulk of the benefits consisted of time savings. The estimated rate of return was comfortably above the test rate of discount of 5 per cent in real terms that had been established in 1984 by the Department of Finance. The study tested the sensitivity of outcomes to different values put on the key elements. Among the different variations, the outcomes were most sensitive to variations in the value of time. While a money value was not put on the value of changes in the environment, a broad indication was given of the likely changes in noise, atmospheric pollution, and the physical environment.

In a subsequent paper, Mansergh (1985) queried these calculated returns on a number of counts. Among the questions raised by Mansergh, taking the Naas study as an example of an approach to cost-benefit analysis in general and its application to road investment in particular, are two that are central to evaluation. Firstly, does project evaluation take adequate account of the return to the exchequer: even if there is a high rate of return to investment, could the acceptance of the project actually worsen the state of the public finances? Secondly, what are the employment implications and are there alternative methods which would be more effective in increasing employment in the

longer term? These are key questions, concerned with two issues of central
concern to economic policy-making in Ireland, the state of the public finances
and the degree of unemployment. They are taken up further, below.

One point, though, should be made immediately. If employment impacts are
to be taken into account when comparing alternative investments, it should be
recognised that there is a limit to the extent to which there can be comparisons
of the net returns between projects that differ considerably in their nature. In
particular, it is questionable to what extent projects that use market prices to
different degrees can be compared: for instance, a traded good and a project in
health care. This was recognised by the National Planning Board (1984, Part
II.4) in the principles that it laid down for public investment planning. Thus,
the best that can be done may be to evaluate projects in such disparate areas,
within a given budget for each area.

In recent years the most contentious areas of transport investment have
concerned, not the inter-urban road network, but urban road investment. While
there are particular difficulties with the evaluation of urban road investment,
it is a pity that no evaluations, if any were done, of the main urban plans of
recent years have been made available. Among other things, evaluations could
have brought out the nature of the implicit values underlying the projects and
the extent to which the main difficulties arising in assessing them were faced.
Among the main areas of difficulty are the following: (a) the need to consider
a range of options, including public transport alternatives; (b) the assessment
of environmental impacts – not just on the natural environment but also on the
built environment, allowing for the additional difficulty that some of the
impacts on the built environment could be irreversible; (c) the social impacts
including those on the stability and location of long-standing communities; (d)
the likelihood that much urban road investment leads to the generation of more
traffic with implications both for congestion elsewhere in the road system and
for the extent of likely time savings.

A further area of difficulty in urban transport appraisal raises an important
general point. This is the link between pricing policies and the appropriate
level of investment. Put at its simplest: urban road users pay below the
incremental cost of their road use (see Barrett and Walsh, 1983). Hence decisions on road investment can be distorted and the benefits from urban
transport investment (which will reflect the number of people prepared to use
the roads at the current set of prices) will be overstated.

A related point came up in one of the classic studies of transport investment,
and indeed of cost-benefit analysis as a whole, that of the Victoria Line in the
London Underground. The initial study was done by Foster and Beesley
(1963). The study worked out the rate of return in cost-benefit terms and
showed that the discounted present value of the Line was positive at different
rates of discount. Several kinds of net benefit were estimated including time

savings, savings in outlays such as the operating costs of road users, and the value put on comfort and convenience. In a subsequent study (Beesley and Foster, 1965), the authors considered the implications for the rate of return, of different assumptions about how the investment was to be financed. The authors found that if the investment was to be financed through the traditional fare policy, that is, if London Transport engaged in a flat-rate percentage increase in fares, there would be a serious loss in net benefits. The second study worked out the implications for the rate of return of different pricing policies. This case raises one of the key areas of difficulty, not least in Ireland: the difference between the net return, calculated in the traditional manner using cost-benefit analysis, and the financial return to the government and its agencies. This is taken up further, below.

The largest single project evaluation exercise that is regularly carried out in Ireland is probably that of industrial projects undertaken by the Industrial Development Authority. Currently the expenditure of IDA grants amounts to approximately 8 per cent of the Public Capital Programme, but this under-states the relative importance of these projects in terms of the economy. One paper (McKeon, 1979-80) outlines the IDA evaluation procedures, at least at the time the paper was given. The steps involved are as follows: (a) a deter-mination of whether the project is commercially viable; (b) a determination of whether the grant paid, together with the costs of infrastructure to the exchequer, falls below a defined fiscal threshold; (c) a test of whether the contribution to the economy (essentially the net benefit in the classic cost-benefit sense, as outlined above) is at an acceptable level in cases (less than 5 per cent of the total, according to the paper) where projects are above the fiscal threshold. At this stage a few comments can be made on this paper; other issues raised are considered below under general problem areas of project appraisal.

Firstly, there is the oddity that the IDA, when considering projects, estimates likely impacts on the environment, yet in the economic evaluation these impacts on the environment are not taken into account. Secondly, there is the relationship between the discount rates used by the IDA and the discount rate used for public projects in general. The rated of discount used by the IDA is a 10 per cent real rate when assessing the fiscal returns. While it might be said in mitigation that the time period involved is a relatively long one, of 15 years, nonetheless this is a very high real rate. By comparison, the Department of Finance test rate of discount, as mentioned above, is 5 per cent in real terms. The UK treasury, not noted for its laxity, in April 1989 increased the required rate of return for nationalised industries from 5 per cent to 8 per cent (while increasing the required rate from 5 per cent to not less than 6 for the non-trading part of the public sector). Thirdly, there is the question of what is meant by commercial viability since in the IDA assessment in most cases it entails viability in the presence of a grant. Fourthly, there must be some concern over the 95 per cent of projects that are not subjected to a'cost-benefit' type appraisal, even in the qualified manner employed by the IDA. Among these are likely to be projects that are commercially viable (in whatever sense of the term one uses) but would show up badly on a full project appraisal.

Before turning to a brief overview of neglected areas of analysis, the guidelines for capital expenditure appraisal, contained in a Department of Finance circular of 1983 (circular 1/83, the appendix to which is reproduced in Dáil Éireann, 1985) should be mentioned. The procedures cover three major areas, namely, all projects costing over £5m; the annual reviews of the five year programmes in telecommunications, roads, sanitary services, health, education and housing; and complex or specialised projects. The procedures require, among other things, that all projects should contain a statement of the objectives of the project or programme, consideration of possible alternative ways in which the objectives of the project or programme could be achieved, a financial assessment covering costs over time in both cash and real (inflation-adjusted) terms and involving exchequer outgoings (both direct and indirect), an assessment of the distribution of the benefits and costs of the project or programme, and consideration of general economic effects on areas such as employment and the balance of payments. These principles are, in general, eminently sound and indeed refer to many of the issues already discussed here. However, the procedures do not highlight the necessity to take account of tax losses, which can be important in particular projects, and curiously only refer to sensitivity analysis when discussing financial flows to the exchequer. The treatment of exchequer effects is taken up below. It would be interesting, to put it at its mildest, to know what the experience of the evaluations has been in the period since this circular was issued.

Finally, in this section, we briefly consider the extent to which particular sectors have been ignored in the evaluation work done to date. Over the past two decades, only a limited number of investment areas have been the focus of published appraisals of capital investment in Ireland. Evaluation work has been notable by its absence in health care, in urban renewal and improvement to the general built environment, in at least some forms of anti-pollution measures and in public training services. Perhaps the greatest deficiency has been the absence of evaluations in the sphere of public expenditure on training. There is a significant amount of public expenditure on this pro-gramme; for example, the 'grant for training' to FÁS is currently some £40m and it would lend itself to appraisal. A number of interesting issues would arise in appraisals of such programmes, including the potential to make comparisons by using a control group: a group of people alike in all respects with the group receiving the 'treatment' (in this case training) except that they do not receive the treatment. In addition, the possibility of 'displacement' effects would arise – whereby people on the programme, coming, for example, from the ranks of the unemployed, would, when trained, displace workers who are in employment. There is also the question of whether, at the margin, publicly-financed programmes provide training services in some cases that would otherwise have been undertaken by private firms, thereby incurring unnecessary losses to the exchequer. Not least, there are potential income distribution impacts. Indeed there is always a potential tension between the use of public training programmes to help groups who are in some sense disadvantaged, and the use of such programmes to improve economic efficiency – that is to ensure that training that would boost aggregate demand actually occurs. Among the benefits of training programmes are the flows of increased incomes from the trainees, compared with the outcomes in the absence of the programme (the 'with-without' criterion). This is where the importance of a control group can come in, since the effects of policy need to be separated from what would have happened in any event.

Problem areas

Now the main problem areas that arise in project appraisal, taking account of the experience outlined above, are briefly considered. These are: shadow prices; the treatment of net revenue or net costs to the exchequer arising from projects; how to deal with risk and uncertainty; and the question of irreversibility in some projects.

Firstly, there is the question of 'shadow prices', mentioned at the outset: cases where prices do not reflect the true costs and benefits (at the margin) to the economy. The most important case that arises relates to the relatively high unemployment rate in Ireland. It could be argued that, in such a case, the extra cost to society of hiring an unemployed person is very low, since little or no output is sacrificed or foregone elsewhere in the economy, the person, say, being hired off the unemployment register.

An adjusted wage, called the 'shadow wage', could be used to calculate the wage bill associated with the project so that it reflected the opportunity cost to society of employing the labour required in the project. There is, however, little agreement as to how to arrive at this shadow wage, although because of high unemployment it is generally set below the market wage. In an extreme case it could be argued that if all the workers employed on the project would otherwise be unemployed, no output would be foregone by employing them on the project and hence the shadow wage for these workers would be zero.

Even if this assumption is accepted, it could be argued that account should be taken of the fact that workers employed on the project increase their consumption as a result of the income which they earn while so employed, and that this represents an increase in the output of consumption goods at the cost of investment goods to the community. Thus, even if it were accepted that those working on the project would otherwise be permanently unemployed, the conclusion would not necessarily be that the appropriate shadow wage would be zero. Furthermore, if there is a wage below which people would voluntarily remain unemployed rather than be employed, the shadow wage may need to be higher than indicated by the opportunity cost of labour.

At the other extreme to the view that the shadow wage is zero, is the view that if the workers in question would be readily re-employed elsewhere in the economy at roughly the same wages as must be paid to hire them for the project, the market wage would be the appropriate measure of their true cost to the project.

In assessing where, between these two extremes, lies the appropriate treatment of the shadow wage, it is important to consider the skill levels of the workforce employed in the project, and the workings of the labour market. Does the workforce on the project come from those who are employed elsewhere? In the case where an evaluation is done of a project which needs state subsidy to survive, one would need to estimate whether the employees could be fairly quickly absorbed into employment elsewhere if they lost their jobs. And, if so, would they in turn displace other workers from employment? In cases where there were unskilled workers who would face prolonged unemployment if they lost their jobs, current earnings from employment overstate the costs to the economy of employing these workers. The appropriate way to deal with this would be to recalculate the company's cost using a shadow wage in place of wages of these workers. This shadow wage would be calculated as the market wage *less* whatever allowance would need to be made for the fact that the value of the output which is displaced elsewhere in the economy by employing these workers may be less than their wage.

The implication of the above is that the shadow price of labour should not be regarded as something that is constant over time or something that is the same for all types of labour. One point of concern is that there is no consensus about the appropriate shadow wage and no guarantee of consistency about the shadow prices used across different public sector projects – and this could lead to distortions in the allocation of resources. It does seem that the shadow price of labour used in IDA evaluations has been low or zero in many cases of grant-aided industry (McKeon, 179-80) and the extent of the undercounting will depend on skill content and conditions in the labour market.

Honohan (1986) has argued that the actual shadow price of labour is much higher than the ratio of the wage rate that is often used. However, one of the planks in his argument has to be questioned. He argues that there is no guarantee that overall employment in a project will increase by as much as direct employment, and that unemployment will not fall in line with any increase in employment, referring to research which suggests that it takes about two new jobs to reduce the level of unemployment by one, even in the short run.

The point about the distinction between the direct increase in employment in a project and the total increase is well-taken; it is another aspect of the points made above about the need to take account of the skill levels and the nature of the labour market. However, the point about the 'slippage' between an increase in employment and a reduction in unemployment does not of itself mean that the shadow wage used has been too high. Among the reasons for this slippage are: (a) people come back from abroad to take up jobs in Ireland, and (b) people who are not counted in the register of the unemployed take up jobs. In case (a), if the aim is to increase total output and employment in Ireland (rather than output per head), the immigration to Ireland is not of itself an indication that the shadow wage is too high. In case (b), in a number of cases the people involved would be regarded as being in the labour force on a wider definition that would include those who had stopped looking actively for work because of discouragement, *or* had been denied unemployment benefit (for instance, on grounds of means-testing).

One way to approach the problem of the shadow wage is to use sensitivity analysis – testing the implications for the outcomes of different discounts applied to the market wage. This was the approach used in a study of natural gas allocation (in particular that component that went to fertiliser production) that did not employ a full-blown cost-benefit analysis (Blackwell *et al.*, 1983). Rather, this study engaged in an examination of various alternatives at the margin. Having started with commercial outcomes, account was taken of wider economic impacts including indirect employment effects and an allowance or a shadow wage. The sensitivity of outcomes of discounts to 10, 20, 30, 40 and 50 per cent from the actual wage bill was assessed. Two plants were investigated; in the highly capital-intensive plant, as would be expected, the discount used had little effect on the outcome. In the other more labour-intensive plant, there was a higher proportion of unskilled workers which meant that outcomes were more sensitive to the discount in that plant.

We now turn to the second of the four problem areas discussed in this section, namely, the question, already raised, about the treatment of net revenue or net costs to the exchequer arising from projects. This is a most complex area, partly because there is sometimes a lack of clarity about the distinction between gross flows to and from the exchequer, net flows to and from the exchequer, and the 'real' net benefits. Some of the flows to and from the exchequer will not affect the net benefits directly although they will have implications for the distribution of income. Take the example above of an evaluation of public training services. If trainees find employment, they will lose unemployment benefit, and gain a gross wage, out of which they will pay direct taxes (income taxes and social insurance contributions); at the same time, taxpayers will gain to the extent that their direct taxes are lower. While this simplified example does not pick up all of the financial flows, it does bring out the difference between the key net benefits (in this case represented by the additional gross wages of trainees who find jobs) and the gross financial flows.

The net financial flows usually mean that there is a net financial cost to the exchequer to ensure that a project occurs. Take the case of a transport project. Having counted up all the benefits and costs (which can include the government as a direct beneficiary, e.g. lower transport costs associated with government transport use), the project may need a government subsidy if is to go ahead. This is a particular case of the point made above in relation to the Victoria Line study: the need to take account of the means used to finance a project. In the case where a net government payment is needed, that will involve additional taxation and, as argued by Honohan (1986), the 'real' costs for the economy of the levying of that taxation should be taken into account. This means that in the case where an increased subsidy needed for a project to occur is exactly balanced by increased tax revenue, there could still be an additional real burden on the economy.

Often the distinction between the income distribution implications of the financial flows and the 'real' economy effects working through the burden of taxation, is not made with sufficient force. While the Department of Finance guidelines refer to income distribution effects, in practice there is a need to distinguish between the initial incidence of taxes and benefits and the final one (dealing with the ultimate beneficiaries and bearers of costs). The latter could be quite different from the former.

There are a number of ways of dealing with this problem. One is to work out the financing implications, followed by the taxation implications and then go back to adjust the net benefit calculations. Another way is to put a limit on the government budget – as a result, not all projects with a positive net benefit would be accepted but those showing a certain minimum benefit-cost ratio would be accepted.

The third of the four problem areas concerns the question of how to deal with risk and uncertainty. Stiglitz (1988) has said that the most common mistake made in dealing with uncertainties is to argue that, in the presence of risk, the government should use a higher rate of discount. The key point is to adjust the flow of net benefits to allow for risk, with risky projects involving a risk premium. The present values can then be worked out using the regular discount rate. Here the Department of Finance guidelines are less satisfactory than one would expect, since they say that the rate of return in a high risk project in a new technological area would have to provide a margin of 7 per cent over the cost of funds. Moreover, the guidelines do not advert to the need to take account of the likelihood that the further ahead the projected flow, the higher the likely degree of uncertainty.

A less formal way of handling uncertainty is to employ sensitivity analysis. Here the sensitivity of outcomes to different values for the key elements (e.g. prices and exchange rates) would be tested.

The final problem area concerns the question, as mentioned above, of irreversibility that can arise in some projects. Instances of this would be cases of 'development' in urban areas involving the destruction of buildings that were irreplaceable, or a project that led to a loss of amenity forever. This issue is likely to be of increasing concern, since as real incomes increase, there tends to be a greater concern with environmental issues, and also there tends to be increased pressure on facilities that are fixed in supply and not replicable (what Hirsch [1977] called 'positional goods'). The problem here involves a lack of symmetry. The option of 'no development' involves the possibility that there could be development at some later stage; while if development occurs, it cannot be reversed. In the context of environmental projects, a method of dealing with this, called the Krutilla-Fisher-Porter approach, has been outlined (OECD, 1989). Without going into detail, the net benefits of development in this approach would be the gross benefits of development, less the development costs, less the net benefits of preservation. In turn, the benefits of preservation are likely to increase over time relative to other benefits in the economy, partly because of the points made above about growing demand for goods such as the experience of natural beauty, and the fixity of supply. Such increase in benefits of preservation is allowed for in this approach.

Summary and conclusions

Given the size of the Public Capital Programme and the importance of efficiency in using resources, there is a strong case to be made for the systematic evaluation of capital projects in the public sector. This chapter has identified areas where there has been a notable lack of disseminated evaluations. The lack of dissemination of evaluations, even when they are made, is unfortunate, partly because it is possible to learn from mistakes. Such learning can take place, for example, by comparing the returns from projects after the event with returns that were predicted in advance.

In some cases, there may not be a need for full cost-benefit analyses. Nor will it always be desirable, since evaluation itself uses up resources. More limited investigations, at least at the outset, can often be useful. This can involve cost-effectiveness analysis. In addition, this work can identify, through the use of sensitivity analysis, the key elements on which the net returns from the project can depend. In turn, this can suggest the issues which could be the subject of more detailed investigation.

The importance of considering appropriate alternatives has been a recurrent theme in this chapter. This is where one of the main skills in project analysis lies. The focus here should be on the key alternatives which exist at the margin, and the principal constraints on achieving improvements in efficiency.

Another theme has been that of trying to ensure some kind of consistency in appraising projects throughout the public sector. Two areas in particular where this has arisen are the choice of discount rate and the shadow price of labour.

Finally, there is need to link together the appropriate pricing of resources and the investment decision. This came up in the study of natural gas allocation mentioned above and in transport work. If pricing policies are distorted, the results of investment appraisal can give the wrong signals.

*

This article was first published in Hardiman, T. and Mulreany, M., (ed.) *Efficiency and Effectiveness in the Public Domain,* Dublin: Institute of Public Administration, 1991

REFERENCES

Barrett, S.D. (1975). 'The Economic Evaluation of Road Investment in the Republic of Ireland, *Journal of the Statistical and Social Inquiry Society of Ireland,* vol. 23, part 3, 1975-76, pp 1-36

Barrett, S.D. and D. Mooney (1984). 'The Naas Motorway Bypass – A Cost-Benefit Analysis', *Quarterly Economic Commentary,* January, pp 21-34

Barrett, S. and B. Walsh (1983). 'The User Pays' Principle: Theory and Applications', in J. Blackwell and F. J. Convery (eds), *Promise and Performance: Irish Environmental Policies Analysed,* Dublin: Resource and Environmental Policy Centre, University College, Dublin

Beesley, M.E. and C.D. Foster (1965). 'The Victoria Line: Social Benefit and Finances, *Journal of the Royal Statistical Society,* Series A, vol. 128, pp 67-88

Blackwell, J., F. Convery, B. M. Walsh, and M. Walsh, (1983). *Natural Resource Allocation and State Enterprise: N.E.T. as a Case Study,* Dublin: Resource and Environmental Policy Centre

Bristow, J.A. and C.F. Fell, (1971). *Bord na Móna: a cost-benefit study,* Dublin: Institute of Public Administration

Challis, D. and B. Davies, (1986). *Case Management in Community Care,* Aldershot: Gower

Dáil Éireann (1985). *Report of the Committee on Public Expenditure: Control of Capital Projects,* Dublin: Stationery Office

Farrell, G.J. and J. Howard, (1975). 'Aspects of Cost-Benefit Analysis of an Arterial Drainage Scheme', Paper at the Institution of Engineers of Ireland, February

Foster, C.D. and M.E. Beesley (1964). 'Estimating the Social Benefit of Constructing an Underground Railway in London', *Journal of the Royal Statistical Society,* Series A, vol. 126, pp 46-78

Goddard, M. (1989). 'The Role of Economics in the Evaluation of Hospice Care', *Health Policy,* vol. 13, pp 19-34

Hirsch, F. (1977). *Social Limits to Growth,* London: Routledge and Kegan Paul

Honohan, P. (1986).'Traps in Appraising Public Projects', *The Irish Banking Review,* Spring, pp 28-35

McKeon, J. (1979). 'The Economic Appraisal of Industrial Projects in Ireland', *Journal of the Statistical and Social Inquiry Society of Ireland,* vol. 24, part 2, 1979-80, pp 119-143

Mansergh, N., (1985).'The Value of Cost-Benefit Analysis of Road Projects', *Quarterly Economic Commentary,* April, pp 36-47.

Mulvey, C. (1970). 'An Application of Cost-Benefit Analysis to the Strategic Shipping Sector', *Journal of the Statistical and Social Inquiry Society of Ireland,* vol. 22, part 3, 1970-71, pp 38-68.

National Planning Board (1984). Proposals For Plan, 1984-87, 1984

O'Donoghue, M. (1968), 'A Cost-Benefit Evaluation of Irish Airlines', *Journal of the Statistical and Social Inquiry Society of Ireland,* vol. 22, part 1, 1968-69, pp. 155-180

Office of Public Works (1978). *River Maigue Drainage Scheme: Cost-Benefit Analysis*

OECD (1989). *Environmental Policy Benefits: Monetary Valuation,* Paris: OECD

Stiglitz, J. E. (1988), *Economics of the Public Sector,* 2nd. ed., New York: Norton

Wright, K.G. (1978). 'Output Measurement in Practice', in A.J. Culyer and K.G. Wright (eds), *Economic Aspects of Health Services,* London: Martin Robertson

3

The Fall and Rise of Cost-Benefit*

PATRICK HONOHAN

Following something of a lull in the early to mid-1980s, there has been a very substantial recovery in academic interest in issues of cost-benefit analysis. The reasons for this evolution are informative and help pinpoint what was less useful about previous work and what is likely to be fruitful in the future. The late 1970s and early 1980s trend towards the substitution of structural reform policies in preference to selective intervention by governments lies at the root of the decline in cost-benefit analysis around that time.

Role of cost-benefit analysis

Fundamentally, cost-benefit is designed to take account of market failures, i.e. of situations where market prices do not correspond to social value.[1] If there were no market failure, then optimising behaviour by profit-seeking enterprises and by individuals in households should result in a socially optimal outcome – no involuntary unemployment, no missed opportunities to get the most out of national economic resources, no unwarranted environmental degradation. But in the presence of market failure the prices prevailing in the market-place do not provide the signals and incentives that will lead to a good outcome. All of the major classical sources of market failure are relevant to the industrial policy problem:

> Externalities: for example, where my behaviour affects your opportunities, resulting in spillover costs or benefits not borne by me. If I am not taking account of (internalising) certain of the costs or benefits of my actions, I will tend to consume or produce what, from society's point of view is too much, or too little (in the sense that others would be willing to subsidise me to produce more or consume less). The relevance to industrial or R&D linkages will be evident.
>
> Absence of relevant property rights: for example, if nobody owns the water-courses or the seafront, then I can degrade the water quality by discharging waste without cost; whereas if the watercourse had an owner she would likely impose a fee that would induce me to curtail my discharges. This kind of situation is increasingly relevant in terms of the location decisions for heavy and other industry.

Monopoly power: for example, I have so much influence over the price I can charge that I will restrict output though marginal cost is below price. This can be potentially relevant in the labour market, where centralised pricing decisions may contribute to unemployment.

Taxation: it is not possible for the Government to raise enough revenue to meet various essential functions that it performs without introducing distortions to economic behaviour. Its high tax burden is a feature which Ireland shares with most modern industrial economies, and the distorting effects of taxation are so often perceived as a major source of economic inefficiency that they cannot be neglected in any list of market failures.

Since market-driven choices may lead to socially inferior outcomes, the cost-benefit analyst attempts to construct a set of 'as if', or shadow prices; these represent the prices which, if they prevailed in the market, would lead enterprises and individuals to make economic choices that correspond to the optimal welfare of all.[2] The use of these shadow prices to guide public investment policy, the policy of state enterprises, and other public interventions, is the goal of cost-benefit. By arranging that the public sector, in its direct economic interventions, behaves as if the shadow prices were in effect, the hope is that the economy as a whole will move closer to the optimum.[3]

Reasons for the decline in the use of cost-benefit

Decline in the use of cost-benefit analysis in the 1970s may be traced to a wider disillusionment with piecemeal state intervention.[4] Why limit oneself to making allowance for market failure in deciding the behaviour of state enterprises and state agencies if the sources of market failure could themselves be eliminated? This was the theme of the structural reform and structural adjustment movements, which were popularly manifested in Thatcherism and Reaganomics, but have actually guided economic policy initiatives since the late 1970s in most countries in the world, to a greater or lesser extent.

These movements were also informed by an abandonment of the assumption that publicly-owned agencies or enterprises would always pursue social goals in a single-minded fashion. Once the relevance of this classic problem of principle and agent was recognised, the technocratic approach of cost-benefit lost some of its attraction.

This is not the place to adjudicate on the success of the attempt to eliminate monopolies, increase competition and lower tax distortions. It is certainly the case that freer trade, the progressive completion of the single market in Europe, and the weakening of trade union power, have lowered the importance of many of the distortions to which cost-benefit solutions had been addressed.

For example, with free trade and elimination of foreign exchange controls, the notion of a shadow price of foreign exchange – once all-important in applications to developing countries, and also sometimes used for Ireland in the past – has lost all relevance.

The development of the international capital market as the residual source of borrowed funds, together with the removal of capital controls, has meant that the world interest rate has largely displaced shadow discount rates based on national rates of time preference or intertemporal substitution.

Despite the higher levels of unemployment which have prevailed since the mid-1970s, even the shadow price of labour has been set close to or at the market wage in the cost-benefit practice of several industrial countries.

The come-back

But cost-benefit has made a come-back. Why? Part of the reason is nothing more than a reaction to its comparative neglect in the mid-1980s. Not everything can be solved by structural adjustment, and government inevitably remains heavily involved in influencing economic activity. The continuing role for government and its agencies in project development and large-scale planning means a continuing need for consistent methods of evaluation which are not merely based on financial profitability. Thus the issue of transport congestion and the value of time saved, safety regulations and the value of a life saved, and such like, continue to require a cost-benefit type approach. The more obvious reason for the return to cost-benefit is the increasing public awareness of environmental issues which have not found satisfactory market solutions, and which inherently call for public policy intervention.[5] In particular it is increasingly private sector investment projects that are now being subjected to cost-benefit analysis, whereas in the past it was mostly public sector projects.[6]

If the shadow price can be worked out analytically, would it not be best for public policy to attempt to push market prices in the direction of the shadow prices, for example through taxation? This is the approach advocated in many environmental contexts, and it has much to recommend it. This solution does require a decision to be taken at the highest levels of government. In the context of the European Union, it may require supranational authority, or at least a co-operative international arrangement. Indeed, a world solution may be required for some large policies such as that relating to CO_2 emissions. It is the consideration that a higher layer of government may be required to achieve the best solution (equalising the shadow and market prices) that ensures a continued role for traditional cost-benefit interventions, i.e. public bodies acting on the basis of shadow prices which differ from market prices.

Layers of government and system-wide impact

Theoreticians have made significant progress in advancing our understanding of how to analyse the economy-wide impact of a cost-benefit procedure.[7] This so-called 'general equilibrium' approach will prove to be an essential component of our approach in this chapter.

An important element of recent theoretical work has been designed to clarify the appropriate behaviour of distinct layers of government which have different instruments at their disposal. Although the full optimum is attainable, it is important, in determining the optimal behaviour of a particular layer of government, to decide in advance what externalities it should take into account in deciding its actions, and what externalities it should leave uncorrected as being the appropriate responsibility of another layer.

The need for operational simplicity

Although the pendulum of political economy, and the emergence of environmental awareness, have been the main driving forces in the cycle of interest in cost-benefit in recent decades, there is another, more practical factor, which has proved to be important, namely the need for simplicity. Project appraisal techniques which had heavy data requirements, and required elaborate and opaque calculations to produce answers – many of which lacked intuitive appeal – were never likely to catch on in practice. Reappraisal by some of the authors of the most widely used cost-benefit manuals has pointed towards the need for a drastic simplification of cost-benefit procedures if they are to be applied in routine situations (such as arise with the industrial development agencies).[8] This message must be taken seriously in the overhaul of industrial policy appraisal procedures.

*

This article is an extract from Honohan, P., *Key Issues of Cost-Benefit Methodology for Irish Industrial Policy*, Dublin: Economic and Social Research Institute, 1998

NOTES

1   There is only a relatively small published literature on Irish cost-benefit, despite many unpublished studies. Gray's (1995) review of standard methodology contains some Irish case studies and references. Boyle (1993) describes the wider process of policy evaluation in an Irish context. There are many textbooks on cost-benefit analysis: a good recent one is Zerbe and Dively (1994). Dréze and Stern (1987) and Squire (1989) are fairly recent surveys at a more technical level. Layard and Glaisters (1994) updated book of readings surveys some of the unresolved or disputed issues. Finally, Department of Finance (1994) and HM Treasury (1991) are official appraisal manuals.

2   A large branch of cost-benefit analysis also considers the distribution of resources
     between individuals as a potential source of deviation from the social optimum
     efficiency. This branch recognises that, even if the economy were producing at
     maximum efficiency, the optimum might not have been achieved if welfare is
     unevenly distributed among members of society. Our approach will, for the most
     part, assume that the problem of distribution is addressed somewhere else in the
     policy structure, and must be taken as given by those involved in industrial policy.
3   One important issue here is that if certain segments of the economy are using
     shadow prices, while other parts of the economy are still responding to market
     prices the outcome could be worse than if all were responding to market prices.
     More sophisticated applications make sure that these general equilibrium
     considerations are taken into account in computing shadow prices for guiding
     public sector decisions.
4   In addition, certain self-serving applications of cost-benefit analysis helped
     discredit the technique in some quarters. The fact that choosing shadow-prices is
     by no means an exact science provided scope for the manipulation of cost-benefit
     techniques to become a potential source of distortion itself.
5   The cutting-edge of applied cost-benefit analysis at present is in the evaluation of
     unmarketable environmental goods, such as clean air and water, biological
     diversity (e.g. preservation of wetlands) and future climate risk. Attempting to
     determine the social value of this kind of thing by survey techniques, asking a
     representative sample of people what value they place on it ('contingent
     valuation'), raises conceptual and practical problems which are very hotly debated
     at present (cf. the debate between Diamond and Hausman, 1994 and Portney,
     1994). The area is likely to become increasingly important in industrial policy in
     Ireland in the future.
6   The present application is a hybrid: analysis of public grant policy directed
     towards influencing private investment decisions – though we do not explicitly
     cover the environmental issues in this paper.
7   Notably in Dréze and Stern (1987, 1990), Hoehn and Randal (1989).
8   Cf. Little and Mirrlees (1991).

REFERENCES

Boyle, R. (1993). *Making Evaluation Relevant: A Study of Policy and Programme
     Evaluation Practice in the Irish Public Sector*, Dublin: Institute of Public
     Administration
Department of Finance (1994). *Guidelines for the Appraisal and Management of
     Capital Expenditure Proposals in the Public Sector*, Dublin: Government Publica-
     tions
Diamond, P.A., and L.A. Hausman (1994). 'Contingent Valuation: Is Some Number
     Better than No Number?', *Journal of Economic Perspectives*, vol. 8, pp 45-64
Dréze, J., and N. Stern (1990). 'The Theory of Cost-Benefit Analysis', in A.J. Auerbach
     and M. Feildstein (eds), *Handbook of Public Economics*, vol. II, Amsterdam: North
     Holland
Dréze, J., and N. Stern (1990). 'Policy Reform, Shadow Prices and Market Prices',
     Journal of Public Economics, vol. 42, pp 1-47.
Gray, A.W., and N. Stern (1990). *EU Structural Funds and Other Public Sector
     Investments*, Dublin: Gill and Macmillan
Hanemann, W.M. (1994). 'Valuing the Environment through Contingent Valuation',
     Journal of Economic Perspectives, vol. 8, pp 19-44

Hoehn, J.P., and A. Randall (1989). 'Too Many Proposals Pass the Benefit-Cost Test', *American Economic Review*, vol. 79, pp 545-551

HM Treasury (1991). *Economic Appraisal in Central Government: A Technical Guide For Government Departments*, London: HMSO

Layard, R., and S. Glaister (eds) (1994). *Cost Benefit Analysis*, 2nd Edition, Cambridge University Press

Little, I.M.D., and J.A. Mirrlees (1991). 'Project Appraisal and Planning Twenty Years on', *World Bank Economic Review*, Proceedings of the World Bank Annual Conference on Development Economics, 1990

Portney, P. (1994). 'The Contingent Valuation Debate: Why Economists Should Care', *Journal of Economic Perspectives*, vol. 8, pp 3-18

Squire, L. (1989). 'Project Evaluation in Theory and Practice', in H. Chenery and T. N. Srinivasan (eds), *Handbook of Development Economics*, vol. II, Amsterdam: North Holland

Zerbe, R.O., Jr. And D.D. Dively (1994). *Benefit-Cost Analysis in Theory and Practice*, New York: Harper-Collins

4

Appraising Capital Expenditure Programmes*

PHILIP BYRNE

Introduction

The purpose of this chapter is to consider the most important techniques for appraising capital expenditure projects, namely, discounted cash flow (DCF) techniques. The chapter will treat the following: the principles of DCF, net present value (NPV), constant annual cash flows, relevant cash flows, internal rate of return (IRR), comparison of NPV and IRR, abandoning projects, sensitivity analysis, replacement theory, project control and evaluation.

The chapter will proceed by outlining basic principles and by using examples to illustrate important issues.

Underlying principles of discounted cash flow

Discounted cash flow is a capital expenditure appraisal technique founded on the concept of time value of money (TVM). People acting rationally prefer money now rather than at some future period of time or, in more formal language, they have a present value preference for money. The basis for this is that €100 now will be worth more than €100 in one year's time.

To understand the notion of TVM, we need to examine the workings of compound interest.

Example 1

An entrepreneur wishes to know the value of €20,000 invested at 10 per cent compounded annually over four years. Suppose we invest €20,000 for four years at 10 per cent per annum, then the compounded future value will be as follows:

Table 4.1: Compounded future values

End of year	Interest earned on investment	Total worth of investment
0	0	20,000
1	$20,000 \times 0.1 = 2,000$	$20,000 + 2,000 = 22,000$
2	$22,000 \times 0.1 = 2,200$	$22,000 + 2,200 = 24,200$
3	$24,200 \times 0.1 = 2,420$	$24,200 + 2,420 = 26,620$
4	$26,620 \times 0.1 = 2,662$	$26,620 + 2,662 = 29,282$

Thus, if you invest €20,000 at 10 per cent compound interest for 4 years, your investment will be worth €29,282 in four years' time. Year 0 in the first column means that no time has yet elapsed. Year 1 means at the end of the first year and so on.

The values in this example could also have been calculated by using the following compound interest formula:

$$FV_n = PV_0(1 + K)^n$$

Where
FV_n = the future value of an investment in n years
PV_0 = the amount invested at the beginning of the period (year 0)
K = the rate of return on the investment
n = the number of years for which the money is invested.

Thus the calculation for €20,000 invested at 10 per cent for three years is:

$$FV_3 = 20,000 (1 + 0.10)^3 = 26,620$$

Therefore given the choice of receiving €20,000 or €26,620 in three years' time we should be indifferent, as we have calculated that the value of €20,000 in three years' time will be €26,620 if we invest it at 10 per cent.

We can manipulate the compound interest formula to form the commonly used discounting formula which allows us to convert future cash flows into their present value.

$$PV_0 = \frac{FV_n}{(1 + K)^n}$$

As can be seen from the foregoing, €1 received today is not the same as €1 received one year from now, because money received today can be used to earn interest over the coming year. Thus €1 in one year's time would be worth €0.9091 today if the interest prevailed at 10 per cent. This is derived as follows:

56

PHILIP BYRNE

$$PV_1 = \frac{1.00}{(1 + 0.10)^1} = 0.9091$$

In Example 1, all of the year-end values are equal as far as TVM is concerned. Thus €22,000 received at the end of year 1 is equivalent to €20,000 received today and invested at 10 per cent (i.e. its present value). We can arrive at this value using the discounting formula as follows:

$$PV_1 = \frac{FV_1}{(1 + 0.10)^1}$$

$$PV_1 = \frac{22,000}{(1.10)^1} = 20,000$$

Net present value (NPV)

Net present value is the result when the initial investment is subtracted from the sum of net future cash flows of money discounted at the appropriate discount rate. If the NPV is positive, it is a financial management indicator of the financial worthiness of the project, and if negative, an indicator of the financial unworthiness of the project.

Establishing the financial worthiness of stand alone projects

Before a net present value can be calculated and analysed, the following steps must be followed:

• Establish the capital project's cash inflows and the possible savings for the enterprise. Examples of inflows are: project revenues, tax receipts, government grants and sale or scrap value of project assets. Examples of savings are: reductions in repair costs and in labour costs.
• Establish all the capital project's outflows. Examples of outflows are: initial investment, tax and working capital investment.
• Establish the life of the project.
• Establish the appropriate discount rate (rate of return). The discount rate is more commonly referred to as the cost of capital (i.e. cost of long-term borrowing).

The following example illustrates how to calculate NPV.

Example 2

Suppose the management of an enterprise is considering purchasing a certain type of machine. The machine which is estimated to have a 4-year life span, has an initial capital cost of €160,000, with a cost of capital of 10 per cent.

Inflows will occur as the machine is expected to achieve labour savings of €110,000 in Year 1 and €100,000 in the subsequent three years, and to have a residual/scrap value of €20,000 in the final year.

Outflows will occur because in addition to the initial investment of €160,000, the expected annual running costs are €50,000 per annum.

Table 4.2 allows us to establish the financial worthiness of the project by calculating the project's NPV. The positive NPV of €21,241 indicates a worthwhile project.

Table 4.2: Financial worthiness of a project

Year	Inflows	Outflows	Net flow	Discount factor	Present value
	€	€	€		€
0	–	(160,000)	(160,000)	$\dfrac{1}{(1+0.10)^0} = 1.0$	(160,000)
1	110,000	(50,000)	60,000	$\dfrac{1}{(1+0.10)^1} = 0.9091$	54,546
2	100,000	(50,000)	50,000	$\dfrac{1}{(1+0.10)^2} = 0.8264$	41,320
3	100,000	(50,000)	50,000	$\dfrac{1}{(1+0.10)^3} = 0.7513$	37,565
4	*120,000	(50,000)	70,000	$\dfrac{1}{(1+0.10)^4} = 0.6830$	47,810
			Net Present Value (NPV) =		21,241

* €120,000 includes €20,000 for scrap value.

In order to calculate the NPV, it is very useful to set out the data in the above tabular format. Discount tables, which are presented in Appendix I at the end of this book, provide a very useful ready reckoner for establishing the discount rate for any period of time.

Constant annual cash inflows

When the annual cash flows are constant, the calculation is relatively simple. Example 3 illustrates this.

Example 3

An enterprise has the opportunity to invest €1,000 in a project which will yield cash inflows of €600 per year for three years. The minimum desired rate of return is 10 per cent. The enterprise wishes to know if it should invest in this project.

The discount factors when the cash flows are the same each year are set out in Appendix I at the end of this book. These tables are known as annuity tables or cumulative present value tables. If you refer to Appendix I you will see that the discount factor for three years at 10 per cent is 2.487.

Table 4.3: Net present value using annuity table

Annual cash inflow	Discount factor	Present value
€		€
600	2.487	1,492
	Less investment cost	(1,000)
	Net Present Value (NPV)	492

The total present value for the period is calculated by multiplying the cash inflow by the discount factor. It is important to bear in mind that Appendix I can only be used when the annual cash flows are the same each year.

The following example is a more sophisticated method of calculating NPV with the use of annuity tables.

Example 4

An enterprise is considering manufacturing a new product which would involve the use of both a new machine (costing €150,000) and an existing machine, which cost €80,000 two years ago and has a current net book value of €60,000. The latter machine has so far been under-utilised and has spare capacity to contribute to the manufacture of the new product.

Annual sales of the product are expected to be 5,000 units, selling at €32.00 per unit.

Unit costs are expected to be:

	€
Direct labour (4 hours @ €2)	8.00
Direct materials	7.00
Fixed costs including depreciation	9.00
	24.00

The project is expected to have a 5-year life, after which the new machine would have a net residual value of €10,000. Because direct labour is continually in short supply, labour resources would have to be diverted from other work which currently earns a contribution of €1.50 per direct labour hour. Working capital requirements would be €10,000 at the outset rising to €15,000 by the end of the first year and remaining at this level until the end of the project, when it will all be recovered. The cost of capital to the enterprise is 20 per cent. The enterprise wishes to know the NPV and whether or not the project is worthwhile.

The relevant cash flows (which will be discussed in more detail in the following section) are as follows:

		€
• Year 0	Purchase of the new machine	(150,000)
• Year 5	Residual value	10,000
• Years 1-5	Contribution from new product	
	5,000 units × € [32 – (8+7))]	85,000
	Contribution foregone	
	5,000 units × 4 hours x €1.50	(30,000)

- The project requires €10,000 of working capital at the outset and a further €5,000 by the end of the first year. These cash outflows reduce the net cash flow for the period to which they relate. When the working capital tied up in the project is 'recovered' at the end of the project, it will provide an extra cash inflow (for example debtors will eventually pay up).

- All other costs, which are past costs, notional accounting costs, or costs which would be incurred anyway without the project, are not relevant to the investment decision.

- The NPV is calculated as follows:

Table 4.4: Net present value of net cash flow using present value and annuity tables

Year	Equipment	Working capital	Contribution	Net cash flow	Discount factor at 20% cost of capital	PV of net cash flow
	€	€	€	€		€
0	(150,000)	(10,000)		(160,000)	1.000	(160,000)
1		(5,000)		(5,000)	0.833	(4,165)
1-5			55,000	55,000	2.991	164,505
5	10,000	15,000		25,000	0.402	10,050
				Net Present Value (NPV)		10,390

The NPV is €10,390 and the project is worthwhile.

Relevant cash flows

Investment decisions, like all other financial decisions, should be analysed in terms of the cash flows directly attributable to them. These cash flows include the incremental cash flows following commencement of the investment.

Before looking at the cash flows that should be included in any discounted cash flow (DCF) analysis, we should note those items that should be excluded.

Depreciation. This is an accounting transaction, not a cash flow. Therefore depreciation charges should be excluded from DCF calculations. If profit figures after depreciation have been provided, the profits need to be converted into cash flows. This is done by adding back depreciation costs.

Apportioned fixed costs. The cost of producing an item may include an apportionment of factory-wide fixed costs using some standard basis for absorption. These should be excluded. Fixed costs may appear as a cash outflow in a DCF calculation, but only if it is known that they will increase as a result of accepting a project. Fixed costs appear in a DCF calculation as a cash saving (inflow) if they will decrease as a result of accepting the project.

Book values of assets. These are not cash flows and must be ignored.

Interest payments. In most cases it can be assumed that the cost of interest has been taken into account by the discounting process. Interest payments should be ignored since to do otherwise would be 'double counting'.

Sunk costs. Any sums that have already been spent or committed and cannot be influenced by the investment decision should be ignored.

The cash flows that should be included in the DCF calculations are those which are specifically incurred as a result of accepting the project and benefits, or losses, foregone as a result of not accepting the project.

Absolute and incremental cash flows

When deciding between two mutually exclusive projects, only one of which can be accepted, two approaches are possible:

- Discount the cash flows of each project separately and compare NPVs; or
- Find the differential (or incremental) cash flow year by year, i.e. the difference between the cash flows of the two projects. Then use the discounted value of those differential cash flows to establish a preference.

Either approach will lead to the same conclusion.

Example 5

Two projects, A and B, are under consideration. Either, but not both, may be accepted. The relevant discount rate is 10 per cent.

This example uses both approaches, namely, discounting each cash flow separately, and discounting relative (incremental or differential) cash flows. The cash flows are as follows:

Time	Project A €	Project B €
0	(1,500)	(2,500)
1	500	500
2	600	800
3	700	1,100
4	500	1,000
5	Nil	500

Discounting each cash flow separately yields the following outcome:

Table 4.5: Discounting separate cash flows

Time	PV factor @ 10%	Project A Cash flow	PV €	Project B Cash flow €	PV €
0	1.00	(1,500)	(1,500)	(2,500)	(2,500)
1	0.9091	500	455	500	455
2	0.8264	600	496	800	661
3	0.7513	700	526	1,100	826
4	0.6830	500	342	1,000	683
5	0.6209	Nil	Nil	500	310
NPV			€319		€435

Project B is preferred because its NPV exceeds that of A by
€ (435 – 319) = €116   €116

Discounting relative cash flows yields the following outcome:

Table 4.6: Discounting relative cash flows

Time	Project A	Project B	Incremental cash flow B – A	PV factor @ 10%	PV of incremental cash flow
0	(1,500)	(2,500)	(1,000)	1.00	(1,000)
1	500	500	Nil	0.9091	Nil
2	600	800	200	0.8264	165
3	700	1,100	400	0.7513	300
4	500	1,000	500	0.6830	341
5	Nil	500	500	0.6209	310
NPV of incremental cash flow					€116

In other words the net present value of the cash flows of project B is €116 greater than those of project A; therefore B is preferred. Both approaches give the same result but the latter provides a useful short-cut to computation when comparing two projects as long as it is known in advance that one must be undertaken.

Example 6

The following example is typical of problems relating to incremental cash flows:

An enterprise has decided to increase its productive capacity to meet an anticipated increase in demand for its products. The extent of this increase in capacity has still to be determined and a management meeting has been called to decide which of the following two mutually exclusive proposals, A or B, should be undertaken. Each proposal has an expected lifetime of ten years.

The following information is available:

	Proposal A €	Proposal B €
Capital expenditure:		
Buildings	50,000	100,000
Plant	200,000	300,000
Installation	10,000	15,000
Net income:		
Annual pre-depreciation profits	70,000	95,000
Other relevant income/expenditure:		
Sales promotion (note (i))	–	15,000
Plant scrap value (note (ii))	10,000	15,000
Buildings disposable value (note (ii))	30,000	60,000
Working capital required over the project life	50,000	65,000

Notes:

(i) An exceptional amount of expenditure on sales promotion of €15,000 will have to be spent in Year 2 of proposal B. This has not been taken into account in calculating pre-depreciation profits.

(ii) The enterprise intends to dispose of the plant and buildings in ten years' time.

The discount rate is 8 per cent. The enterprise would like to know which of the alternatives is preferable.

Since the decision has been made to increase capacity (i.e. 'to do nothing' is not an alternative), the easiest approach is to discount the incremental cash flows.

The tabular approach is still appropriate, particularly as the project lasts for 10 years.

Table 4.7: Discounting incremental cash flows

Time		A €,000	B €,000	B – A €,000	8% Factor	PV €,000
0	Capital expenditure	(260)	(415)	(155)	1.00	(155)
0	Working capital	(50)	(65)	(15)	1.00	(15)
2	Promotion	–	(15)	(15)	0.8573	(12.860)
1-10	Net income	70	95	25	6.7100	167.75
10	Scrap proceeds	40	75	35	0.4632	16.212
10	Working capital	50	65	15	0.4632	6.948
				Net Present Value (€,000)		8.05

The present value of proposal B exceeds that of proposal A by €8,050 at 8 per cent and therefore proposal B is preferred.

The foregoing example makes two assumptions. Firstly it assumes that the disposal value of buildings is realistic and that all other figures have been realistically appraised. Secondly it assumes that expenditure on working capital is incurred at the beginning of the project life and recovered at the end.

The incremental approach is effective in comparing two projects when one must be chosen. It may not, however, be reliable when neither project need be chosen. For example, if two projects both had negative NPVs the incremental approach would favour the project with the 'least negative' NPV. Of course, a manager with the freedom not to choose would in this case choose neither.

Internal rate of return (IRR)

For so-called conventional projects, i.e. those where a single cash outflow is followed by subsequent cash inflows, it is often useful to compute the internal rate of return (IRR) of the project. The internal rate of return is that discount rate which gives a net present value of zero.

It is sometimes known as the yield, or DCF yield, or internal yield, but these terms may lead to confusion and their use is not recommended.

In general, it is necessary to compute the IRR by trial and error, that is to compute NPVs at various discount rates until the discount rate which gives an NPV of zero is found.

The IRR can be thought of as the maximum rate of interest that can be paid on the finance for a project without making a loss.

Example 7

An enterprise wishes to make a capital investment of €1.5m but is unsure whether to invest in one of two machines each costing that amount. The net cash inflows from the two projects are as follows:

Time	1	2	3
Machine X (€,000)	900	600	500
Machine Y (€,000)	700	700	700

The enterprise wishes in the first instance to find the IRR of machine X.

At a discount rate of 10 per cent, the net present value is:

$$-€1,500,000 \quad \frac{€900,000}{1.10} + \frac{€600,000}{(1.10)^2} + \frac{€500,000}{(1.10)^3} = -€189,707$$

The aim is to find the discount rate that gives an NPV of zero. Since the project has a positive NPV at 10 per cent, the later cash flows have not been reduced (discounted) enough and a higher discount rate must be chosen; try 20 per cent.

At a discount rate of 20 per cent the NPV is calculated as follows:

$$-€1,500,000 + \frac{€900,000}{1.20} + \frac{€600,000}{(1.20)^2} + \frac{€500,000}{(1.20)^3} = -€43,981$$

This is clearly closer to the IRR than 10 per cent, but not that close. One can continue to try discount rates between 10 and 20 per cent or else use a short-cut.

- NPV has fallen from a positive €189,707 to a negative €43,981 (by €233,688) as the discount rate has increased by 10 per cent (from 10 per cent to 20 per cent). This is a fall of €23,369 per percentage point increase.
- To find the IRR the NPV needs to fall another €189,707.
- To achieve this, the discount rate must be increased by:

$$\frac{€189,707}{€23,369} = 8.12 \text{ percentage points}$$

- Therefore the IRR is 10% + 8.12% = 18.12%

This approach, known as interpolation, is one of a number of approaches that may be taken to calculating the IRR and is the only one to be considered here. The approach we have used can be generalised as follows:

$$IRR = A + \left(\frac{N_A}{N_A - N_B} \right)(B - A)$$

where
A = lower discount rate = 10%
B = higher discount rate = 20%
N_A = NPV at rate A = €189,707
N_B = NPV at rate B = − €43,981

Using this formula we derive the IRR for the foregoing example as follows:

$$10\% + \left(\frac{189,707}{189.707 - 43,981} \right)(20\% - 10\%) = 18.12\%$$

Figure 4.1 illustrates in the case of example 7, the relationship between NPV and the discount rate along with the determination of IRR. It shows that the NPV is zero at 18.12 per cent which is therefore the IRR.

Figure 4.1: The NPV and the discount rate

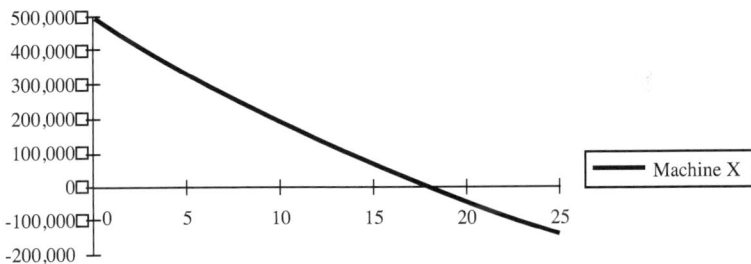

Net present value and internal rate of return

Different types of investment decision

We have considered two different DCF methods: NPV and IRR. When used to analyse a project, the decision is easily made:

• If a project has a positive NPV it should be accepted.
• If a project has an IRR greater than the required rate of return, accept it.

Since the two DCF methods are based on the same underlying principle – the time value of money — one would expect them to give identical investment decisions. This is not always so.

Different types of investment decision can be identified, namely decisions on

- single investment
- mutually exclusive investments
- projects with multiple yields.

The two DCF methods may not always give the same conclusion. The different types of decision are considered in turn.

Single investment decision

When deciding only whether or not to accept a single capital project, no ambiguity arises. A project will be accepted if it has a positive NPV; if it has a positive NPV then it will have an IRR that is greater than the required rate of return. Figure 4.1 above illustrates the point.

Mutually exclusive investments

Organisations may often face decisions in which only one of two or more investments can be undertaken; these are called mutually exclusive investment decisions. If NPV is used, the project with the highest NPV is chosen. If IRR is used, the project with the highest IRR is chosen. In these circumstances NPV and IRR may give conflicting recommendations. This is illustrated in the following example.

Example 8

An enterprise is considering two short-term investment opportunities, project A and project B, which have the following cash flows.

Project	Time	
	0	1
Project A (€,000)	(200)	240
Project B (€,000)	(100)	125

The enterprise has a cost of capital of 10 per cent and it wishes to find the NPVs and IRRs of the two projects. These are calculated as follows:

	NPV €,000	IRR %
Project A: $-200 + \dfrac{240}{1.10}$	18.18	20
Project B: $-100 + \dfrac{125}{1.10}$	13.64	25

The IRRs could be found either by trial and error or by using the interpolation formula introduced above. It is easier to notice that project A, over 1 year, earns €40,000 on an investment of €200,000 (a 20 per cent return) whilst project B earns €25,000 on €100,000 (25 per cent).

Project A has the higher NPV whilst B has the higher IRR and there is clearly a conflict between the two methods.

This conflict can be seen in graphical form. If the NPVs of the two projects were calculated for a range of discount rates and a graph of NPVs against the discount rate plotted on the same axes it would look as shown in Figure 4.2.

Figure 4.2: NPV v Discount rate for mutually exclusive projects

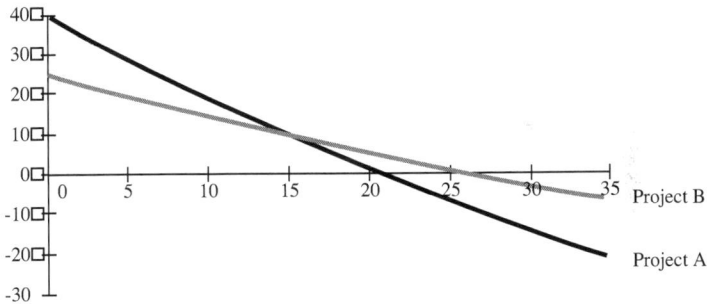

Each graph slopes downwards indicating that the NPV decreases as the discount rate increases for a 'conventional' project. The line representing project A starts at €40,000 (i.e. €240,000 – €200,000); the line representing project B starts at €25,000 (ie €125,000 – €100,000). The lines cut the horizontal axis in their IRRs of 20 per cent and 25 per cent and intersect at approximately 15 per cent. Project B has the higher IRR, whereas at the cost of capital of 10 per cent (in fact of any rate below 15 per cent) project A has the higher NPV.

Although NPV and IRR are based on the same principle of time value of money they are calculated in very different ways and there is no reason why they should give the same ranking for mutually exclusive projects.

Project A is preferred because it provides an incremental benefit of €4,540 (i.e. €18,180-€13,640) over project B when discounted at 10 per cent.

In general, for mutually exclusive projects the NPV method is preferred to the IRR. The NPV method, by choosing the project with the greatest net benefit in current money terms, ensures the largest contribution to the value of an enterprise. The IRR method, as shown in the example above, can choose a project which will add less value than is possible to the enterprise. The IRR method does not take cognizance of the size of a project and may favour an unsuitably small project simply because of its higher rate of return.

Projects with multiple yields

If mutually exclusive investments provide one reason why the IRR should not be used as a principal investment appraisal method, projects with multiple yields reduce IRR's status still further.

A weakness of the IRR method is that projects may either have no IRR or several IRRs as illustrated in the following example.

Example 9

Consider the following projects with cash flows over a three year period.

Table 4.8: Projects with irregular IRR

Time	Project A €	Project B €	Project C €
0	(5,000)	(10,000)	(100,000)
1	2,000	23,000	360,000
2	2,000	(13,200)	(431,000)
3	2,000	(1,000)	171,600

An enterprise wishes to know the NPV of these projects over the range 0–40 per cent at 5 per cent intervals and to see the results on three separate graphs.

Table 4.9: NPVs at 5 per cent intervals

Rate	0	5	10	15	20	25	30	35	40
NPVA	1,000	447	(26)	(434)	(787)	(1,096)	(1,368)	(1,608)	(1,822)
NPVB	(1,200)	(931)	(750)	(637)	(579)	(560)	(574)	(613)	(670)
NPVC	600	162	0	(25)	0	19	0	(76)	(219)

The three graphs are shown below.

Figure 4.3: Project A

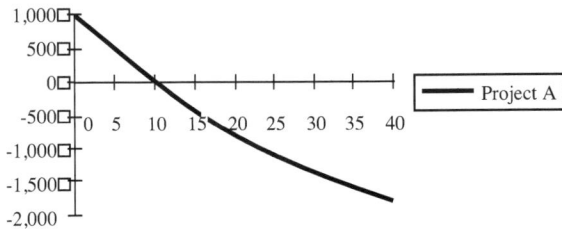

Project A is a 'conventional' project, with one outflow followed by several net inflows and shows the expected pattern of NPV decreasing as the discount rate increases. Table 4.9 shows that Project A has one IRR at just under 10 per cent.

Figure 4.4: Project B

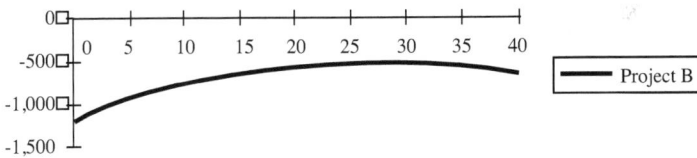

Project B has no IRR. Project B's cash flows could be described as unconventional with outflows of a significant size appearing at the beginning and end of the 'project' (which is always unprofitable but is least unprofitable at 25 per cent).

Figure 4.5: Project C

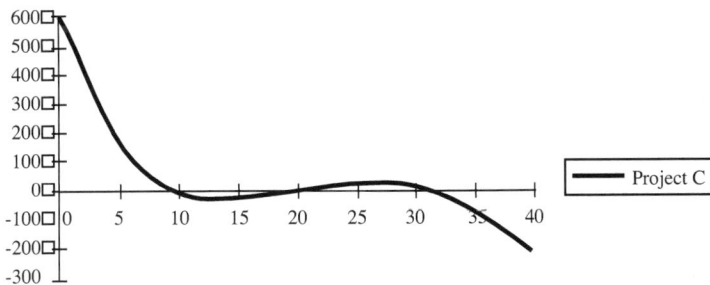

Project C's cash flows alternate between being outflows and inflows and the graph of the NPV and IRR alternatively falls and rises. Project C has three IRRs, at 10, 20 and 30 per cent.

The feature of projects which causes the graph of the NPV and the discount rate to change from the standard shape, as shown by Project A, is more than one 'change in sign'. Project A had an outflow followed by inflows (one change in sign), whereas Project B had outflows, then inflows (a first change in sign), but then further outflows (a second change in sign).

There may be as many IRRs as there are changes in sign in the cash flows. Clearly Project C has three changes in sign and has three IRRs, although Project B has two changes in sign but no IRRs.

If Project B's cash flows were adjusted to delete the last outflow then there would be two IRRs. We can call this scenario Project D which can be represented graphically as follows.

Figure 4.6: Project D

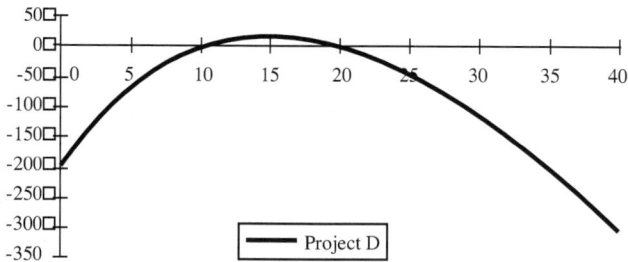

This type of cash flow pattern might occur with projects such as mining or oil exploration. An initial investment is followed by receipts from sales for a few years but at the end of the project the sizeable cost of reparations or shutdowns has a major effect on the project.

Clearly it is difficult to use the IRR method in these circumstances. Attempts can be made to modify the cash flows in such a way as to be able to find a single IRR without invalidating the analysis. However, this is cumbersome. Multiple yields merely provide further evidence that the NPV method is superior to IRR. Despite having several IRRs, projects will have only one NPV at the required rate of return.

Finally, we might note that the NPV method should be preferred in periods of interest rate volatility. Interest rate changes can easily be incorporated into NPV calculations. It is more difficult to allow for interest rate changes in IRR calculations because the IRR is based on an average rate of return over the life of a project.

Abandoning projects

Relevant costs and the decision to abandon

During our initial consideration of project appraisal, we noted that past costs were irrelevant to any decision about the future of a project. This remains true for those occasions when an enterprise has started a project and must decide whether it should continue with it or abandon it. The only relevant costs are future costs: these must be compared with future revenues to decide on viability or abandonment. Decision-makers in enterprises are often reluctant to abandon projects which are underway because it may reflect poorly on past decisions; however true this may be, it would be even worse to compound errors by making further poor decisions. Projects, therefore, must be kept constantly under review.

Cash flow patterns and the decision to abandon

We shall now consider two basic patterns of cash flow: firstly, negative cash flows followed by positive ones and secondly, a mixture of positive and negative cash flows throughout a project's life.

The first is the 'conventional' pattern, where, for example, a factory is built and then used to manufacture goods which will recoup the outlay as in the following:

Table 4.10: Conventional cash flows

Period	0	1	2	3	4	5	6
Cash Flow €,000s	−500	−1,000	−200	+750	+600	+500	+400

In this example, it is unlikely that the project would be abandoned before period 3, unless it transpired that estimates of inflows were wildly inaccurate and that future cash flow expenditure would not be sufficiently covered by future cash inflows. When period 3 is reached, there would seem to be little point in abandoning the project, as it is expected to generate net inflows from then on.

It is, of course, important to keep estimates under review to gauge their accuracy. It would probably be fatal for the project, for instance, if at period 3 a net outflow of €100,000 was achieved instead of an expected inflow of €750,000, as this would clearly indicate that the estimated revenues were seriously inaccurate.

The second pattern, namely a mixture of positive and negative cash flows throughout a project's life, might take the following form:

Table 4.11: Positive and negative cash flows

Period	0	1	2	3	4	5	6
Cash Flow €,000s	−100	+150	−70	+60	+80	−100	+150

Such a flow might occur, for example, if substantial replacements were necessary in periods 2 and 5.

This project would not be abandoned immediately after a negative cash flow, if positive flows were expected in later periods. Thus, we would not abandon it in period 2 or 5. We would have to consider at period 1, whether we should proceed to period 3 or 4; and at period 4, whether we should proceed to period 6.

Factors in the decision to abandon

The following considerations must be taken into account in deciding whether to continue or abandon a project:

• The costs of proceeding with the project

• The revenues associated with the project

• Revenues which would arise if the project were abandoned

• Other projects, which may be either alternatives to the project under consideration, or more profitable uses of funds tied up in the project under review.

Each of these factors must be consciously assessed at each stage of a project's life, and if it is seen that abandoning the project would be more beneficial than proceeding with it, then a decision to abandon must be made.

Example 10

An enterprise with a cost of capital of 10 per cent is undertaking a capital project with estimated cash flows from the outset as in Table 4.10 above:

Assume that the enterprise has made an initial investment of €390,000 rather than the €500,000 forecast. It is approaching the end of the first year and €1m is just about to be spent. The managers are happy about the accuracy of the inflows originally forecast for periods 3 to 6 of the project. However, they now believe that the outflow in period 2 is more likely to amount to €450,000 rather than the original estimate of €200,000. The enterprise wishes to know whether the project should be abandoned before the €1m is spent.

Table 4.12: Net cash profile

Period	1	2	3	4	5	6
Cash flow €,000s	−1,000	−450	+750	+600	+500	+400
10% discount factor	1.00	0.9091	0.8264	0.7513	0.6830	0.6209
Present value (€,000)	−1,000	−409.1	+619.8	+450.8	+341.5	+248.36

The NPV is therefore €251,360, so the project still has a positive expected NPV and therefore should not be abandoned.

Sensitivity analysis

A notable problem with any capital investment decision is that the figure reached in any calculation (a positive or negative NPV) is only as reliable as the estimates used to produce that figure.

One way of providing useful supplementary information for an investment decision is to consider a range of figures for various estimates and establish whether these give positive or negative NPVs. This exercise, sometimes referred to as posing 'what if?' questions, is relatively easy to perform with spreadsheet packages. However, it is important to be able to determine what variations in estimates are reasonable and what are unlikely. This analysis is usually applied to one estimate at a time although it can be applied to each estimate simultaneously.

A more concise form of analysis takes each estimate in turn and assesses the percentage change required to change an investment decision. It is customary to apply the analysis to single estimates although, if any relationship between variables is known, it can be applied to groups of figures. It is this form of sensitivity analysis that is considered here.

Example 11

An enterprise is considering investing €500,000 in equipment to produce a new type of ball. Sales of the product are expected to continue for three years, at the end of which the equipment will have a scrap value of €80,000. Sales revenue of €600,000 per annum will be generated at a variable cost of €350,000. Annual fixed costs will increase by €40,000 if this investment is accepted.

The enterprise wishes:
(a) to determine whether, on the basis of the estimates given, the project should be undertaken assuming that all cash flows occur at annual intervals and that the cost of capital is 15 per cent; and

(b) to find the percentage changes required in the following estimates for the
     investment decision to change:

   • initial investment
   • scrap value
   • selling price
   • sales volume
   • cost of capital.

The first question can be answered with the aid of Table 4.13.

Table 4.13: Initial investment decision

Period	Cash flow	15% Discount factor	Present value	€,000
0	Equipment	(500)	1.00	(500)
1–3	Revenue	600	2,28	1,368
1–3	Variable costs	(350)	2.28	(798)
1–3	Fixed costs	(40)	2.28	(91)
3	Scrap value	80	0.66	53

The NPV is therefore €32,000 and the project, on the basis of these estimates,
should be accepted.

The second question requires the use of sensitivity analysis. In order to find
the percentage change required in an estimate which would change an
investment decision, we will calculate:

$$\frac{\text{NPV of the project}}{\text{PV of the estimate in question}}$$

• Initial investment
  For the decision to change, the NPV must fall by €32,000. For this to occur
  the cost of the equipment must rise by €32,000. This is a rise of:

$$\frac{32,000}{500,000} \times 100 = 6.4\%$$

• Scrap value
  If the NPV is to fall by €32,000, the present value of scrap proceeds must
  fall by €32,000. The PV of scrap proceeds is currently €53,000; it must fall
  by:

$$\frac{32,000}{53,000} \times 100 = 60.37\%$$

(This would bring the scrap proceeds down by 60.37 per cent to €32,000; the PV of the scrap proceeds would be €21,000, i.e. a reduction of €32,000).

- Sales price
  If sales price varies, sales revenue will vary (assuming no effect on demand). If the NPV of the project is to fall by €32,000, the selling price must fall by:

$$\frac{32,000}{1,368,000} \times 100 = 2.3\%$$

- Sales volume
  If sales volume falls, total revenue and total variable costs fall; if the NPV is to fall by €32,000, volume must fall by:

$$\frac{32,000}{1,368,000 - 798,000} \times 100 = 5.6\%$$

- Cost of capital
  If NPV is to fall, cost of capital must rise; the figure to which the cost of capital has to rise, that gives an NPV of zero, is the project's IRR. To find the IRR we can commence by calculating the NPV at say 17 per cent by using summarised cash flows. The net cash inflow is €210,000 (i.e. €600,000 – (€350,000 + €40,000)).

$$NPV\ (\text{€,}000) = -500 + [210 \times 2.21] + [80 \times 0.62]$$
$$= 13.7$$

The IRR is a little more than 17 per cent, possibly 18 per cent. Using the formula introduced earlier in the chapter we get:

$$IRR = A + \left(\frac{NA}{N_A - N_B}\right)(B - A)$$

$$IRR = 15 + \left(\frac{32}{32 - 14}\right)(17 - 15)$$

$$= 18.55\%$$

The cost of capital would have to increase from 15 per cent to 18.55 per cent to cause the investment decision to change.

Replacement theory

The nature of replacement theory

Replacement theory is concerned with the decision to replace existing operating assets. The two questions to be answered are, when should the existing equipment be replaced? and what should be the replacement policy thereafter (i.e. the future replacement cycle)?

It is difficult to determine the replacement policy for existing assets in isolation, because that decision will be dependent on the cost of the future replacements, as will be demonstrated in the sections which follow.

Factors in replacement decisions

The factors to be considered include:

- Capital cost of new equipment. The higher costs of equipment will have to be balanced against known or possible technical improvements.

- Operating costs. Operating costs will be expected to increase as the machinery deteriorates over time. This is referred to as operating inferiority, and is the result of:
  - increased repair and maintenance costs
  - loss of production due to 'down-time' resulting from increased repair and maintenance time
  - lower quality and quantity of output.

- Resale value. The extent to which old equipment can be traded in for new.

- Taxation and investment incentives.

- Inflation. Both the change in the general price level, and relative movements in the prices of input and outputs.

Replacement techniques

There are various replacement techniques of which we will examine the lowest common multiple and equivalent annual cost approaches.

Lowest common multiple (LCM)

The lowest common multiple is the smallest number divisible by each of two or more numbers: 12 is the lowest common multiple of 2, 3, 4, and 6. Using this method the lowest common multiple of the various replacement cycles is computed and the present value of costs over this period is computed. Then the cost of replacement cycles is compared, e.g. the cost of 3 × 2 year cycles is compared with 2 × 3 year cycles.

The method rapidly becomes unwieldy. For a machine which can be replaced every five or seven years the lowest common multiple is thirty-five years.

Equivalent annual cost (EAC)

The neatest solution is to compute the present value of costs over one cycle and then turn it into an equivalent annual cost by the use of an annuity factor. Thus, the costs associated with any particular cycle can be considered as equivalent to having to pay this EAC every year throughout the cycle and throughout subsequent cycles. This will be made clearer by use of the following example.

Example 12

An enterprise must decide on replacement policy for vans. A van costs €12,000 and the following additional information applies:

Table 4.14: Trade-in allowance

Interval between replacement (years)	Trade-in allowance €
1	9,000
2	7,500
3	7,000

Table 4.15: Maintenance cost

Age at year end	Maintenance cost paid at year end €
Year of replacement	Nil
1	2,000
2	3,000

The enterprise wishes to know the optimal replacement policy at a cost of capital of 15 per cent. There are no maintenance costs in the year of replacement. In what follows, to simplify the calculation, we will ignore taxation and inflation.

It is assumed that a brand new van is owned from the beginning to the end of the cycle. We will now use the three techniques introduced above.

Lowest common multiple (LCM)

Since replacement is possible every one, two or three years the LCM is six and hence a six year period will be considered. First we will consider the case of replacement every year. The necessary information is laid out in Table 4.16.

Table 4.16: Replacement each year

Period	Capital cost (€)	Trade-in allowance (€)	Maintenance (€)	Net cost (€)	15% factor (€)	PV (€)
0	(12,000)	–	–	(12,000)	1.0000	(12,000)
1	(12,000)	9,000	–	(3,000)	0.8696	(2,608.80)
2	(12,000)	9,000	–	(3,000)	0.7561	(2,268.30)
3	(12,000)	9,000	–	(3,000)	0.6575	(1,972.50)
4	(12,000)	9,000	–	(3,000)	0.5718	(1,715.40)
5	(12,000)	9,000	–	(3,000)	0.4972	(1,491.60)
6	(12,000)	9,000	–	(3,000)	0.4323	(1,296.90)

The NPV is, therefore, (€23,353.50).

Next, we consider the case of replacement every other year. The necessary information is laid out in Table 4.17.

Table 4.17: Replacement every other year

Period	Capital cost (€)	Trade-in allowance (€)	Maintenance (€)	Net cost (€)	15% factor (€)	PV (€)
0	(12,000)	–	–	(12,000)	1.00	(12,000)
1	–	–	(2,000)	(2,000)	0.8697	(1,739.2)
2	(12,000)	7,500	–	(4,500)	0.7561	(3,420.45)
3	–	–	(2,000)	(2,000)	0.6575	(1,315)
4	(12,000)	7,500	–	(4,500)	0.5718	(2,573.1)
5	–	–	(2,000)	(2,000)	0.4972	(994.4)
6	(12,000)	7,500	–	(4,500)	0.4323	(1,945.35)

The NPV is therefore (€24,091.7).

In the case of replacement every third year, the necessary information is laid out in Table 4.18.

Table 4.18: Replacement every third year

Period	Capital cost (€)	Trade-in allowance (€)	Maintenance (€)	Net cost (€)	15% factor (€)	PV (€)
0	(12,000)	–	–	(12,000)	1.00	(12,000)
1	–	–	(2,000)	(2,000)	0.8696	(1,739.2)
2	–	–	(3,000)	(3,000)	0.7561	(2,268.3)
3	(12,000)	7,000	–	(5,000)	0.6575	(3,287.5)
4	–	–	(2,000)	(2,000)	0.5718	(1,143.6)
5	–	–	(3,000)	(3,000)	0.4972	(1,491.6)
6	(12,000)	7,000	–	(5,000)	0.4323	(2,161.5)

The NPV is therefore (€24,1091.7).

We can conclude therefore that annual replacement has the lowest present value of costs.

Equivalent annual cost (EAC)

The costs incurred over a single cycle are computed and the equivalent annual costs are shown in Table 4.19.

Table 4.19: Equivalent annual cost

Replacement	NPV of a single cycle	Annuity Factor	Equivalent annual cost $\left(\dfrac{\text{NPV}}{\text{annuity factor}}\right)$
Every year	$-€12,000 + \dfrac{€9,000}{1.15}$ $= -€4,174$	0.8696	$\dfrac{-€4,174}{0.8696} = €4,799.9$
Every 2 years	$-€12,000 - \dfrac{€2,000}{1.15}$ $+ \dfrac{€7,500}{(1.15)^2} = -€8,068$	1.626	$\dfrac{-€8,068}{1.626} = -€4,961.9$
Every 3 years	$-€12,000 - \dfrac{€2,000}{1.15}$ $\dfrac{-€3,000}{(1.15)^2} + \dfrac{€7,000}{(1.15)^3}$ $= -€11,405$	2.283	$\dfrac{-€11,405}{2.283} = -€4,995.6$

Comparing the three replacement choices, therefore, the optimal replacement period is every year (as it was in the previous instances).

Example 13

A company with cost of capital of 12 per cent wishes to determine the optimum replacement policy for its computers. Each computer costs €5,000 and can either be traded-in at the end of the first year for €3,000 (no maintenance cost paid) or at the end of the second year for €2,000 (€500 maintenance paid after one year). The company wishes to know the equivalent annual cost of each policy and which should be implemented. The calculation proceeds as follows:

Replacement every year:

NPV of one cycle $\quad = -€5,000 \dfrac{€3,000}{(1.12)} + \quad\quad = -€2,321.5$

Equivalent annual cost $\quad = \dfrac{-€2,321.5}{0.8929} \quad\quad = -€2,599.9$

Replacement every other
year NPV of one cycle $\quad = -€5,000 - \dfrac{€500}{(1.12)} + \dfrac{€2,000}{(1.12)^2} \quad = -€3,852$

Equivalent annual cost $\quad = \dfrac{€(3,852)}{1.69} \quad\quad = -€2,279.3$

Therefore replacing every two years is the cheaper option.

Conclusion

In this chapter we discussed how DCF techniques can be used to appraise capital projects. These techniques are treated in greater depth in texts listed in the references below. The capital investment techniques must of course be considered within the overall process of project control. Project decisions involving capital expenditure will affect the direction and pace of an enterprise's future growth, or perhaps, its very survival. If a wrong decision is made, it will be difficult to correct, particularly where special purpose plant is involved.

Of all the decisions taken by management, those concerned with investment are the most crucial: once made, they may fix the future of an enterprise in terms of its technological status, cost structure and the market effort required.

Once the product has been selected and the plant built, the enterprise is committed to the cost structure which accompanies them.

In order to control investment decisions, a capital expenditure committee may be formed, either as a sub-committee of the budget committee or as a separate meeting of the entire budget committee.

The functions of such a committee are to co-ordinate capital expenditure policy, appraise and authorise capital expenditure on specific projects and review actual expenditure on capital projects against the budget.

Capital expenditure requiring approval by the committee must be formulated by the managers. The amount of detail should be stipulated by the committee along the following lines.

- An outline of the project, including the budget classification and how it is linked, if at all, with other projects

- The reason for the expenditure – if a new project – and the departments affected along with an assessment of intangible benefits or disadvantages

- The amount of capital expenditure required (fixed and working capital), including a breakdown by budget periods, and an estimate of any work required within the enterprise

- A complete statement of incremental costs and revenue arising from the project, and the budget periods affected, along with an assessment of the effect of taxation

- The estimated life of the project

- An assessment of risks to which the project is sensitive – political, economic, competitive, natural hazards and so forth

- An identification of projects which are feasible alternatives along with comparative data

- The effect of postponement or rejection of the project.

Strict control of large projects must be maintained and the accountant must submit periodic reports to top management on progress and cost. A typical report would include such data as:

- Budgeted cost of the project, date started and scheduled completion date

- Cost and over- or under-expenditure to date

- Estimated cost to completion, and estimated final over- or under-expenditure

- Estimated completion date and details of penalties, if any.

The capital expenditure committee will seek explanations for any overspending that may have arisen. Where projects are incomplete and actual expenditure exceeds the authorisation, additional authority must be sought to complete the project. In so doing, the committee must consider the value of the project as it then stands and the additional value that will be gained by completing it, compared with the additional expenditure to completion.

A vital consideration is the adequacy of funds available. Where existing projects are overspending their allocation, other, perhaps more desirable projects may be delayed. When reviewing progress, therefore, the committee must consider the funds available, in the light of which it may become necessary to revise the order or priority in which funds are awarded to projects.

On completion of a project, an investigation should be undertaken to examine its profitability and compare it with the plan. Such investigations hold managers accountable and discourage them from spending money on doubtful projects. Moreover, it may be possible over a period of years to discern a trend of reliability in the estimates of various managers. If a similar project is undertaken in the future, the recently completed project will provide a useful basis for estimation.

This article was first published in Mulreany, M., (ed.) *Economic & Financial Evaluation: Measurement, Meaning and Management,* Dublin: Institute of Public Administration, 1999

REFERENCES

Anthony, R.N., J. Dearden and N.M. Bedford (1989). *Management Control Systems,* Illinois: R.D. Irwin

Bendry, M., R. Hussey and C. West (1996). *Accounting and Finance in Business,* London Letts Education

Brealey, R. and S. Myers (1991). *Principles of Corporate Finance,* Maidenhead: McGraw Hill

Broadbent, M., and J. Cullen (1994). *Managing Financial Resources,* London: Butterworth, Heinemann

Clarke, P.J. (1994). *Accounting Information for Managers,* Dublin: Oak Tree Press Publishing

Drury, C. (1996). *Management and Cost Accounting,* London: International Thomson Publishing

Fitzgerald, R. (1992). *Practical Business Finance,* London: Kogan Page Ltd

Franks, J.R. and H.H. Scholefield (1979). *Corporate Financial Management,* Aldershot: Gower Press

Gadella, J.W. (1996). 'Post-Auditing the Capital Investment Decision', *Management Accounting,* November, pp. 36-40

Glynn, J. (1987) *Public Sector Financial Control and Accounting,* Oxford: Basil Blackwell

Horngren, C. T., G. Foster and S.M. Datar (1997). *Cost Accounting: A Managerial Emphasis*, Englewood Cliffs: Prentice Hall Inc

Lucey, T. (1996). *Management Accounting*, London: D.P. Publications

Mott, G. (1991). *Management Accounting for Decision Makers*, London: Pitman

5

Elements of Appraisal*

DEPARTMENT OF FINANCE

These guidelines are intended to serve as a broad review of the main features of project appraisal and not as a detailed technical manual on the techniques involved.

Appraisal

The basic purpose of systematic appraisal is to achieve better investment decisions. The following step-by-step approach to the selection and appraisal of investment projects is intended to provide operational guidance to those considering projects involving the use of public resources. Given the wide variety of projects in the public sector, adaptations to suit particular circumstances may be required.

The diverse nature and impact of the wide range of projects across the public sector means that legitimate comparisons on a cross-sectoral basis may be difficult to make. Comparisons within relatively homogeneous areas of investment, such as between alternative courses of action within a programme, are more easily derived.

Needs and objectives

An important task of any public sector organisation is continually to reassess needs and objectives. New projects should only be undertaken where there is a clearly established public need for the product or service provided; existing services should be reviewed to ensure that the kind of service provided is the kind of service required and is on the appropriate scale. The aim should be, subject to resource constraints, to avoid 'bottlenecks', and also to avoid costly and wasteful over-supply, and/or under-utilisation of resources.

An objective is the explicit intended result of a particular programme or project, measured as precisely as possible. For example, there may be a need to improve traffic flow on a road. To state the objective of works on that road as being 'to reduce average journey times' would be unsatisfactory since it would not provide a basis for judging whether investment proposed to improve the road would produce sufficient benefit. Something more explicit is needed. 'To reduce average journey times between Town A and Town B by X per cent by the year 2000' is a precise objective. It assists in addressing such questions as: what are the various ways in which this objective can be reached? what costs and what results can be expected from each alternative course of action? and are the benefits sufficient to justify the costs?

Project and programme objectives should be expressed in terms of the benefits they are expected to provide and those whom they are intended to benefit. For example, road building programmes are not ends in themselves; they must be seen in the light of the needs of the economy as a whole and of the target groups for which the programmes cater (for example, freight traffic, tourist traffic, commuters, etc).

There is a need for realism in setting objectives. Where programmes have multiple objectives it is necessary to be clear about the relative importance of each and how this should be reflected in resource allocation and in the appraisal process.

Objectives should be expressed in a way which will facilitate consideration and analysis of alternative ways of achieving them. They should not be so expressed as to point to only one solution. For example, population growth may put pressure on the schools in a particular area and an objective might be expressed as being 'to build new schools in the area' to meet this pressure. The objective 'to provide school places to meet population growth within the area' would provide a basis for considering alternative ways of achieving this objective, such as the provision of new schools, the expansion of existing schools, on a permanent or temporary basis, or making better use of the existing stock of schools by provision of special transport (school bussing) arrangements.

Constraints

There will invariably be constraints in reaching objectives. There will normally be resource constraints. There may be technical constraints; for instance, there may be only a limited number of ways in which a product can be made, or a service delivered. Constraints may also arise as a result of previous policy or investment decisions, but these may be amenable to change. Constraints must also be explored, and fully taken account of, because they will limit the range of solutions which are feasible or acceptable.

The following is a checklist of the kinds of constraint which typically should be considered in appraising a proposal:

- financial

- technological

- legal/regulatory

- environmental

- physical inputs/raw materials

- availability of manpower and skills

- time

- administrative/managerial ability

- distributional (e.g. between regions, income groups, etc)

- social

- land use planning

- co-operation required from other interests

- general policy considerations.

Options

All realistic ways of achieving stated objectives should be identified and examined critically. This should be done with a completely open mind and should always include the option of 'doing nothing' or 'doing the minimum'. Different scales of the same response should be included as separate options, where appropriate. 'There should be no presumption that public sector responses are the only ones available; options which involve, or rely totally on, the private sector should also be considered. The alternatives should be described in such a way that the essentials of each alternative, and the differences between them, are clear.

Considering the possible alternatives in the light of the constraints will usually lead to the conclusion that some of the alternatives are not feasible. Others may conflict with existing policies. Where a conflict with existing policies occurs, it should be brought to the attention of decision-makers who then have the opportunity to review those policies. This may result in a change of policy, or in the widening of the focus of investigation. It may be inappropriate to proceed further with appraisal of alternatives until the policy issues are reviewed.

Objectivity is important in considering options. There is a danger that the selection of options may be manipulated in order to make a case for a course of action which is already favoured. For example, options for which there is a very weak case may be put forward in order to make a poor option look good. If the poor option is the best available it should be considered alone on its own merits.

Analysis of options

Different forms of analysis provide different kinds of information about investment proposals, and it is important to identify clearly, and to agree with the Sanctioning Authority, which forms of analysis are appropriate. The chief criterion used in deciding on the appropriate forms of analysis is whether or not the project is to be operated on a commercial basis (see Figure 5.1). Before discussing these forms of analysis, it is necessary first to consider a number of methodological issues which are common to some or all of them.

Discounting

For most forms of analysis, a critical issue is how to evaluate costs and benefits which occur at different points in time. Resources are said to have a time value, i.e. a given sum of money (cost, benefit or imputed value) is normally perceived to be worth more today than the same amount at a later date, even after taking inflation into account. Money values occurring at different points in time are converted to values at a common point in time through the process of discounting.

Analytic techniques

A variety of techniques to evaluate options is available. These appraisal techniques can be applied in a variety of forms of analysis. The main techniques used (most of which involve discounting in one form or another) are as follows:

Net present value (NPV) method

Revenues of a project are estimated, net of outgoings, and then are discounted and compared with the initial investment. The preferred option is that with the highest positive net present value.

Internal rate of return (IRR) method

The IRR is the discount rate which, when applied to net revenues of a project sets them equal to the initial investment. The preferred option is that with the IRR greatest in excess of a specified rate of return.

Figure 5.1: Identifying the appropriate type of analysis

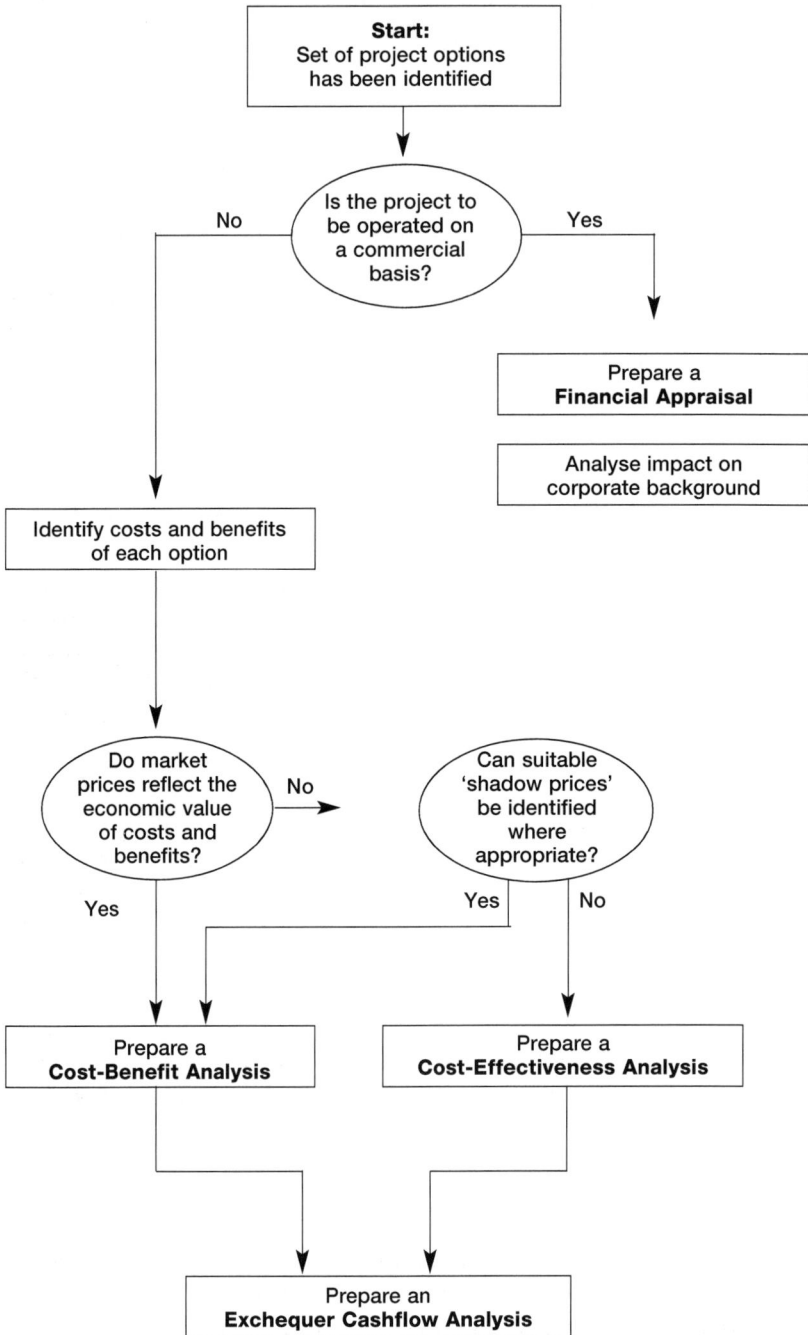

Benefit-cost ratio

The benefit-cost ratio is the discounted net revenues divided by the initial investment. The preferred option is that with the ratio greatest in excess of 1.

Payback and discounted payback

These methods identify how long it will take to pay back the amounts invested.

More details about these methodologies may be found in standard textbooks on financial analysis.

The choice of a discount rate is crucial to the application of most of the techniques listed above. This depends on the form of analysis being undertaken. In discussing each form of analysis below, the appropriate discount rate to apply is indicated.

Importance of NPV method

Applying different evaluation techniques to the same basic data may yield contradictory conclusions. In choosing between options A and B, the NPV method may suggest that A is preferable, while the IRR method may suggest that B is preferable. In such cases, the results indicated by the NPV method are more dependable. For this reason, the NPV method should always be used where money values over time need to be evaluated. However, the other techniques yield useful additional information and may therefore be worth undertaking also.

Appraisal of commercial projects

While the main thrust of the evaluation of commercial projects will be the financial appraisal as described below, major investment proposals in commercial state bodies should be considered against their corporate backgrounds. Issues that can usefully be addressed include:

- Would the investment involve a change in the overall corporate thrust of the body and is this advisable? What changes in the body's policies, organisation and personnel resources would be called for by the investment and is it feasible to put them in place sufficiently quickly?

- Would the investment be compatible with the body's corporate plan and, if not, should the plan, or the investment, be changed?

- Can the investment be financed without creating undue financial risk for the body? Could gearing (the ratio between debt and equity) become excessive? Could other necessary investments be crowded out?

- Are competitors planning or likely to undertake similar investments and what effect could this have on the profitability of, and case for, the investment?

- What effect will the investment have on the body's ability to remunerate its shareholders?

Assumptions about market growth, future prices for the firm's products/ services and for its inputs, interest rates and exchange rates (where relevant) should be closely examined. An assessment of the scale and distribution of the costs and benefits of the investment may also be undertaken, if relevant.

The financial restructuring of a commercial state body, involving capital injection or commitments (e.g. loan guarantees) by the state, normally requires a total review of its operations.

Circumstances differ so much that this document could not usefully attempt to give guidance save to say that the assumptions made in any restructuring plan on key variables, on targets and on actions should be realistic.

Financial appraisal

The key financial elements in appraising commercial projects are as follows:

Commercial cash flow analysis

This identifies the amount and timing of the cash inflows and outflows associated with each project option and discounts them to their net present value.

The discount rate should be appropriate to the organisation's cost of capital, the risk profile of the project and any other relevant factors. The rate used, and the rationale for its use, should be set out clearly in the project documentation.

Profit and loss account projections

These should show the impact of the project on the main revenues and costs of the organisation and should include a commentary where necessary.

The period of the projections should be appropriate to the life of the project.

Balance sheet projections

These should show the impact of the project on the finances of the organisation, with particular emphasis on its working capital, debt and reserves. Again, a commentary should be included where necessary.

The period of the projections should be the same as for the profit and loss account projections.

These key elements may be supplemented by other forms of analysis (internal rate of return, benefit/cost ratio, payback period etc.) where appropriate.

Sensitivity analysis of the project should also be undertaken, examining the effect on the key financial elements of varying the main assumptions of the project (including the discount rate) across an appropriate range.

Appraisal of non-commercial projects

In the case of non-commercial projects, two forms of analysis are required. These are (i) either cost-benefit or cost-effectiveness analysis and (ii) Exchequer cashflow analysis.

These forms of analysis assist in:

- establishing if there is a sufficient economic or social case for a proposal

- identifying whether or not the proposal under consideration can be afforded

- providing a basis for choosing between differing options and

- ranking projects in order within programmes.

Cost-benefit or cost-effectiveness analysis?

There are two basic forms of economic analysis, one of which should be applied in the appraisal of each non-commercial investment proposal:

Cost-benefit analysis

The general principle of cost-benefit analysis (CBA) is to assess whether or not the social and economic benefits associated with a project are greater than its social and economic costs.

Cost-effectiveness analysis

Cost-effectiveness analysis (CEA) compares the costs of different ways of achieving a particular objective. A choice can then be made as to which of these options (which all achieve the same or similar ends) is preferable.

Cost-benefit and cost-effectiveness analysis are very similar. Ideally, cost-benefit analysis would always be undertaken. However, there are situations where significant costs or benefits associated with a project cannot be quantified or valued and where this occurs cost-effectiveness analysis may have to be relied on.

Whether undertaking cost-benefit or cost-effectiveness analysis, a number of important considerations arise:

- There may be significant costs or benefits which do not affect the Sponsoring Agency but which are important to other persons or agencies or to society in general. These are usually called 'externalities' (i.e. they are external to the sponsor's direct concerns).

- There may be no market prices available for evaluating some costs or benefits associated with project options as they may not be traded items.

- In some cases, though resources consumed and outputs produced may be traded, the prices may not reflect the real value to society of those resources or outputs.

Externalities

Externalities arise in a number of ways. For instance, the benefits from a particular investment may make it attractive to the Sponsoring Agency but at a cost to others, due, for example, to the need to provide back-up infrastructure such as roads, water supply or waste treatment facilities.

Shadow prices

It is sometimes argued that distortions exist in the market prices for resources used in projects, or for the outputs of projects. The implication is that some other price, usually called a 'shadow' price (i.e. a price attributed to a good or factor on the basis that it is more appropriate than its market price) should be used. For example, when there is high unemployment, it could be argued that people employed in a project would not otherwise be employed in a productive way, and that the market cost of employing them should be replaced by a lower shadow price.

However, market prices are generally reliable and, normally, verifiable. They generally provide the appropriate basis for valuing a project's costs and benefits; they should be used, unless there are clear and convincing reasons that they are inappropriate and also that it is possible to derive shadow prices using a sound means of calculation.

If shadow prices are used, market prices, if available, should be applied also. If the analysis on both bases lead to differing conclusions, reliance should be placed on results using shadow prices only where it can be clearly justified.

Test discount rate (TDR)

The same basic discount rate (usually called the test discount rate or TDR) should be used in all cost-benefit and cost-effectiveness analyses of public sector projects. The recommended TDR is 5 per cent in real terms. By real terms is meant that, before discounting, all nominal flows of costs and benefits should be deflated by the expected level of general price inflation.

It may be appropriate from time to time, due to significant changes in real interest rates and in the rate of return on investments in Ireland, to vary the level at which the TDR is set. When such revisions are required, the Department of Finance will notify the Departments, Offices and public bodies concerned accordingly.

Cost-benefit analysis (CBA)

In cost-benefit analysis all of the relevant costs and benefits, including indirect costs and benefits, are taken into account. Cash values, based on market prices (or shadow prices, where no appropriate market price exists) are placed on all costs and benefits and the time at which these costs/benefits occur is identified. The analytic techniques outlined above (i.e. NPV method, IRR method, etc) are applied using the TDR.

The general principle of cost-benefit analysis is that a project is desirable if social benefits are greater than social costs. However, meeting this test may not necessarily show that a project should proceed, since other projects competing for the same limited funds may have a higher net present value.

It is vital that cost-benefit analysis is objective. Its conclusions should not be prejudged. It should not be used as a device to buttress a case already favoured, for or against a proposal. Factors of questionable or limited relevance to a project should not be brought into an analysis in order to bias the results in a preferred direction.

Cost-effectiveness analysis (CEA)

It is difficult to measure the value to society of public investment in social infrastructure (e.g. schools and hospitals) because the outputs may be difficult to specify accurately, and to quantify, and are frequently not marketed. In cases like these, the cost of the various alternative options should first be determined in monetary terms (although the benefits need not be). A choice can then be made as to which of the options (if they all achieve much the same effects) is preferable. CEA is not a basis for deciding whether or not a project should be undertaken. Rather, it is concerned with the relative costs of the various options available for achieving a particular objective.

Evaluating options in CEA is best done by applying the principles of the NPV method to the stream of cash outflows or costs. The recurring costs of using facilities as well as the capital cost of creating them should be taken into account, particularly if they differ between alternative options. Usually, the aim will be to select the option which minimises the net present cost.

There is a particular need for consistency in the assumptions and parameters adopted for CBA and CEA appraisals.

Appraising investment proposals within a single policy area

CBA and CEA can significantly assist the process of establishing investment priorities between projects which are similar in nature provided that:

- consistent parameter values are used

- there is a consistent practice on the factors properly to be taken into account in analysis. (The remarks made above concerning factors of questionable or limited relevance apply here.)

Establishment of parameter values for non-market items (e.g. time savings in respect of transport developments) should be as rigorous as possible.

Comparison of investment proposals across sectors/expenditure programmes

The comparison across sectors of investment proposals using cost-benefit analysis is difficult. However, it is important that the maximum degree of comparability is achieved. It is partly for this reason that the use of market rather than shadow prices is advocated. If shadow prices are used, it is important that the same, or at least not greatly divergent, shadow prices are used in different programme areas. If radically different shadow prices are used, the results of analyses cannot be validly compared and they provide no guide to investment priorities. Users of shadow prices are encouraged to consult as widely as possible, including consultation with the Department of Finance, in the interests of achieving consistency in the matter.

Unquantifiable benefits

It is not always possible to quantify and value all benefits or costs of a particular project option. This may result in a situation where one option would be judged preferable if estimated cash values only are taken into account. A different option may have a lower cash value but may bring additional non-cash benefits or have lower non-cash costs. When this occurs, results should be presented in a form which allows the decision-maker to choose whether the additional non-cash benefits (or lower non-cash costs) are worth the loss in cash value which is involved in taking the second option.

An example of this is the treatment of pollution. Pollution involves social costs, which may be impossible to value in monetary terms. Information should be given in analysis to enable decision-makers to judge whether the differences between the costed net social benefits of alternative projects are outweighed by differences in their uncosted pollution effects.

Exchequer cashflow analysis

Exchequer cashflow analysis should take into account flows both directly and indirectly associated with proposals, identifying the years in which the flows occur.

Direct cashflows include Exchequer expenditure on building works, employment, planning costs, equity participation, grants and so on, and income from such items as user charges and dividends. Additional expenditures for which the Sponsoring Agency is not responsible, but which a project will necessarily involve, should be included. EU finance passing through the Exchequer should be included. EU finance going directly to a body from the EU Commission need not be included in Exchequer cashflow analysis; however, it should be included in a separate cashflow analysis which should also be made available to the Sponsoring Agency.

Indirect Exchequer cashflows (e.g. savings on unemployment payments, additional tax revenues) may be relevant but are not as amenable to reliable costing. For instance, it is normally inappropriate to assume that income tax receipts from the workers employed in a project are attributable to any substantial extent to that project. To do so would overlook the fact that similar Exchequer income would derive from the use of the same resources in alternative ways. Similar considerations apply to savings on unemployment payments.

Any amounts attributed to indirect cashflows should be based on estimates of the extra costs or revenues over and above those that would arise in the absence of the project. The assumptions used in estimating indirect cashflows should be consistent with those used in the economic analysis. Indirect Exchequer income should not be viewed as an important factor in favour of a project given the difficulty in estimating it reliably.

*

This article is an extract from *Guidelines for the Appraisal and Management of Capital Expenditure Proposals in the Public Sector*, Dublin: Department of Finance, 1994

6

Proposed Working Rules for Cost-Benefit Analysis*

COMMUNITY SUPPORT FRAMEWORK EVALUATION UNIT

Section 1: Introduction

Outline of the document

This chapter is divided into three sections. The first section is the introduction, which includes two specific recommendations on essentially procedural matters relating to cost-benefit analysis. The second section consists of the proposed working rules themselves. The third section consists of a discussion of selected issues, where we felt it would be useful to explain the thinking behind the working rules.

Background

This chapter has been prepared at the request of the Community Support Framework (CSF) Monitoring Committee[1] following an earlier review by this Unit of cost-benefit analysis in the CSF[2] as well as the criticisms in the CSF mid-term evaluation[3] of a number of cost-benefit studies of Structural Funds projects.

In our earlier review paper, we examined a range of cost-benefit studies commissioned under the CSF[4] and detected general problems arising from a lack of consistency in the main parameters used and a tendency towards undue optimism in the estimation of socio-economic benefits. Specific weaknesses included the use of unrealistically low shadow wage rates, lack of clarity in identification of the counterfactual, use of baseline scenarios of doubtful plausibility, as well as problems with the treatment of taxation and the choice of discount rate. Many of the criticisms we made were echoed in the ESRI's mid-term evaluation of the CSF. The ESRI also drew attention to the difficulties inherent in the commissioning process for cost-benefit studies. They noted that the studies are generally commissioned by the sponsoring department or agency and that a political decision to undertake the project has often been taken in advance of the cost-benefit analysis. Except where a standard appraisal system exists, as in the industry and transport areas, the ESRI recommended that cost-benefit analyses should be commissioned by the CSF Evaluation Unit. They also recommended that they be undertaken prior to a public commitment being made to the project.

Objectives and applicability

Our objective with this document is to present a set of working rules which will lead to more consistency and rigour in future cost-benefit analysis applications and hence to better informed decision-making.

The working rules are intended for use by analysts and consultants undertaking future cost-benefit analyses. Necessarily, therefore, the intended users also include government departments and agencies which commission cost-benefit analyses or undertake them internally. The rules will act as a checklist for steering the work of cost-benefit analysts. This document is not intended as a guide or manual on the conduct of cost-benefit analysis.

Given our CSF context, the working rules were drafted to apply to Structural Fund investments where a cost-benefit analysis is required under the relevant regulations.[5] However, we recommend that they should also be applied, as appropriate, to other areas of public expenditure. Indeed, given the fungibility (or interchangeability) of money, the distinction between Structural Funds and Exchequer funds has no economic significance at the margin.[6]

The working rules should be read in conjunction with the relevant guides which have been prepared by the Department of Finance[7] and the European Commission.[8] The Department of Finance guide deals with the different stages of project appraisal and management. The Commission guide aims to assist officials in assessing projects and to inform experts of the Commission's requirements for cost-benefit studies. It outlines the relevant Structural Fund regulations, lists the main elements required in a cost-benefit study and provides specific guidance in respect of a number of sectors.

We also draw the reader's attention here to the two more detailed papers on cost-benefit appraisal which have been prepared for the transport[9] and industry[10] sectors. These papers should be consulted on sector-specific issues such as the valuation of accident and time savings (transport) and the treatment of deadweight effects (industry).

Approach taken

In preparing these working rules, we have undertaken an extensive review of international and domestic literature on cost-benefit analysis as well as related financial and economic literature (see bibliography). In particular, we have drawn heavily on the work of domestic experts such as Alan Gray and Patrick Honohan, international organisations such as the World Bank and the European Investment Bank and the guidelines prepared by the European Commission.

Concluding comments and recommendations

The application of the working rules should lead to more consistent and rigorous cost-benefit analysis. However, the rules clearly do not obviate the need for the analyst to exercise critical judgement in any individual study.

In parallel with the application of these working rules, improved administrative procedures for cost-benefit analysis need to be put in place. We have two recommendations in this respect, as follows:

- Where no standard appraisal methodology exists, a cost-benefit appraisal should be commissioned by an agency which is independent of the sponsoring department or state body.

- Where a standard appraisal methodology does exist (as is the case for certain investments in the transport and industry areas), it should be subject to periodic independent review. Similarly, the working rules which follow in Section 2 of this document, and particularly the parameter values set out in Rules 15, 17 and 18, should be periodically reviewed.

We note that Recommendation 1 above has already been put forward by the CSF mid-term evaluator.

Section 2: Proposed working rules for cost-benefit analysis

1. **Timing**: Cost-benefit analysis is a decision support tool. It should be undertaken at an early stage in the project selection process before any commitment, provisional or otherwise, has been entered into.

2. **Project identification**: A project subject to appraisal must be a clearly identified unit of analysis with all elements of the project being taken into account.[11] For example, in the case of an industrial project, any necessary additional supporting infrastructure requirements such as roads, water

supply etc., should be taken into account. A single cost-benefit analysis should not be undertaken for a group of projects which are not interdependent.

3. **Financial viability**: A cost-benefit analysis of a commercial or productive sector project should include a financial appraisal. A clear link should be established between the financial appraisal and the cost-benefit calculation in such a way that private and social benefits and costs are easily and separately identifiable.

4. **Counterfactual**: A cost-benefit study should clearly identify and examine a counterfactual (or alternative option) for comparison with the project under appraisal. The counterfactual involves an assumption (or set of assumptions) about the future state of the world in the absence of the project. Commonly used counterfactuals include the 'do nothing' and 'do minimum' options.

5. **Project rationale/strategic objectives**: The analyst should rigorously interrogate the rationale/strategic objectives of the project as put forward by its sponsors. This will assist the analyst in identifying the main socio-economic benefits and costs which can realistically be attributed to the project.

6. **Measures of net project benefit**: Net Present Value (NPV) or Internal Rate of Return (IRR) should be used as the measure(s) of net project benefit in both the financial and cost-benefit analyses. However, the analyst should be aware of the technical pitfalls associated with the 1RR.[12]

7. **Appraisal/timeframe**: The appraisal/timeframe should be the estimated economically useful life of the project. Productive sector projects should generally be appraised over a 10-year period. Infrastructure projects should generally be appraised over a 20-year period. Residual values and/or decommissioning costs at the end of the project's useful life should be included in the analysis.

8. **Estimation of project demand and costs**: It is important that demand and cost projections put forward by a project's sponsor should not be accepted at face value. Projections should be assessed rigorously and included in the appraisal at their mean expected values. Where necessary, analysts should obtain independent expert validation of projections.

Cost overruns are a particular problem. An examination of cost escalation on similar projects can help identify the potential for such overruns. A provision for contingent costs should also be considered.[13] A final reassessment of demand and costs should be undertaken if there is a significant time-lag between the appraisal and commissioning of the project.

9. **Identification of benefits and costs**: Only those benefits and costs which arise as a consequence of a decision to proceed with the project should be included in the appraisal. Where a benefit is included in the appraisal, the corresponding cost should also be taken into account.

10. **Displacement**: The possibility of the project displacing other economic activity should be specifically examined. The net benefit arising from the proposed project should be reduced in proportion to the estimated amount of the displaced activity.

11. **Estimation of value-added (income/employment effects)**: The net socio-economic benefit of a project consists of the additional value-added arising less the social opportunity cost of the resources involved plus the net social benefit or cost arising from externalities. The value-added element of this equation (definitions and calculation) is dealt with below. Externalities are covered in Rule 12. Rule 13 deals with the portion of value-added which goes to the Exchequer, i.e. taxes. Rules 15, 16 and 17 detail the shadow prices which should be used in calculating social opportunity cost.

   (i) *Definitions:* The additional value-added generated by a project is equivalent to the additional profit and wage income arising (corresponding to the additional employment of enterprise and labour). The additional value-added is generally classified in terms of three effects: the direct effect, the indirect effect and the induced effect. The direct effect consists of the additional profit and wage income directly created by the project. The indirect effect consists of the additional profit and wage income generated by the project's purchases of materials. The induced effect represents value-added resulting from expenditure out of the additional income arising through the direct and indirect effects.

   (ii) *Estimation of direct and indirect effects:* Direct (income or employment) effects should generally be calculated on the basis of estimates in the project proposal (subject to validation by the analyst). Indirect effects (and direct effects if they cannot be estimated reliably from the proposal) should be estimated using multipliers based on the CSO's input-output tables.[14] Care should be taken not to double-count direct effects when using these multipliers.

(iii) Induced effects: Induced effects should not be included in the analysis unless it is demonstrated that they have been calculated on the basis of a rigorous methodology using data for the Irish economy.

12. **Externalities**: Externalities are benefits or costs which affect third parties who are not charged for the benefit or compensated for the cost. External benefits include public good effects and beneficial spillover effects for third parties (e.g. new tourist facilities may benefit local businesses).[15] External costs include congestion effects and pollution. Only those externalities which represent a significant project outcome and which can be valued on the basis of a reliable, well-established methodology should be included in the actual cost-benefit calculation. Significant externalities which cannot be given a monetary value should be excluded from the cost-benefit calculation but nonetheless fully assessed in the cost-benefit report in such a way as to ensure their full consideration in the decision-making process.

13. **Taxes and subsidies**: To the extent that the economic activity arising from the project will be additional (i.e. not displaced), the tax revenues arising, including PRSI, should be included as a benefit.[16] (Care should be taken to avoid double-counting in this regard; taxation is a portion of the total value-added (benefit) generated by the project; it is not a benefit in addition to the total value-added generated.) Grant-aid and subsidies to the project should be included as a cost. Exchequer cash flows (taxes and grants) should be shown separately from other cash flows.

14. **Market and shadow prices**: As they typically best reflect the opportunity cost of the project's inputs, market prices should always be used in cost-benefit analysis unless there is a clear reason for doing otherwise. Shadow prices should be used where market prices do not reflect opportunity costs due to some clearly identified market failure.

15. **Shadow price of labour**: As per Rule 14 above, labour costs should generally be included at market prices unless an explicit case is made in the cost-benefit report for an alternative approach. (Such a case should be based on objective, quantifiable criteria, including national or regional labour market conditions.) In any event, the shadow wage used should not be less than 80 per cent of the market wage.

Where a shadow wage of less than the market wage is used, the appraisal should contain a sensitivity analysis on the basis of a shadow wage of 100 per cent.

In all cases, labour costs in respect of overtime hours should be included at the market rate.

16. **Shadow price of profit**: The shadow price of profit should reflect the opportunity cost of the capital in its best alternative use. This will typically imply a shadow price of 100 per cent except in circumstances where super-normal or windfall profits arise.

17. **Shadow price of public funds**: In order to take account of the distortionary effects of taxation, a shadow price of public funds of 150 per cent should be applied to Exchequer cash flows (taxes, grants and subsidies) to make them commensurate with private cash flows.

18. **Discount rate**: For *consistency across* appraisals, the official discount rate, as stipulated by the Department of Finance, should be used in all cases to take account of time preference.

19. **Treatment of risk and uncertainty**: The risk that project benefits and costs might deviate from their mean expected values should be assessed by undertaking sensitivity analysis (to check the impact of changes in endogenous assumptions) and scenario analysis (focusing on changes in exogenous factors). (See also reference to sensitivity analysis in Rule 15.) Where appropriate, the analyst should draw attention to the risk that a project may result in an irreversible loss of amenity which would preclude more beneficial future projects.

Section 3: Discussion of selected working rules

In this section of the document, we discuss certain key issues which have arisen in the course of our preparation of the working rules. In the case of most of the working rules, the reasoning behind them is self-evident. Accordingly, we focus here only on those rules which represent a departure from current practice or where we feel it is necessary to explain the basis of our conclusions. These are as follows: Rule 15 – Shadow Price of Labour, Rule 17 – Shadow Price of Public Funds, Rules 18 and 19 – the Discount Rate and the Treatment of Risk and Uncertainty.

Shadow price of labour

In Rule 15, we recommend that the shadow price of labour used in cost-benefit analysis should equate to the market wage except where there is a clear case for a different approach. In any event, a minimum shadow wage of not less than 80 per cent of the market wage should apply. With the exception of the appraisal model used by the industrial development agencies, this rule represents a significant departure from practice in Ireland up to now since much lower shadow wage rates have generally been used.[17] However, the recommendation brings us more closely into line with international practice.[18] The implications of the recommendation will be significant as the difference between the market wage and the shadow wage has usually formed a large part of the net socio-economic benefit demonstrated in cost-benefit studies.

In arriving at this recommendation, we have been guided by relevant literature, in particular by the work of Patrick Honohan. In his work on the development of an appraisal model for the industrial development agencies, Honohan, on the basis of research findings on the relationship between changes in employment and unemployment, concluded that a shadow wage of 80 per cent of the average actual wage should be used. (For larger projects, he suggested that sensitivity analysis using a shadow wage of 100 per cent of the market wage should be undertaken.) We have also been guided by the pronounced tightening of the labour market in recent years. The unemployment rate, which provides a measure of the extent to which there are labour resources with a low or zero opportunity cost, has fallen by some seven percentage points to 7.8 per cent in the four years to April, 1998, declining subsequently to just 6.4 per cent of the labour force in the final quarter of 1998.[19] We have also borne in mind the increasing reliance on immigration as a source of labour supply[20] and increasing evidence of unfilled vacancies in the economy.

Finally, we recommend that labour costs in respect of overtime work should always be included at the market wage or higher. Overtime wages are typically higher than normal market wages, reflecting the opportunity cost of leisure foregone. Labour inputs for a project are often accounted for in terms of full-time equivalents which may include standard and overtime labour units. It is important that a shadow wage is not applied to labour units which are receiving overtime rates.

Shadow price of public funds

In Rule 17, we recommend that a shadow price of 150 per cent be applied to Exchequer cash flows (taxes, subsidies and grants) to take account of the distortionary effect of taxation.[21]

Taxation gives rise to economic distortions by altering the incentives facing economic agents, leading to changes in their behaviour and reduced economic activity. For this reason, the shadow price of public funds is greater than one. Put another way, a €1 private benefit resulting from a €1 grant raised by extra taxation does not imply a neutral result for the economy. The distortionary costs imposed by the additional taxation must be taken into account. As Devarajan *et al* argue '[If] [these costs] are omitted, and public costs and private benefits are treated equally, the net present value of ... projects will be systematically overestimated'.[22] In practice, the distortionary costs can be incorporated in cost-benefit analysis by adjusting public benefits and costs by a factor to make them commensurate with private benefits and costs. Economic theory suggests that the distortionary costs of taxation vary roughly in line with the square of the marginal tax rate. Drawing on earlier research estimates for this parameter in Ireland in the mid-1980s, and taking into account reductions in marginal tax rates in the interim, Honohan (1998)[23] recommends the application of a shadow cost of public funds parameter of 1.5 (i.e. a shadow price of 150 per cent) in the appraisal model for the industrial development agencies. This forms the basis for Rule 17.

Aside from in the industrial sector, the use of a shadow cost of public funds parameter will represent a departure for the practice of cost-benefit analysis in Ireland. We are aware that the application of Rule 17 will imply a more rigorous form of appraisal being applied to those expenditure areas which are subject to cost-benefit analysis than to those areas which are not. We take it as given that rigorous project appraisal criteria should be applied across all relevant public expenditure. Furthermore, on this basis, Rule 17 applies as much in the case of a project funded solely by the Exchequer as it does in the case of a project funded under the Structural Funds. Again, the fungibility of money renders distinction between the different sources of funding somewhat meaningless at the margin.

The discount rate and the treatment of risk and uncertainty

The approach encapsulated in Rules 18 and 19 is that the discount rate should be used to take account of time preference only, with risk and uncertainty explicitly dealt with by undertaking appropriate sensitivity and scenario analyses.

There are different views on whether the discount rate should be used to account for risk aversion. Based on modern portfolio theory, the usual practice for private sector investment appraisal is to add a risk premium to the discount rate. On the other hand, Arrow and Lind[24] argue that public sector projects should use a risk-free discount rate. Gray (1995)[25] recommends against using the discount rate to account for risk on the basis that such an approach assumes that risks are compounding over time and in the same way for all costs and benefits, which can lead to a bias against long-term investments. He also notes that use of a higher discount rate to assess alternative cost streams will actually favour the more risky project. Having considered the matter in detail, we have come to the view that the inclusion of factors for both risk aversion and time preference in one single discount rate is an unsatisfactory approach.

There is no theoretical consensus on what the appropriate time preference rate for society should be. It is likely to differ from that of the individual for reasons such as length of life and imperfect information.[26] The approach which is generally used in practice is to use the real rate of interest on government gilts. This has the advantage of being readily available. In fact, the development of international capital markets and the removal of exchange controls means that such market rates should more accurately reflect social time preference rates, thereby avoiding the need to develop a notional or shadow discount rate.[27] The real rates used in the EU are generally between 3 per cent and 10 per cent.[28] The Department of Finance currently recommends a real rate of 5 per cent.[29] We recommend that the rate set centrally by the Department of Finance should be used in all future cost-benefit appraisals. This approach is also recommended by Saerbeck (European Investment Bank)[30] who argues that '[In] practice, many countries have an officially agreed discount rate, which although it may not be theoretically precise does have the advantage that all projects are measured by the same benchmark. So if such an official rate is available, it should always be used'.

*
This article was first produced as a report by the Community Support Framework Evaluation Unit in 1999.

NOTES

1   The package of mid-term review decisions taken by the Committee at its meeting of 29th July 1997 included a provision that the CSF Evaluation Unit 'produce ... a paper on cost-benefit analysis for the benefit of implementing departments and agencies'.

2   CSF Evaluation Unit, *Cost-Benefit Analysis in the Community Support Framework: A Critical Review*, June, 1997.

3   Honohan, P. (ed.), *EU Structural Funds in Ireland: A Mid-Term Evaluation of the CSF 1994-99*, ESR Policy Research Series, Paper No. 31, 1997.

4   The cost-benefit studies reviewed concerned the peat-fired power station, the proposed National Convention Centre at the RDS, the development of the National Museum of Ireland at Collins' Barracks, and national primary roads and rail infrastructure.

5   The new (1999) Structural Funds Regulations require that a cost-benefit appraisal be undertaken in the case of any project for which the total cost is greater than EUR 50 million.

6   Some of those projects which are funded under the Structural Funds are likely to have taken place anyway, funded by the Exchequer. (From the perspective of the EU, this can be characterised as a deadweight element.) Accordingly, the effect of Structural Funds can be to release Exchequer resources to fund other projects which might not have taken place in the absence of Structural Funds. Following this logic, the marginal project which Structural Funds may actually be funding is ostensibly funded by the Exchequer, while the project which would have gone ahead anyway is ostensibly funded from Structural Funds.

7   Department of Finance, *Guidelines for the Appraisal and Management of Capital Expenditure Proposals in the Public Sector,* July, 1994.

8   European Commission, DG XVI, *Guide to Cost-Benefit Analysis of Major Projects in the Context of EC Regional Policy,* 1997 Edition.

9   DKM Economic Consultants, *CBA Parameter Values and Application Rules for Transport Infrastructure Projects,* 1994.

10 Honohan, R., *Key Issues of Cost-benefit Methodology for Irish Industrial Policy,* ERSI General Research Series No. 172, November, 1998.

11 The Structural Fund Regulations (EC No 6959/99) define major projects as those 'which comprise an economically indivisible series of works fulfilling a precise technical function and which have clearly identified aims'.

12 For discussion, see chapter two in Gray, A.W., *EU Structural Funds and Other Public Sector Investments – A Guide to Evaluation Methods,* 1995.

13 For guidance on examining costs of infrastructure projects, the analyst should see European Commission, DGXVI, *Understanding and Monitoring the Cost-Determining Factors of Infrastructure Projects – A User's Guide,* April, 1998.

14 The multipliers from the CSO's input-output tables give the *average* input content for output by economic sector. Caution should be exercised when using multipliers from or based on these tables as they are generally only available after a long time-lag and may need to be updated to take account of price and productivity changes which have occurred in the interim. Account needs to be taken also of the current state of the economic cycle and of capacity constraints in the economy or in particular sectors. The multipliers can be distorted by sector-specific shocks. Generally speaking, it is important to bear in mind that a cost-benefit study is concerned with the project's marginal contribution whereas the tables give sector-wide average values.

15 As appropriate, the social benefits arising from spillover effects should be calculated in accordance with Rule 11.

16 In certain cases, indirect taxes contain a significant corrective component, e.g. in the case of excise duty on cigarettes. Such a component does not represent net benefit.

17 See CSF Evaluation Unit, 1997 and Honohan, 1997, op. cit.

18 For instance, Honohan, 1998, op. cit., points out that Canada and the UK use shadow wage rates of 95 per cent and 100 per cent respectively.

19 Indicators of potential labour supply also point to a tightening in the labour market with the broadest measure reported by the CSO (S3), declining by 5 percentage points to 10.6 per cent in the year to November 1998.

20 For example, gross immigration amounted to an estimated 44,000 persons in the year ending April 1998. Of this figure, 35,000 persons were in the age category 15-64, which effectively corresponds to working age.

21 While additional public expenditure can be financed through additional borrowing in the short-run, this will ultimately give rise to a tax burden on future generations.

Accordingly, all public expenditure can be looked upon as being funded from taxation.

22 Devarajan, S., Squire, L., and Suthiwart-Narueput, S., 'Beyond Rate of Return: Reorienting Project Appraisal', *The World Bank Research Observer,* vol. 12, no. 1, February, 1997.
23 Honohan, 1998, op. cit.
24 Arrow, K.J., and Lind, R. C., Chapter 4 in *Cost-Benefit Analysis*, 2nd Edition, Cambridge University Press, 1994, Edited by Layard, R. and Glaister, S.
25 Gray, 1995, op.cit.
26 See Stiglitz, J.E., Chapter 3 in *Cost-Benfit Analysis*, 2nd Edition, Cambridge University Press, 1994, Edited by Layard, R. and Glaister, S.
27 Honohan, 1998, op. cit.
28 European Commission, DGXVI, 1997, op. cit.
29 Department of Finance, 1994, op. cit.
30 Saerbeck, R., 'Economic Appraisal of Projects – Guidelines for a Simplified Cost Benefit Analysis', *Investment Bank Papers*, No. 15, December, 1990.

REFERENCES

Brealey, R.A. and S.C. Myers, *Principles of Corporate Finance,* Third EditionCopeland, T.E. and J.F. Weston. *Financial Theory and Corporate Policy,* 3rd Edition, Addison Wesley

CSF Evaluation Unit (1997). *Cost-Benefit Analysis in the Community Support Framework: A Critical Review,* June

CSF Evaluation Unit (1998). *Review of Ongoing Evaluation Function in the CSF,* October

Deane, B. and E. Henry (1993). 'The Economic Impact of Tourism', *Irish Banking Review* Winter

Department of Finance (1994). *Guidelines for the Appraisal and Management of Capital Expenditure Proposals in the Public Sector,* July

Devarajan, S., L. Squire and S. Suthiwart-Narueput (1997). 'Beyond Rate of Return: Reorienting Project Appraisal', *The World Bank Research Observer,* vol. 12, no. 1, February

DKM Economic Consultants (1994). *CBA Parameter Values and Application Rules for Transport Infrastructure Projects*

European Commission, DG XVI (1997). *Guide to Cost-Benefit Analysis of Major Projects in the Context of EC Regional* Policy

European Commission, DGXVI (1998). *Understanding and Monitoring the Cost-Determining Factors of Infrastructure Projects – A User's Guide,* April

Gray, A.W. (1995). *EU Structural Funds and Other Public Sector Investments – A Guide to Evaluation Methods*

Harberger, A.C. (1997) 'New Frontiers in Project Evaluation?, A Comment on Devarajan, Squire and Suthiwart-Narueput', *The World Bank Research Observer,* vol. 12, no. 1, February

HM Treasury (1997). *The Green Book, Appraisal and Evaluation in Central Government,* HMSO

Honohan, P. (1996). *Methodological Issues in Evaluation of Irish Industrial Policy,* ESRI Working Paper 69, January

Honohan, P. (ed.) (1997). EU *Structural Funds in Ireland: A Mid-Term Evaluation of the CSF 1994-99,* Policy Research Series, No. 31, Dublin: The Economic and Social Research Institute

Honohan P. (1998). *Key Issues of Cost-Benefit Methodology for Irish Industrial Policy,* ESRI General Research Series no. 172, November

Honohan, P. (1994). 'Traps in Appraising Public Projects', *Irish Banking Review,* Spring

Layard, R. and S. Glaister (1994). *Cost-Benefit Analysis,* 2nd Edition, Cambridge University Press

Nas, T.F. (1996). *Cost-Benefit Analysis, Theory and Application,* Sage Publications

Saerbeck, R. (1990). 'Economic Appraisal of Projects – Guidelines for a Simplified Cost Benefit Analysis', *European Investment Bank Papers, No. 15,* December

7

Cost-Benefit Analysis in the Community Support Framework: A Critical Review*

COMMUNITY SUPPORT FRAMEWORK EVALUATION UNIT

Section One: Introduction

Objectives of this study

Project appraisal is concerned with the optimal allocation of scarce resources. Its objective is to improve the quality and effectiveness of investment. The importance of this task hardly requires justification. Inadequate prior appraisal can lead to projects being chosen that provide low or even negative returns. Moreover, alternatives that could provide better returns might be overlooked. Poor quality investment ultimately represents a waste of resources with consequences for living standards and employment.

Improving the effectiveness of the Structural Funds in meeting their objectives means minimising bad investment decisions. This concern is reflected in several different articles of the Structural Funds regulations. It is also evident in the European Commission's guide to Cost-Benefit Analysis (1997). Poor quality investment will affect growth in the poorer regions, thus hindering convergence in per capita incomes and the attainment of regional policy objectives. Indirectly, it places an unnecessary burden on taxpayers from the more prosperous regions. From the Commission's perspective, the increase in the amount of Structural Funding in recent years has focused attention on this issue. Under the present round funds will total about ECU 150 billion, up considerably on funding under the previous agreement. There is also ECU 16 billion allocated under the Cohesion Fund. In total this represents a large level of investment which is mainly concentrated in Spain, Portugal, Greece, Italy and Ireland.

Naturally, the national authorities seek the highest possible return from public investment (a concern reflected in the project appraisal guidelines of the Department of Finance). Good project appraisal techniques are required to assist the optimal allocation of resources irrespective of how investment is funded. The issues that arise in the context of investment co-funded by the European Commission are relevant for investment funded exclusively by the national taxpayer. Accordingly, the conclusions and recommendations of this paper have implications for public sector investment generally.

Large scale infrastructural projects are an important part of the Community Support Framework for Ireland (CSF), 1994-1999. The success of these projects has a crucial bearing on its overall impact. Against this background, this paper examines the economic appraisal of projects funded under the CSF. The study is limited to a number of infrastructural projects funded under the Operational Programmes for Transport, Economic Infrastructure and Tourism. An examination of the appraisal of five different projects is undertaken. A separate section is devoted to each one. The methodological approach adopted for each is critically assessed, with due regard given to the complexity of the issues and the constraints within which the evaluation took place.

We are principally concerned with whether the appraisal has been undertaken in accordance with good practice. The identification of the project, the establishment of the counterfactual against which the proposed investment is judged and the extent of the sensitivity analysis will be examined. However, a key focus will be the treatment of costs and benefits in both the financial analysis and the cost-benefit analysis (CBA). For the latter the treatment of shadow costs, in particular of labour, and employment, income and tax multipliers will take up the bulk of our discussion. This is due to the apparent sensitivity of the results to assumptions on these issues.

The objectives of this paper are clear: it is hoped that gaps identified in present practices can lead to better project appraisals in the future.

Appraisal of public sector investment

These are similarities between the financial appraisal of private sector investment and the appraisal of investments funded from the public purse. Both involve the identification of costs and benefits and the estimation and assignment of monetary values for each element. The sums of these costs and benefits are compared after an appropriate adjustment for the time value of money. Decisions are based on maximising returns given finite resources.

Public sector project appraisal is more complex, though, for a number of reasons. Public projects are commonly geared towards the attainment of multi-objectives. Road investment, for example, seeks to reduce journey times and improve road safety. Complementarity between multi-objectives can lead to decisions involving complex trade-offs.

In contrast to financial appraisal, which considers the costs and benefits to the firm undertaking the investment, a CBA considers the wider implications for society as a whole. This involves aggregating the costs and benefits to individuals not directly involved in the investment decisions. This has implications for the pricing of inputs and outputs. In the appraisal of private investment, market prices are usually adequate. For many public projects, however, a market for the output might not exist. Alternatively, market prices – most notably for labour – might not be representative of the true costs and benefits to society as a whole. These prices require adjustment to more accurately reflect their opportunity or resource cost.

We will take account of the complexity of these issues in evaluating the robustness of the studies reviewed in sections 3-7 of this paper. Section 2 expands on the above discussion by briefly examining some of the main issues such studies ought to address. It will draw heavily on the various guides to CBA and some of the literature in the area. There are a number of specific issues which arise in the evaluation of Structural Funds Programmes. These will be discussed in the remainder of this section.

Institutional context

The appraisal of projects must take account of the administrative structure within which decisions take place. Account must also be taken of the precise resource allocation question being addressed. We deal with this issue first.

The purpose of project appraisal is to optimise the allocation of resources. It is evident that funding is not sufficient to finance all projects that may be considered worthwhile. It is essential to prioritise activities to be funded on the basis of agreed criteria. A project appraisal system might therefore be asked to answer a number of completely different questions. In broad terms the requirements will depend on the extent to which it is required for:

- ranking projects which are completely different in nature (e.g. environment *v* transport)

- ranking projects in the same general area (e.g. road *v* rail investment)

- ranking projects in the same specific area (e.g. road investment)

- ranking projects which are alternatives to achieving the same objective (e.g. different ways to by-pass a town)

- ranking projects of a similar type but with different objectives (e.g. water supply schemes which seek to improve water quality or increase capacity).

In essence the decision-making process within the Structural Funds area takes place at two broad levels. At the macro level agreement is reached on the indicative allocations across different areas. The first two points above might fall into this category. Within these allocations decisions are made on the projects to be funded.

For the purposes of this paper we will consider a small sub-set of the questions listed above. In the roads area, for example, a systematic approach has been developed to the appraisal of projects. Rates of return are calculated for proposed projects which are competing for funds within a particular programme. Clear guidelines have been set and each of the projects is appraised according to a consistent set of criteria. This enables a valid comparison of projects. But it does place particular demands on the project appraisal – for example the need to develop comparable data sources.

Most project appraisal relates, however, to once-off projects which are not, by definition, competing for funding against similar projects with a finite budget allocation. The bulk of the appraisals examined in this paper are of this variety. In these circumstances the crucial issue is whether the benefits of the proposed investment outweigh the costs to society as a whole. In an ideal scenario the project rate of return ought to be compared with the returns from alternative projects. If higher returns exist for projects elsewhere, whether within or across Programmes, funds should be re-allocated accordingly.

The reality, though, is that such comparisons are not made. For these projects, therefore, a positive net present value is sufficient to trigger a favourable decision. This has obvious consequences for the nature of the appraisal undertaken. As ranking of projects is not a requirement, ensuring a comparability of assessment through applying a similar evaluation methodology is not seen to be as important.

This is a weakness of project appraisal to which we will return often throughout this paper. Although comparisons with other potential projects are not formally made, account must be taken of the opportunity costs of funds in the treatment of costs and benefits in an appraisal. For example, the employment gains associated with a project are generally included as a benefit on the basis that the opportunity cost of labour is low. However, alternative uses of the funds also have positive employment impacts.

Again, we will return to this point later. However, it must be noted that the way in which an appraisal is undertaken depends on how the results are used. We take the somewhat purist view that, as far as is possible, common guidelines should apply to project evaluation. This reflects the point made above that there is an associated opportunity cost of a project to be funded from the same exchequer or EU source. Moreover, in the absence of such guidelines, it may be too easy to develop assumptions which overstate the true benefits of a project.

Finally, a particular project will give rise to a number of different benefits to society as a whole. Not all of these benefits will be linked to the objectives of the Programmes from which they are funded. A question arises as to whether these benefits ought to be included in assessing the project's overall return. On balance we believe that all costs and benefits should be included.

Wider administrative issues

There are a number of administrative questions of relevance to this area which we will briefly outline here but which are not touched upon again in the report. A key element of project selection and appraisal is the relationship between the agent implementing/ sponsoring the project and the decision-making body. This context has a strong impact on the process. In the Environmental Services area, for example, there are a number of projects competing for funding within a fixed budget. Initially, each local authority ranks project proposals according to priority on foot of an assessment of water and sanitary needs. The Department of the Environment subsequently chooses the projects to be funded from the lists submitted.

A related issue is when the actual appraisal should take place. From an administrative perspective, it is impractical for sponsoring agencies to conduct appraisal of each potential project identified. There is an obvious need for some form of initial screening. There are problems with this inasmuch as potentially worthwhile projects might not be submitted to the final decision-making body. The initial screening process will determine the quality of projects from which the department must ultimately make its final choices. Maximising the returns from the investment programme will, therefore, depend in part on the quality of this process.

Another consideration is the different objectives of the project sponsoring agency and the decision-making body. The primary focus of the former is the maximisation of funds. This can lead to circumstances where there is a clear incentive to exaggerate a project's net benefit. This in turn can lead to poor decision-making where verification of benefits is difficult.

The programme-based approach

Structural Funds are dispersed through nine Operational Programmes which comprise the CSF for Ireland. Project appraisal under the CSF gives rise to a number of particular issues due to the programme-based environment in which EU assistance is provided. These are examined briefly here.

Investment decisions are considered at two levels. Firstly, there is the establishment of priorities and allocation of funds within and across Operational Programmes (OPs). This is the subject of a negotiated process involving the National Authorities and the European Commission. Secondly, there is the selection of projects consistent with these agreed priorities and plans. This paper is concerned with the latter of these two questions.

Operational Programmes are in essence applications for assistance under the various Structural Funds. The Programmes contain an agreed set of objectives focused on a particular sector or priority. They include the strategy and analysis underpinning the investment plans. For the infrastructural OPs an indicative list of projects for which assistance might be sought are included. However, the projects listed are not necessarily those that will be submitted or approved for EU assistance. Within these plans the national authorities have considerable discretion in relation to the selection of projects that meet the objectives of the programme.[1]

However, for infrastructural projects which cost more than ECU 25 million (and for productive investment, projects which cost more than ECU 15 million) a cost-benefit study must be undertaken. These requirements will be examined in detail in the next section.

As discussed earlier, the decision-making process operates at two levels: the agreement of the programme document and the selection of projects consistent with the agreed priorities and plans contained therein. In some cases project appraisal begins and ends with the agreement of the programme document: the investment plans are acted upon in the absence of further formal appraisal. Projects are chosen from the small number that are consistent with the programme's objectives. The requirements of the Commission, in relation to larger projects, and of certain Monitoring Committees as noted, can make it slightly more complicated.

Accordingly, reaching agreement on the strategy within the CSF and the supporting OPs determines to a large extent the projects which receive funding. The evaluation of plans prior to inclusion in the programme document, therefore, becomes crucial. The need for these ex-ante appraisals of both Programmes and CSFs are part of the Commission regulations. These state 'that in order to ensure the effectiveness of Community assistance, measures taken for structural purposes shall be subject to appraisal, monitoring and after implementation, evaluation'.

In accordance with the regulations, prior appraisal of each of the Programmes took place. It is not our intention to examine the quality of these studies or the extent to which they influenced the final shape of the Programme. Our focus is on how projects are selected to meet programme priorities; we do not propose to examine the basis for the initial allocation of funds.

There is, though, a clear link between project appraisal at a micro level and issues related to the initial allocation of resources across measures and programmes. For example, high project rates of return estimated for roads investment assist agreements in favour of more road arguments. Moreover, any attempt to develop more sophisticated methods of capital budgeting would rely on project data and estimated returns at a micro level.

In reality, there are enormous practical difficulties with a budgeting approach based on cross-sectoral estimates of returns. Even with a CBA framework sectoral characteristics can undermine comparisons. For example, investment in road transport and environmental services are fundamentally different. Even within programmes, difficulties arise (e.g. assessing the relative merits of investment in different modes of transport). Despite these constraints a systematic approach to resource allocation can focus attention on the priority of maximising investment returns.

Section Two: Issues in cost-benefit analysis

Introduction

This section contains a broad sweep of the main issues in cost-benefit analysis. The main appraisal techniques are briefly outlined. This is followed by a discussion of the Commission guidelines on cost-benefit analysis which outline the main elements that ought to be included in an appraisal. In addition some of the more important issues are examined in detail. It is hoped to offer some broad conclusions on how these should be treated. The purpose of this section is to provide a basis for judging the appraisals subsequently reviewed.[2]

Appraisal techniques

There are different types of evaluation techniques that can be used to appraise public sector investments. No technique is appropriate for every situation. Nor is there a technique which acts as a complete substitute for the application of some form of judgement. The most appropriate technique will depend in part on the question to be asked and how the results are to be used.

The type of project to be appraised is also important. A full CBA of environmental projects, for example, is difficult due to the measurement of benefits linked to environmental improvements. Multi-objectives or a lack of clarity in the specification of objectives also influence the choice of technique. Data availability is an additional factor.

There are three main types of appraisal techniques: cost-effectiveness, multi-criteria analysis and cost-benefit analysis.

Cost-effectiveness aims to choose the most cost-effective way of achieving an objective. Only costs are calculated as the output or benefit of a project is fixed. It is only appropriate where the project has a single well-defined objective.

Multi-criteria analysis is in many ways more complex than the other techniques. This technique assesses and scores projects (but not on a monetary basis) against a number of specified criteria. Weights are attached to each criteria, summed and discounted to arrive at the present value of benefits. This is then compared with the present value of costs. Rankings can be developed using this approach but it cannot be used to determine whether a project would provide a net benefit to society. It is appropriate for projects of a similar type with multi-objectives.

Cost-benefit analysis seeks to measure the discounted values of all costs and benefits over the lifetime of a project. The valuation of costs and benefits is the main task involved. Shadow prices are used where market prices do not adequately reflect the true value of the resource to society due to distortions or externalities. When market prices do not differ from shadow prices, the calculation of discounted costs and benefits basically becomes a financial appraisal. CBA has its limitations but in many respects is the most comprehensive approach.

Issues in cost-benefit analysis

Project objectives

Appraisal studies must clearly identify the unit of analysis and the key socio-economic objectives that the project seeks to effect. These objectives should be related to the overall objectives of the Structural Funds. This is particularly relevant from the perspective of the Commission. Objectives must also be logically related to the project and expressed clearly.

There are cases where a project has several objectives. The primary objective of investment in rail infrastructure is to reduce journey times and the costs of transport, thus increasing access to markets and improving industrial competitiveness. An indirect benefit is to maintain employment in the railways as an overall objective of the Structural Funds is to increase employment. A dilemma arises in deciding the relative weighting to attach to these various objectives. For example if the benefits from journey times do not cover the costs of the investment should the secondary benefits be included in calculating the overall total costs and benefits of the project?

There are differing views on this issue. It could be argued that these secondary benefits apply to all capital projects inasmuch as alternatives to the proposal might yield similar results depending on the employment-intensive-ness of the investment. On this basis they should be excluded. However, a key objective of evaluation is to show the net benefit/loss to society from the investment, pointing to their inclusion. Comparisons with alternatives can be made if consistent underlying assumptions are adopted.

There is an additional issue of importance which is not considered in the guidelines. A project may lead to benefits which are not related to the Structural Funds' objectives. Investment in the road network seeks to reduce journey times for all road users. A monetary value based on wage rates is assigned to these savings, disaggregating between business and other users.[3] The objective of the investment is to improve competitiveness by reducing transport costs. Accordingly, should benefits to private car users be included? These benefits are analogous to increases in consumer surplus with no impact on competitiveness. While this might be considered a goal of national policy (and represents a welfare gain) it does not sit easily with the Structural Fund's objectives.

As mentioned above it is our view that all costs and benefits must be included. As will be discussed in Section 6 all time savings are included in the evaluation of road projects. Their exclusion, though, would not affect investment decisions given the high rates of return on this investment. Nonetheless it could be important for other projects where the benefits are less clear.

Feasibility and option analysis

Appraisals must also indicate that the project is the best feasible option and that other alternatives have been considered. This is particularly important given that a CBA might show that the project has a positive net benefit but might not be the best available option. This gives rise to two separate questions. Firstly, does the study indicate that alternatives have been considered? Secondly, is the project feasible?

This second question is usually answered by undertaking a financial appraisal. This seeks to establish whether the project will be adequately financed by calculating an annual inflow and outflow cash statement. The project's costs and benefits should be forecast over its economically useful life with an estimated internal financial return. For infrastructural projects a period of not less than 20 years may be appropriate.

A financial appraisal should contain information on physical inputs and outputs on an annual basis. Prices must be given to items either in constant or current terms. A financial appraisal differs from a CBA as the latter considers the wider societal impacts of a project. However, if market prices adequately reflect economic costs a financial appraisal may be sufficient.

For most evaluations reviewed in this paper, except in the transport area, both a financial appraisal and CBA are required. It is desirable that the appraisal develops a clear link between the two. In essence inputs/outputs and their respective prices in the financial appraisal provide the starting point for the estimation of the project's wider costs and benefits. The next step is: adjust market prices to take account of these effects.

Shadow prices

Including shadow prices, which differ from market prices, in a CBA will affect the net social value of the project. If shadow prices used are lower than market prices when estimating costs, the social value of the project increases compared with its private value. The estimated shadow cost of labour is particularly important. Adjusting the market wage rate on the basis of the low opportunity cost of labour is a common feature of the evaluations reviewed in this paper. Moreover, this adjustment explains a significant part of the estimated socio-economic benefits of these projects.

In general it is recommended that market prices be used in a CBA. The guidelines suggest that the full social costs and benefit of a project will not be captured by market prices when any of the following factors are relevant:

- actual prices are distorted by monopolies, trade restrictions, etc

- wages are not linked to labour productivity

- taxes or subsidies influence price structure

- there are externalities

- there are non-monetary effects, including environmental impact.

The rationale for correcting these distortions is that investment decisions on the basis of these shadow prices will lead to a more efficient allocation of resources. This is on the basis of some notional economy-wide social welfare function. In other words, assuming that the market wage for labour does not reflect its true opportunity cost, using this wage will lead to a lower level of investment than is optimal. As noted in Gray (1995) a comparison of financial and economic appraisals gives an indication of the degree of market distortions and externalities.[4]

The guidelines stress that the valuation of shadow prices ought to be prudent and consistent but no particular approach or specific indicators are suggested. This is an omission, particularly in relation to the shadow price of labour.

It is clear that key decisions about shadow prices are common to project appraisals across sectors. A lack of consistency in the application of shadow prices can undermine the usefulness of appraisal particularly when it seeks to identify the relative attractiveness of projects competing for limited resources. Failure to adhere to common criteria would represent a fundamental weakness of the appraisal system. In order to overcome such pitfalls it has been suggested (Gray, 1995; Fitzpatrick, 1993) that common guidelines on shadow prices, and other issues, are required.

Shadow price of labour

A key issue in economic appraisal is whether to adjust the market price of labour and if so by how much. A considerable part of project benefits is usually accounted for by the gap between the shadow and market price of labour. This reflects the view that the social opportunity cost of labour is low due to high unemployment. This cost is defined as the value of the alternative employment that an individual employed on the project could find without affecting the employment prospects of others in the labour market.

On the basis of this definition, and under certain assumptions about the Irish labour market, it is possible to recommend a shadow price of labour significantly lower than the market rate. Assuming the existence of structural unemployment and no displacement or other effects as a result of employment increases associated with an investment proposal, the economic cost is equal to the value of leisure foregone. This implies that the increase in employment is matched by a corresponding fall in unemployment. It also assumes that jobs are filled either directly by the unemployed workers or by individuals employed elsewhere who will be replaced by unemployed workers.

The characteristics of the Irish labour market do not fit easily with this framework. There are many additional different issues and factors to be considered. Most of these have been covered extensively in two recent papers (Gray, 1995; Honohan, 1995). We do not intend to cover this ground once more. Instead we identify a few key issues and offer some tentative conclusions on the appropriate shadow cost of labour.

Relationship between employment and unemployment

A key issue is the sensitivity of unemployment to changes in employment. If unemployment does not change in response to employment changes, this calls into question the view that the opportunity cost of labour is low and that the shadow cost of labour is much below the market rate.

It is clear that at a macro level there is not a one-to-one relationship between changes in employment and unemployment. This pattern has been clear for some time. Indeed, recent Labour Force Survey data indicates that the increases in employment required to reduce unemployment by a given amount is rising. This also applies at project level. The reasons for this however are varied and its implications for the shadow cost of labour will depend in part on which of these explanations is valid.

Macro-economic impacts

In a tight labour market higher employment due to investment could affect labour costs with implications for employment elsewhere in the economy.

There is no concrete evidence to suggest that this has actually occurred. However, in the late 1990s there is increasing evidence of labour shortages appearing in certain sectors of the Irish economy. In the tourism sector, to take just one example, there are unfilled vacancies. This would increase the probability that a proposed project would have adverse employment effects. This puts upward pressure on the opportunity cost of labour.

Account should therefore be taken of the skills profiles of the jobs to be created. High unemployment amongst construction workers would suggest a low opportunity cost for construction employment associated with a project. It would be appropriate to take the opposite view for employment requiring skills in short supply. There are no clear rules to apply in deciding the appropriate shadow prices to assign. Generally, skilled labour would have a higher opportunity cost than unskilled on the basis that unemployment is higher amongst the latter groups. However, this is not always the case.

Inward migration and higher labour force participation

Inward migration and higher labour force participation also explain the lack of a one-to-one relationship between changes in employment and unemployment. Labour mobility raises a particularly complex question. What opportunity cost should be assigned to employment filled by workers from another country? As noted by Gray (1995), a key factor is whether those employed were previously unemployed abroad. If they were employed it is suggested that market prices should be used. This implies no increase in the net social value of the project due to this additional employment.

An alternative approach might be valid. Higher employment filled by returned emigrants, for example, represents a benefit to the economy as policy aims to encourage returned emigrants. In addition, there is no conflict with efforts to reduce unemployment as returned emigrants are unlikely to reduce the employment prospects of unemployed workers. Therefore, regardless of the previous employment status of returned emigrants, these employment gains might be included as a benefit.

Obviously, higher labour force participation will also offset the unemployment impact of higher employment. It has been suggested that the economic impact will be the same as if unemployment declined except for different assumptions about the value of leisure. On this basis the lack of a one-to-one relationship between changes in employment and unemployment does not necessarily point to a high opportunity cost of labour. It is of course relevant but its implications may depend on the explanatory factors.

An important issue relates to the level at which the analysis is undertaken. For Structural Funds Programmes the national perspective should be adopted. However, local labour market conditions ought to be considered. This can have significant implications for estimating shadow prices. An investment in a particular location might attract unemployed workers from outside. Although an objective of the project is to improve the employment prospects of local unemployed workers, taking a national perspective dictates that the same price should apply to both categories of workers.

Choosing the shadow cost of labour

Our brief discussion of this issue gives some indication of the complexity involved. Some of the relevant factors have been outlined. A complete list of the factors taken from Gray (1995) is included as follows:

- the national level of unemployment
- the forecasts for future levels of unemployment and labour force growth rates
- the skill levels and other labour force characteristics
- the degree to which skill shortages exist
- the regional location of the project and the local labour market features
- the degree of national and international labour force mobility
- the extent to which the project causes a loss of output or employment elsewhere in the economy
- the extent of direct versus indirect labour inputs
- the degree to which labour costs represent wage levels or taxes
- the extent of overtime assumed
- the level of taxes and subsidies involved.

It would not be practical nor, we suggest, possible to collect the necessary information on each of these factors for each appraisal. However, there is an obvious need for detailed research on this issue. This could provide the basis for a clear set of guidelines which could be adapted to match individual circumstances.

In the absence of further research it is not possible to reach firm conclusions on this issue. Gray (1995) suggests that the 'national unemployment rate is probably the minimum percentage of labour inputs that would have no opportunity cost'. He adds that it is difficult to envisage circumstances where nearly all of those employed in a project would have no opportunity cost and suggests that a shadow price of labour of between 40 and 90 per cent of market prices is appropriate.

Patrick Honohan (1995) looked at this issue in some detail in seeking to derive a new methodology for appraising industrial projects. He used an econometric model to estimate the reduction in unemployment resulting from an expansion in industrial employment on the basis that this relationship must be established in order to determine the shadow price of labour.

The analysis suggests that unemployment is reduced by only about 20 per cent of the increase in jobs which indicates that on average 80 per cent of the new jobs created by a project are filled by workers other than the unemployed. If the opportunity cost assigned to the unemployed is zero, then Honohan suggests a shadow wage equivalent to 80 per cent of the actual wage. This contrasts with a figure of 15 per cent used previously.[5]

We have expressed doubts about placing too much emphasis on the weak relationship between changes in employment and unemployment without further analysis. High labour mobility between Ireland and abroad is a factor to be considered. Although the opportunity cost of these workers might be high, a case could be made for including the additional employment filled by mobile workers as a benefit to the Irish economy. This could be achieved through a lower shadow price of labour. Higher labour force participation is an additional factor; the economic impacts could be the same as if the jobs were filled by unemployed workers.

It is clear, though, that the existence of unemployment does not, per se, justify a low opportunity cost of labour. Account must be taken of other factors some of which have been discussed here. In the Irish labour market changes in employment are not fully reflected in unemployment as not all vacancies are filled by the unemployed. This is in part related to the skills required for these jobs.

It is difficult to justify a shadow cost of labour which is below 50 per cent. More research is required, in particular building on the work of Honohan. On balance it would seem that a shadow cost of labour of between 50 and 80 per cent of market prices is appropriate.

Income/employment multiplier

In estimating the additional employment generated by a project, income/employment multipliers can be used. In contrast to shadow prices, using multipliers adds directly to the estimated benefits. The income multiplier, for example, is the ratio of the change in national income resulting from the expenditure. Expenditure on a project will lead to indirect income and employment benefits. The purchases of goods and services due to construction and on-going activity of a project is such an impact. It is also common for appraisals to include the impact of expenditure by those employed directly on the project.

There are two main questions to be addressed: which multiplier effects to be included and what parameter estimates to use. There are many potential multiplier effects depending on the nature of the project. Deciding on which effects to include is quite complex. While clear guidelines are not available, each evaluation should adhere to reasonable and prudent parameter estimates and underlying assumptions.

Estimates of the multiplier effects are usually derived from input-output tables. While this methodology is well-known, estimating the magnitudes of these impacts is far from certain. A key issue is the opportunity cost of resources. Account should be taken of capacity constraints in the economy. If the economy is operating at, or close to, full capacity, resources might not be idle. In such circumstances external impacts might not be included. In addition, the open nature of the Irish economy is a factor to be considered.

The inclusion of multiplier effects is a common feature of CBA which can have a crucial bearing on the estimated benefits of a project. However, there is a tendency to over-estimate these effects, highlighting the need for a consistent methodology. This is particularly important if the appraisals are used to compare the returns on several projects and where the size of the multiplier effects may vary according to the project.

Taxation

The treatment of taxation is another issue of relevance. In terms of its impact on the overall results, however, it is not as important as the issues already discussed. The guidelines suggest that prices should be net of VAT and that transfer payments be omitted. There are examples where the inclusion of taxation could amount to double-counting, but it should be possible to safeguard against this occurring. The most important point is that the treatment of taxation is consistent.

Discounting and the economic rate of return

The guidelines suggest that a real discount rate of 5 per cent may be appropriate. Arguments for and against this figure can be made. However, it is our view that this is a reasonable figure. It is also consistent with the Department of Finance guidelines.

The overall results can be presented in many ways. It is suggested that the Economic Rate of Return be used. Interestingly, the Commission guidelines argue that the net social benefits should include an increase in aggregate real income, a reduction in regional disparities and a reduction in unemployment. The first criterion will be satisfied if the project shows a positive net present value. The second criterion is a bit ambitious as it requires a comparison with projects from other countries. The final criterion is normally satisfied by adjusting market prices as discussed.

Other issues and sensitivity analysis

There are many potential external costs and benefits of a project which have not been discussed here. Every attempt should be made to include in the appraisal all factors relevant to the decision-making process. There are two caveats, however. Firstly, it is not possible to place a monetary value on each factor. Nonetheless the relevant factors ought to be included; it is a matter for others to decide how they should be weighted in the decision-making process.

Secondly, the impact of an investment might have wider implications that cannot be incorporated in a rigorous manner into the analysis. This has been accepted as a limitation of this type of exercise. A complete and rigorous analysis of each investment would require a macro-economic model to simulate the effects. Even analysing investment within a particular sector, such as transport for example, is difficult. The returns on a road investment could be affected by a reduction in journey times on competing modes such as rail. As a rule the wider context of investments must be considered.

Finally, a sensitivity analysis is an integral part of any appraisal. The robustness of results should be tested against several sets of assumptions. Project appraisal is more art than science. The uncertainty attached to the estimation of costs and benefits is not in dispute. A sensitivity analysis is essential to add weight to the validity of the assumptions and the results attained. It is important that the baseline against which the different scenarios will be compared is the most appropriate. A clear identification of the project should indicate the most appropriate baseline.

Department of Finance guidelines

Guidelines governing the appraisal of individual projects are also issued by the Department of Finance. These are included in a publication entitled *Guidelines for the Appraisal and Management of Capital Expenditure Proposals in the Public Sector (1994)*. The guide aims to assist officials concerned with capital projects.

The report notes that there are several stages to project appraisal and management. Appraisal is divided into preliminary and detailed. The former aims to assess if the project has sufficient merit to justify a full and detailed appraisal while the detailed study provides the basis for a decision on whether to drop a project or to approve it in principle. Planning involves detailed planning and costing of the project. Implementation requires clear arrangements for monitoring and cost control. Finally, the guide suggests that as a final step a post-project review should be undertaken.

Only part of this guide is devoted to the issue of appraising projects. The guide provides a broad view of some of the issues. It is particularly strong on the need for a consistent approach to parameter values and the factors to be taken into account in an appraisal. It suggests that the Department of Finance should be consulted on the appropriate shadow prices to use.

Section Three: The Peat-Fired Power Station

Introduction

This section examines the CBA of the proposal to build a peat-fired power station in the East Midlands. This review does not examine all aspects of the appraisal undertaken, but concentrates on a number of key methodological issues considered to be of importance. Before examining the detail of the appraisal, the background to the project is outlined. There is also a brief discussion of some relevant evaluation issues.

Background

The proposal to build a 123 MW peat-fired power station is included in the Economic Infrastructure Operational Programme under the Energy Sub-programme. At an estimated cost of 111.4 MECU it is one of the largest infrastructural projects under the CSF. The EU agreed to provide up to 26 MECU in grant aid.

This proposal to build a peat-fired station has been subject to considerable analysis. In addition to the work of the Department of Transport, Energy and Communications, and the two semi-state organisations involved, Bord na Móna and the ESB, several external consultants were employed to examine aspects of the proposal. In June 1993 Bord na Móna commissioned IVO to carry out a full feasibility study.

The socio-economic dimension was subsequently analysed by Blackwell and Associates (1993). This study suggested that in the vicinity of the new peat station there would be a total of 500 additional jobs (divided equally between permanent and seasonal) in peat extraction for a period of approximately 25 years. This contrasts with the alternative power plants using imported fuels which would provide no additional employment. These two studies are not examined here. The focus is on the CBA by NERA, the National Economic Research Associates (1995) which formed the basis for the successful application to the EU for grant aid. It should be borne in mind that NERA's analysis of the project's employment effects draws on the analysis by Blackwell and Associates.

Evaluation issues

Evaluating the viability of the proposed plant is a complex task. There are several overlapping issues. Some are exclusively technical in nature: how efficient are the different energy plants? what is the likely future demand for electricity and what is the present capacity of the system? An evaluation seeking to establish the likely future demand for electricity and the most cost-effective way of meeting that demand, would probably go no further than finding answers to the above questions. However, the objectives go beyond minimising the costs of energy production. The key elements, as first suggested by Bord na Móna in its 1991-1996 Corporate Plan, are:

- the continued use of indigenous fuels in our energy mix

- the creation of additional employment in the Midlands area

- the achievement of target sales of milled peat by Bord na Móna in order to help secure the company's viability.

This latter point is a key element of the decision to proceed with the plant. Bord na Móna has undergone significant rationalisation, with employment falling from around 6,000 in 1984 to around 2,300 currently. The government plan for the viability of the company, which allows for investment of £120 million over three years, is based on the assumption that sales will equal 3 million tonnes of milled peat per annum over the next number of years. The development of a new plant is an integral part of this plan. With older peat power stations reaching the end of their operating lives, this sales target would not be met without the 1 million tonnes that would be absorbed by the new plant.

Cost-benefit analysis

Introduction

As the cost of the project is greater than 25 MECU, a detailed CBA was commissioned. NERA were appointed to undertake the study and they submitted their report in January 1995. The terms of reference for the study were to determine the overall social and economic costs and benefits of the investment, paying particular attention to its regional impact and impact generally, including the environmental aspects.

In summary, the main findings of the report were as follows:

- There is a need for new capacity by the end of this decade on the basis of the ESB's projections.

- Including the new peat plant as part of the investment plan to meet this higher electricity demand will increase costs by approximately £25 million compared with the best alternative without the peat plant included.

- The socio-economic benefits of the peat station and associated peat production will be approximately £36 million when compared with the alternative generation plant strategy on the basis of the assumptions used.

- In the absence of new discoveries, peat will be Ireland's main indigenous energy source in the future. Building the plant reduces our exposure to fossil fuel price volatility.

Each of the main questions were examined, namely, the need for greater generating capacity, economic appraisal of alternative planting strategies, socio-economic effects, diversity and security of supply and environmental effects. The analysis of future electricity needs is straightforward and, accordingly, is not commented upon here. Likewise the examination of environmental effects and the diversity and security of supply are not discussed in detail, the latter being confined to the sensitivity analysis where the impact of fuel price changes is considered. The main elements of the study to be examined are the economic appraisal of the alternative plants and the socio-economic analysis, sections 4 and 5 of the study respectively. These are discussed below.

Economic appraisal of alternative planting strategies

The economic appraisal involves examining the costs of producing electricity with the peat-fired power station compared with the best alternative strategy. The consultants develop a model to examine the cost decisions to build and despatch generating units to meet demand over the next twenty years.[6] The analysis of costs requires a number of assumptions to be made regarding the price of fossil fuels, the future demand for electricity and the technical and costs characteristics of all existing and potential plants. Data from the ESB and Bord na Móna are used in all cases.

An analysis of the costs of the alternatives indicates that the option with the peat plant costs £24.5 million more than the ESB plan without the peat plant. This is in 1993 prices, net present valued at 10 per cent over a 25-year period from 1996 and includes connection and local authority costs. Fuel costs and other operating and maintenance costs are broadly the same for both plans while capital costs account for most of the difference. This reflects the different capital investment plans under the two scenarios with both timing and costs influencing the estimated net present values.

Without expert knowledge of the electricity generating sector, it is difficult to comment on the detail of this analysis. However, it seems that the alternative option to meet future electricity needs in the absence of the new plant has been thoroughly examined. The sensitivity analysis illustrates, though, that minor adjustments to the assumptions can lead to a significant change in the overall cost differential between the two alternatives considered.

Discount rate

A real discount rate of 10 per cent is used in the baseline scenario instead of the figure of 5 per cent normally used. The report states that the ESB use this higher figure. It is also suggested that a rate of 15 per cent, closer to normal commercial practice, would be more appropriate. Following from the discussion in section 2 we would disagree with this as a consistent approach to appraisal is required. Using a higher figure might be justified in circumstances where the project is deemed to be carrying a higher risk than is normal. However, in discussing the benefits of the project there is no mention of the likely risk attached to the forecasts.

The time profile of the costs is particularly crucial in this study. In comparing the costs of the alternative planting strategies the profile of the plants required to meet future electricity demands is the key question. If a new plant is delayed by a year compared with the alternative scenario, the present value of the costs is reduced due to an additional year of discounting. The sensitivity analysis reveals that the choice of discount rate is crucial. For example, discounting using the 5 per cent rate increases the cost differential between the two strategies from £24.5m to £45.4m expressed in terms of present values. However, the overall impact on net present values is small.

Using a 5 per cent rate ensures a consistent approach to the evaluation of projects being funded from the same budgetary source. In the absence of any convincing case in favour of using the higher discount rate, the failure to adhere to this basic parameter represents a weakness of the report.

Socio-economic effects

This section examines whether there is a socio-economic benefit of building the peat-fired station compared with the alternative option of a gas-fired station. By its nature this type of exercise is quite arbitrary. It involves establishing the extent of inter-sectoral linkages and quantifying the final direct and indirect impact of a project on employment and income either nationally or in a particular region. This implicitly involves developing a theoretical framework of the economy within which the project can be analysed. Furthermore, it requires a quantification of the relationships based on the assumptions adopted.

Theoretical framework

The theoretical framework outlined in the report assumes that the project will have no macroeconomic impacts. Jobs created in the East Midlands region will not displace jobs elsewhere. A 'constant pressure of demand' is assumed, implying that the level of demand in the Midlands will have no bearing on the rate of inflation (and activity) in Ireland as a whole. In addition, it is assumed that the employment in this region is principally related to demand in the peat industry and shows little variation with demand generally.

Much of the analysis in this section does not seem to be particularly relevant to the subsequent CBA. It is at times confusing and unclear. As such, it hinders our ability to fully appreciate the extent of the analysis and the related assumptions.

The key question relates to the establishment of the counterfactual. In the context of the labour input, we are concerned with deciding how to value the opportunity cost of the labour associated with the new plant including both direct and indirect demands. The conclusions reached clearly influence the way in which wider income and employment multiplier effects are treated. However, these questions are not explicitly addressed. From our perspective at least, it is difficult to reconcile the theoretical framework developed with the subsequent socio-economic analysis. Its implications for the assumptions adopted which inform the estimation of the project's benefits are not immediately obvious, and are not explained in sufficient detail. More broadly, the 'constant demand of pressure' assumption, on which the framework rests, does not derive from established cost-benefit theory.

Shadow cost of labour

Notwithstanding the above, the framework seems to imply that increases in employment arising from the proposed plant will lead to a corresponding fall in unemployment for the region with no consequences for the region's total labour force or the wider economy. All of the employment gains associated with the plant are included as a benefit except for an allowance for displacement effects. This suggests that the assumed opportunity cost of the labour employed is close to zero (i.e. persons employed as a result of the plant would not find employment elsewhere).

An adjustment is made for the fact that the peat jobs might replace employment that would otherwise exist in the region. The rationale for this displacement effect is not very well developed. The rate is set at 5 per cent, but again no explanation is provided for this figure. The assumption regarding the shadow cost of labour is at variance with the views outlined in section 2 above. While the characteristics of the midlands region might warrant some adjustment to the national opportunity cost of labour, no rationale is developed for this low figure.[7] In summary, this methodological approach is unconvincing and clearly calls into question the results obtained given the importance of socio-economic benefits in justifying the project.

Measuring employment benefits

Employment effects associated with the peat plant, both direct and indirect, are included in the calculations of the project's gross socio-economic value. These are employment effects associated with:

- the construction of the power station and its operation
- the preparation and extraction of peat during the plant's operational phase
- industrial linkages and other activity as a result of higher household income.

The report states that no allowance is made for the fact that some of the higher estimated income will be spent on imported goods. The report considers this to be irrelevant given the macroeconomic assumptions, but again the explanation is not very convincing.

The gross socio-economic benefit of the project is, therefore, considered to be the additional income associated with the direct and indirect employment created in the peat area, as outlined above, except for an adjustment of 5 per cent for job displacement. This figure is also net of income tax and unemployment payments as it is assumed that the increase in employment leads to a one-for-one fall in unemployment.

This estimated level of income is, thus, additional to the levels that occur if the peat power station does not go ahead. This alternative level of employment is supplied by Bord na Móna and included in the study by Blackwell and Associates. Overall, on the basis of the baseline assumption this indicates that the net present value of additions to GDP arising from the peat plant discounted at 10 percent is £36.1m.

Sensitivity analysis

In the baseline scenario, this additional income arising from the proposed peat plant is not compared with the additions to GDP that would arise as a result of the alternative strategy of building a gas-fired station. This is, however, considered in the sensitivity analysis. It indicates that the socio-economic benefits of the gas-fired station are only £6.2m compared with £36.1m for the peat station. This differential is explained by the fact that the fuel for the gas station is imported and accordingly has no positive employment effects.

The explanation given for not including this more relevant comparison in the baseline scenario is unclear. The report seems to suggest that for the alternative strategy the employment effects should not be considered because the background assumption of 'constant demand pressure' does not hold. However, the gas-fired station must be built somewhere and these socio-economic benefits ought to be included, a fact subsequently recognised in the sensitivity analysis.

Overall, the sensitivity analysis is comprehensive. Several different assumptions about discount rates, the number of jobs created, unemployment payments and the job displacement rate are tested. These show that the results are particularly sensitive to changes in the underlying assumptions. Under more optimistic employment scenarios for the area (i.e. higher displacement rates) the socio-economic benefits of the peat station decline considerably. Including the benefits of the gas station they become negative.

Conclusions

Overall the theoretical framework for this study is inadequately developed. The 'constant pressure of demand' assumption is an unusual one in CBA and its link with the subsequent analysis in the estimation of socio-economic benefits is at times unclear. As such it is difficult to follow elements of the report. Apart from commenting on the methodology used, this is a criticism of the report. Moreover, it would seem that much of the analysis is inappropriate in an Irish context.

The treatment of the shadow cost of labour is questionable. It seems that all of the additional employment arising from the plant, both direct and indirect, except for 5 per cent due to displacement, is attributed as a benefit. Greater allowance ought to have been made for displacement and the existence of alternative employment possibilities. The likelihood that higher employment in the area will affect migration with implications for the relationship between employment and unemployment should have been considered. The implied opportunity cost of labour included in this study is too pessimistic.

We would also question the choice of assumptions in the baseline scenario. The discount rate of 5 per cent should have been used. The explanations for not using this rate are unconvincing. In the baseline scenario the socio-economic benefits of the peat station should have been compared with the similar, albeit lower, benefits arising from the gas-fired option. This is a more relevant comparison.

The detailed sensitivity analysis partly compensates for deficiencies elsewhere in the report. The analysis of future electricity needs and the different strategies to meet these needs is also a positive feature of the report. Environmental concerns are also covered well.

In overall terms, we have an unfavourable view of this report, in particular the estimation of the project's overall return. It is our view that the cost-benefit methodology does not stand up to close scrutiny. It is important to note, however, that not all relevant factors were included in the CBA. For energy policy the diversity of supply is a key issue. It is difficult to fully incorporate considerations of this variety in a cost-benefit framework.

Section Four: National Convention Centre

Introduction

This section examines the appraisal of the proposed National Convention Centre (NCC) in Dublin. Some brief comments on the background are included initially followed by an analysis of the appraisal by ECOTEC Research and Consulting Ltd (1996).[8]

Background

Sub-Programme 2 of the Tourism Operational Programme contains a proposal to establish a large dedicated convention centre capable of handling up to 2,000 delegates. This is a response to the view that Ireland's development as a venue for major conferences is constrained by the lack of such a facility. This proposal sought to encourage private sector investment with a 50 per cent grant rate from the European Regional Development Fund.

However, an invitation to the private sector to submit bids on this basis failed to attract suitable proposals. This failure encouraged the national authorities to consider a bid from the Royal Dublin Society (RDS) based on a 75 per cent grant rate. This proposal was to build a 2,000 seater conference centre without an operating subsidy at an estimated capital cost of £33m.

Cost-benefit analysis

Introduction

ECOTEC Research and Consulting Limited in conjunction with Ventures Consultancy and WS Atkins Transport Consultants were appointed by Bord Fáilte to undertake a CBA of this proposal. This task required a number of different elements:

- an evaluation of the market projections for the proposed centre

- a review of the environmental implications of the project and its potential external costs

- an analysis of the project's financial projections to determine its viability and the need for grant support

- an assessment of the external benefits of the project based upon standard socio-economic and cost-benefit criteria.

The report is divided into a number of sections: market context and scenario, financial performance, external economic and other impacts and other issues. It should be noted that, unlike other appraisals, no alternative is considered. This is not in accordance with standard cost-benefit practice but may reflect the background to the project.

Market context and scenario

The analysis of the market context and future scenarios is a crucial element of the study. An increase in overseas conference delegates as a result of the proposed centre is forecast on the basis of two separate studies, one produced for the RDS business plan and an independent evaluation of the potential market by Ventures Consultancy.[9] Both suggest there is scope to attract further large international conferences in Ireland on the basis that the centre will provide better facilities than existing conference facilities. An increase in Ireland's share of larger conferences is forecast on the basis of the small number of these conferences attracted at the moment, the size of the European market and the market potential that exists.

Without knowledge of the sector, it is difficult to examine the validity of this analysis. It is, however, an extremely detailed and comprehensive examination of the market for conference business.

Financial analysis

The financial analysis was carried out in accordance with the Commission guidelines. The main revenue and expenditure items associated with the project are included.

We have two minor points of criticism. Firstly, the annual costs and benefits are examined only for the first 10 years. It is common for large-scale projects of this nature to be appraised over a longer time horizon of perhaps about 20 years. Secondly, and more importantly, there is some confusion about the conclusions of the financial analysis. The report suggests that grant aid of 75 per cent or about £25m in cash terms is required to make the proposal viable. It also states that the project will only make a positive contribution to the RDS under the most optimistic scenarios (i.e. when the net present value is between £23.7m and £41m). This seems to question the viability of the project even with the 75 per cent grant except in the most favourable of circumstances. A more realistic conclusion based on the evidence in the report points to the need for a higher grant in order to guarantee commercial viability.

Economic and other impacts

A CBA differs from a financial analysis because the wider or external benefits of a project to society as a whole are assessed. The inclusion of these wider impacts provides the basis for government assistance. It is normal for a CBA to build on the work of the financial appraisal which includes the basic information on the quantity and prices of inputs and outputs. For this study these linkages are not very well-defined. The external project impacts are assessed with little reference to the preceding analysis. In overall terms this part of the report suffers from a lack of clarity. In a number of instances it is difficult to understand the basis for the calculations. This is a particular problem in seeking to reconcile the micro detail with the overall estimated net present values.

The external benefits equal the sum of the increase in income, both employment-related and profits but mainly employment, arising from the project's different economic impacts. These include the direct temporary impact arising during the Centre's construction, the impact of the Centre's day-to-day operation, the impact of delegate-expenditure spend and the indirect, induced and exchequer benefits. These represent the main socio-economic benefit of the project. The calculation of each is discussed below but, as noted, there is some confusion over how these numbers were attained.

Construction impacts

Temporary construction employment is valued at £41m in wages and salaries. This is based on 1,127 person years at £14,700 each for two and a half years. The profits of construction firms are set at 10.8 per cent of turnover, equivalent to £3.6m.

On-going impact of the centre

The direct impact of the centre includes both on and off-site temporary employment. It is estimated that 13 additional jobs will result from the operation of the centre. Services and goods purchased by the centre will generate further employment of about 40 full-time temporary jobs by year 5.

Impacts of delegate expenditure

Further employment will result from delegates' expenditure on transport, meals and beverages etc. These effects are discussed in some detail, but a precise figure for the employment impact is not provided in the text. In a subsequent table, there is a figure for direct employment off-site of 588 in year 5, which we assume is the employment impact of the delegate expenditure. Increases in tourism profits are again included at around 5 per cent of turnover, in contrast to 10.8 per cent for construction profits.

Indirect and induced benefits

The study also takes account of the multiplier impact of these various employment effects to gauge the total increase in employment/income as a result of the project. For example, businesses which benefit directly from increased conference business and visitor spend will in turn purchase goods and services, providing an indirect employment benefit. The report uses a ratio of direct to indirect and induced employment of 1:1.8 (i.e. the employment multiplier) although it is suggested that this figure is too high. On the basis of the RDS figures, this leads to employment of 514 in year 5 (i.e. 80 per cent of direct employment on and off-site).

Overall results

The present value of the project's benefits are derived by assigning income values for the relevant years to the different elements outlined above. The main findings listed below are expressed in terms of present values discounted at 5 per cent over a 25-year period.[10]

- additional income to the RDS of £17.5m to £24m

- profits of between £6m-£10m in the tourism sector in Dublin[11]

- generation of income of between £50m-£80m due to additional employment in the tourism and construction sectors

- social value of creating jobs of between £3.3m-£5.1m

- tax payments to the Irish exchequer of between £75m-£114m.

The present value of the project's costs is in the range £49m to £59m. On reasonable assumptions, according to the report, the benefits easily outweigh the costs – even ignoring the exchequer benefits. While traffic congestion would add to costs the favourable conclusion of the analysis would not be altered. While the general approach of the appraisal seems to be well-based there are some deficiencies. As noted earlier, in parts the report is not sufficiently clear, in particular the linkages between the micro-level of the project's benefits and overall estimated present values. The report also lacks a separate sensitivity analysis; the estimation of a range of values for the different effects does not work as well.

The treatment of the employment benefits is the report's main weakness which has implications for the robustness of the findings. Income derived from the employment spin-offs is the main benefit of the proposed project. All of the employment resulting from the project is classified as a benefit implying an opportunity cost of labour of zero. The consultants rationalise this on the assumption that general unemployment will continue at high levels and that the opportunity cost of labour is low and that individuals attach no disutility to work. As discussed in section 2, while unemployment in Ireland is undoubtedly high, this fact alone does not imply a low opportunity cost of labour.

To suggest that the vacancies resulting from the investment will be filled exclusively by the unemployed, as implied in the report, is not credible. Recent anecdotal evidence from sources within the tourism industry suggests that labour shortages already exist. Increased employment arising from the centre would have effects in other parts of the economy with potentially adverse consequences for employment.

There is also an additional value placed on the 'social value of creating jobs'. This is estimated to be between £3.3m-£5.1m. No rationale is provided for the inclusion of this element as a benefit. It is unclear how it differs from the other employment effects included in the analysis.

Exchequer payments

The consultants suggest that taxation increases associated with the higher income and profits generated might be included in the estimation of benefits. The present value of these benefits is calculated to be between £75m-£114m although the basis for this calculation is not clear. The consultants suggest that the inclusion of these benefits would to a large extent represent 'double counting'. We would agree with this view.

Conclusions

While there are a number of methodological weaknesses as outlined above, this represents a reasonable economic appraisal of the proposal considering the difficulty of this type of study. The market context for the project is discussed in detail. However, the report does not contain a formal sensitivity analysis. Estimates of impact are calculated within ranges. This is an omission. Different scenarios should be tested during the sensitivity analysis from which comparisons with the baseline can be drawn.

A comprehensive financial analysis is undertaken. All the different elements that ought to be included are present, although the detailed analysis does not feed directly into the subsequent CBA. A discount rate of 5 per cent is used in both instances. However, the costs and benefits are analysed over a 25-year period for the CBA, which is appropriate for this type of project, but over only 10 years for the financial analysis.

The estimation of the project's external benefits is very detailed. The discussion on the impact of the centre, both direct and indirect, seems reasonable. The standard multipliers for the tourism sector are used, subject to adjustment where deemed appropriate. These adjustments are in most cases justified. This part of the report does suffer, however, from a lack of clarity. The basis for some of the estimations is not easily identifiable. In particular the link between the micro analysis and the aggregated net present values figures estimated is weak, even with the inclusion of tables containing the calculations.

On a more fundamental level the assumed opportunity cost of labour is too low. As noted, the existence of unemployment is not sufficient to support this assumption. The Irish labour market is characterised by structural problems manifested in apparent skills mismatches. This implies that the socio-economic benefits of the centre might have been exaggerated. We are not in a position to state whether the report's favourable conclusion would be altered by this. Nonetheless, in common with other evaluations reviewed it is a serious methodological weakness.

Regarding exchequer benefits it is our view that their inclusion would represent a double counting of benefits.

Section Five: The National Museum of Ireland at Collins Barracks

Introduction

This section examines the proposal to develop Collins Barracks as part of the National Museum. The main focus is on the treatment of costs and benefits in the appraisal.

Background

National cultural institutions are considered to be an important element of Ireland's tourism product. Their development is an important part of the Operational Programme (OP) for Tourism.

Investment in the National Museum is earmarked under the OP. It is accepted that the museum required additional space to develop its full potential and make the maximum contribution to Ireland's tourism industry.

Cost-benefit analysis

The CBA was undertaken by TECNECON economic consultants (1997). It was received by the Department of Arts, Culture and the Gaeltacht in February 1995. At the time of writing the report had not been considered and, as a consequence, a final decision on funding for the project had not been taken.

We deal with the main sections of the report in turn. Unlike other studies reviewed the EU Guidelines on CBA are closely followed. This gives rise to a clear and logical structure in which all of the main issues are examined. The clarity of the report compares favourably with others reviewed, particularly in relation to the assumptions underpinning the project's estimated costs and benefits.

Project identification and objectives

The need to develop museum capability and capacity is the project's main objective with the Collins Barracks proposal as the means to achieving this. The project is considered in the context of the existing institutions to which it is adding new capacity. This approach to the nature of the project, with which we agree, has implications for the appraisal. For example, the development of Collins Barracks will release buildings used at the moment for storage space. These effects are offset against the costs of the project.

For any project, the benefits are related to its stated objectives. This project addressed both tourism and cultural and heritage objectives. As the project is funded under the Tourism OP, tourism objectives take precedence.

The principal objectives of the project are to enable the National Museum to:

- contribute towards an increase in tourism income and employment in Ireland
- educate Irish people and visitors to Ireland concerning Irish history and culture
- conserve existing and future collections
- meet its obligations to archaeological and other collections on behalf of the nation.

There were also supplementary objectives such as a redistribution of tourism activity within Dublin.

Alternatives to the project

The report outlines the do-nothing and do-minimum options against which the proposal should be appraised. The do-nothing option was not available in this instance as such a strategy would involve a loss of artefacts which is considered unacceptable. The do-minimum option relates solely to increasing the available storage space. In present value terms discounted at 5 per cent over the lifetime of the costs this was estimated at £11.676m. This cost represents the baseline against which the additional cost of developing the Barracks is judged, although the proposal offers benefits in addition to providing more storage space.

Financial analysis

The financial appraisal is in line with recommended practice. A five per cent discount rate is applied to costs and benefits over a 50-year time period. This time period is longer than for most projects but does not seem exceptional for a museum.

Capital costs

Capital costs are estimated to be £31.2m. These include an allowance for inflation, VAT and PRSI. When these factors are netted out, the present value is computed to be £24.116m in 1996 prices. These costs are then compared with the cost of the do-minimum scenario which are considered savings if the Collins Barracks option is undertaken. Accordingly, these savings are set off against the capital costs of the project.

Recurring costs

Recurring costs include operating costs, wages and salaries, security and the maintenance of building. Operating costs are adjusted to take account of potential savings elsewhere in the system. Wages costs are adjusted in a similar fashion. In addition, costs are adjusted for VAT and the PRSI element associated with the labour content of costs. It is correctly stated that any divergence between private and social costs is a matter for the CBA. Accordingly, distortions between market prices and resource costs are not addressed in the financial analysis.

As admission is free, revenues include only receipts from sales at the museum. It is clear that costs outweigh the benefits. However no conclusions are offered arising from the analysis. A profile of losses on an annual basis is not provided while Internal Rates of Return are not calculated. Nevertheless, this part of the report is of a high quality.

Socio-economic costs and benefits

In calculating capital costs for the CBA, market prices are not adjusted using shadow prices for labour or materials. It is suggested that there is no evidence of market distortions which would invalidate the use of market prices. However, in calculating the benefits of the project, employment gains are included. This implies that market prices do not reflect the resource cost of these inputs. In this case this is reflected in the calculation of benefits rather than adjusting costs although the impact on the result is the same.

Total costs, including both capital and recurring costs, are the same as in the financial costs. Recurring costs are not adjusted for the potential low opportunity costs of labour in the vicinity of the project. These are, however, considered later as a benefit. The possibility of traffic congestion as a result of the project is considered, but it is not felt to be a significant factor.

There are a number of benefits arising from the project. Tourism benefits are the most important. These include net additional tourism income, and less tangible effects such as improved perceptions of Ireland as a cultural and heritage destination.

Net additional visitors

The main benefit of the project arises from visitors who would not have come in the absence of the project and those visitors who extend their stay in order to visit the museum. Strict displacement and additionality criteria are applied. Nonetheless, gross expenditure from the project is expected to be between £1.284m and £4.644m for a given year depending on high or low estimates of visitor numbers. The total expenditure estimated is a function of the number of visitors, the length of stay and daily expenditure.

In addition there is the expenditure by non-additional visitors. This involves the displacement of an activity with a low or zero expenditure with a visit to the museum which might involve a higher level of expenditure. It should be noted that the projections are based on a range of estimates of future growth. Growth rates of between 5-10 per cent for the next 15 years are used which, although in line with recent years, seem to be overly optimistic considering the capacity constraints facing the sector. On balance, we believe this assumption is questionable.

Tourism income and employment multipliers

Given the existence of unemployed resources in the economy, the report believes that tourism multipliers can be used to estimate the final value to the economy of the project. Multipliers ranging from 0.5 to 0.65 are based on a study in Scotland. These are different to numbers used for comparable Irish studies, however.

Overall results

The net present values have been assessed over a 50-year period at a real discount rate of 5 per cent. The report shows the estimated present values of income generated under different assumptions about visitor numbers, income multipliers and future growth rates. In general, the project only has an estimated positive return under the 'high visitor numbers' scenario.

Other benefits

These figures do not include all the likely benefits of the project. Employment effects and employment multiplier impacts as a result of the current expenditure of the museum on wages and salaries and the purchase of goods and services are excluded.

The positive benefits of redistributing tourism expenditure and impact on urban regeneration are also factors which need to be considered. In common with the benefits outlined in the above paragraph, these are not included in the estimation of overall benefits. It is estimated that about 70-100 jobs will be created in the immediate vicinity of the project. These will have a further knock-on effect throughout the economy, although some of these impacts would already have been included in the overall analysis. Finally, the construction of the barracks will have a positive employment impact.

There are also heritage and education benefits and conservation benefits. These are best considered as merit goods and the report does not assign to them a monetary value.

The other benefits outlined above have not been included in the actual calculation of the project's benefits. Undoubtedly it is not possible to place a monetary value on the merit good aspects of this project. However, the omission of the socio-economic benefits, for which values can be computed, is surprising – in particular as employment effects of the capital and the recurring costs, in addition to the indirect and induced multiplier effects, are normally included in this type of analysis.

Report's conclusions

The consultants conclude that on the basis of a range of realistic assumptions the project generates a positive net present value. A key assumption is that the project is marketed sufficiently to attain the high level of visitors required, although these marketing costs are not included in the estimations. There are also, however, merit good and urban regeneration aspects which add to the overall acceptability of the project.

Conclusions

This represents a good quality project evaluation. The report follows a clear structure and covers most of the main issues. The assumptions in relation to the treatment of costs and benefits are clearly defined and, in general, stand up to scrutiny.

We would question the projections of visitor numbers attracted to Ireland on account of the museum's development. They seem to be optimistic, although it is accepted that such projections are by their nature difficult to formulate. This may cast doubt on the overall results. On the other hand, the exclusion from the calculations of some benefits outlined above which ought to be included would tend to work in favour of the project.

The discount rates used adhere to the guidelines while the time period over which the benefits are discounted seems reasonable. The identification of the project and the establishment of a counterfactual against which the project is used, is a positive aspect of the report. The consultants display a clear understanding of the opportunity costs of resources in the formulation of the counterfactual. This provides a basis for the analysis in the bulk of the report. The linkages between the financial analysis and the CBA are clear. A sensitivity analysis is also included and the different assumptions tested are a valuable addition to the report.

In the CBA the costs included in the financial analysis are not generally adjusted to account for distortions. In the calculation of benefits, a judgement on the opportunity costs is implicitly made: an employment multiplier is applied to the estimated first round income effects of the project on the basis that there are unemployed resources in the economy. A multiplier figure based on Scottish data is used. It is clear that this figure was not altered to reflect the consultants' view on the shadow cost of labour in Ireland. The absence of a discussion on the relevance of this issue for the appraisal is a weakness of the report.

Notwithstanding some of the slightly critical comments, and accepting the problems inherent in such work, the report is soundly based and compares favourably with other studies. It is our view that the report benefited from close adherence to the EU project appraisal guidelines.

Section Six: National Primary Roads

Introduction

A key element under the Operational Programme for Transport is investment in the primary road network. Appraisal of proposed projects by the National Roads Authority (NRA) is undertaken according to a common methodology. The same approach to calculating rates of return is applied to all projects. The application to the Commission for assistance is based on these estimates.

The appraisal of road projects under the CSF is different to other evaluations reviewed in this study. In contrast to other sectors there are a large number of projects to be evaluated. This leads to the requirement for a practical and routine approach which can produce comparable rates of return. These calculations are carried out by the NRA rather than external consultants which is the norm for other projects.

CBA of road projects in Ireland was first introduced in 1985 with the adoption of a modified version of a model used in the UK. In response to requirements under the 1989-1993 CSF, a new methodology was developed by Dr James Crowley of UCD. This was subsequently added to by DKM, the external evaluator to the programme, with the production of a set of parameter values and application rules to be followed in appraising all projects in the transport area. Drawing heavily on international experience these guidelines outline the costs and benefits to be included and appropriate parameter values. This section will focus on the work by DKM. This follows a brief outline of the objectives of these road projects.

Project selection

The National Roads Authority (NRA) has responsibility for selecting major national primary road projects under the Supporting National Economic Development sub-programme. In accordance with the integrated approach to developing the road network, at least 70 per cent of the total expenditure on national primary roads must be allocated to the four main strategic corridors. The under-developed condition of much of the road network clearly defines the priority areas for improvement. This simplifies the selection task faced by the NRA.

The primary roads investment strategy is implemented through two principal measures: major improvements and integrated network improvements. The major improvement measure aims for:

- a substantial improvement of the inter-urban network linking major urban centres, ports and airports

- the elimination of traffic bottlenecks by means of town by-passes

- the reduction of urban congestion by providing new river crossings, ring-roads and relief roads.

In choosing major schemes the NRA considers the impact the project will have on improving the road network (e.g. time savings for long distance travel), the project's rate of return and the carriageway condition as indicated by vertical and horizontal alignment and safety record. Some degree of regional balance is also considered.

Impact spreadsheets are prepared for proposed projects. These include a description of the scheme; the internal rate of return (if available); the existing geometrics, capacity, pavement condition, traffic levels and accident record, and a description of the roads' characteristics on completion. These spreadsheets provide the information which forms the basis for the decision to proceed with the project. Environmental and engineering factors complement the estimated rates of return.

Parameter values and application rules

The basic rules used to appraise national road projects are detailed in a report by DKM.[12] The DKM report sought to develop CBA parameter values and application rules for use across the transport sector. A principal requirement was to produce a set of rules that would enable comparability of results across sectors. The international and domestic experience of appraising projects in this area is reflected in the report.

The report proposed a set of working rules which are included at Table 7.1

Table 7.1: Proposed Working Rules for Cost Benefit Analysis

Proposed Working Rule 1: Working time should be valued (in 1994 prices) at £9.20 per hour.

Proposed Working Rule 2: Non-work time should be valued (in 1994 prices) at £3.70 per hour.

Proposed Working Rule 3: This value should apply equally for large and small time savings and for urban and rural areas.

Proposed Working Rule 4: Adjustments should be made only where the project involves a traffic pattern very different from the average, for example, a school bus service.

Proposed Working Rule 5: Where accident costs are deemed to be important, the following values (at 1994 prices) should be used: fatality, £750,000; non-fatal injury, £25,000; damage only, £1,500.

Proposed Working Rule 6: Savings in vehicle operating costs should be at 10p per km for cars, at 1994 prices, with a 50 per cent premium for larger vehicles.

Proposed Working Rule 7: Projects where benefits are reasonably certain, such as public utility-type projects, should use a discount rate (for benefits) as recommended by the Department of Finance. Where benefits are less certain, for example, projects which finance operators in competitive markets, a higher rate should be explicitly specified in the evaluation. How much higher is a matter of choice by the analyst, but it should be explicit.

Table 7.1: Proposed Working Rules for Cost Benefit Analysis (contd.)

Proposed Working Rule 8: Where there is uncertainty about costs, a sensitivity analysis should be conducted.

Proposed Working Rule 9: A qualitative assessment of environmental impact should be prepared alongside the CBA analysis.

Proposed Working Rule 10: The unit of analysis (the project) should be specified so as to distinguish projects from Programmes. All of the ancillary sub-projects unavoidably required should be included.

Proposed Working Rule 11: The CBA analysis should experiment with alternative starting dates.

Proposed Working Rule 12: The option of closure of a route, or discontinuation of a service, should be amongst the options considered in some transport investments.

Proposed Working Rule 13: When user benefits have been fully accounted for, analysts should avoid double-counting through the inclusion of other projected occurrences which are induced by these user benefits.

It is difficult to find fault with these rules. They are based on well-known and tested approaches suitably adopted for domestic circumstances. The first six rules concern the valuation of benefits. In the absence of market prices the value to be placed on roads investment is equated with the imputed value of reductions in journey times. This is judged to be the value of working and non-working time depending on the nature of the journey undertaken.

This technique has been criticised in the past with suggestions that it overstates the benefits of road investment. For certain routes the validity of these assumptions could be tested by tolling. This would ascertain whether motorists are really willing to pay for the time savings as assumed.

The validity of apportioning time savings on private journeys as a benefit, given the specific economic development objective of Structural Funds, is debatable. While the links with economic objectives are hard to establish, they represent legitimate goals of national policy resulting from road improvements. Accordingly, they should be included.

It is noted that the market price of labour is considered to be appropriate in valuing construction costs. This is different to other approaches examined which used a shadow price well below the market price. Noting the labour-intensive nature of construction this would significantly increase the estimated returns. As discussed in some detail in section 2 we are sceptical of such an approach. It is clear, though, that different values are being used for different appraisals. In the absence of a clear justification this is difficult to defend as the opportunity cost of the investment funds is the same and should be evaluated as far as is possible on the same basis.

In general terms the estimation of rates of return follows these guidelines. It is worth noting that accident costs are not included in the NRA methodology. The exclusion of this factor underestimates the calculated rates of return. The calculations also assume traffic growth of 3 per cent while no allowance is made for the fact that real wages are rising over time thereby increasing the real value of time savings. As noted in the mid-term evaluation report[13] these factors would add to the calculated rates of return. Environmental factors are omitted which could have either a positive or negative impact.

Conclusions

The rules and parameter values developed in this area provide clear guidelines as to the most appropriate way to appraise projects. While sets of assumptions, particularly in this area, are always open to interpretation the guidelines seem reasonable. There are some queries over the inclusion of certain benefits and the value to be placed on time savings. These are, however, not on a par with some of the serious methodological problems encountered when appraising projects in other areas.

It seems that implementation of the guidelines is the norm. There are question marks about the estimation of construction costs and the consideration of alternative options.

Section Seven: Rail Infrastructure

Introduction

The Transport Operational Programme contains a plan for rail infrastructure and rolling stock investment of £288m in 1996 prices over the period 1994-1999. The bulk of the investment is on track and signalling (£165.7m), divided into signalling (£17.5m) and track renewal and track equipment (£148.2m). The balance of the funding (£122.5m) is earmarked for rolling stock investment. Regional and Cohesion funding was sought for the implementation of this plan.

This development programme was subject to an evaluation by CIÉ. This was undertaken at two levels. Firstly, the economic returns on a range of options for the future development of the railway were examined. Secondly, the evaluation extended to a detailed analysis of a number of rail lines.

Goodbody Economic Consultants (1996) were commissioned to examine the CIÉ evaluation, making corrections as deemed appropriate, and subsequently re-estimating the expected rates of return. This constituted a re-evaluation of the plan focusing in particular on a line-by-line analysis. This section reviews this study which is, in essence, additional to the original work of CIÉ and a series of earlier studies. The section is in two parts; one reviews the analysis by the consultants of the CIÉ evaluation of the proposed investments, the other presents revised estimates.

CIÉ economic evaluation

Overall view

The CIÉ investment plan was devised after consideration of a range of alternative options for the railways. These ranged from closure to a full-scale development plan. A do-minimum option which included a programme of improvements was compared with a development option which represented an acceleration of the renewal option. Both the do-minimum option and the development option provided a greater return than the various closure scenarios, with the development option producing the highest NPV.

Goodbodys conclude that the NPVs for the full railway system are very small. The robustness of the CIÉ results are questioned due to the inclusion of employment maintenance as a significant benefit of retaining the railways. In common with other studies reviewed, though as we have seen there is some debate on this issue, it is assumed that many of the redundant workers would not find alternative employment and, accordingly, the price of labour is reduced to reflect this.

Subsequent to the above analysis a line-by-line evaluation was also undertaken by CIÉ. The methodology used was also considered by Goodbodys to be weak. The analysis assumed that the viability of the railway was dependent upon a substantial level of investment. The proposed investment plan to be evaluated assumed expenditure pre-2000 compared with the do-minimum scenario of postponing investment beyond 2000. Accordingly, the analysis evaluated the effect of bringing forward investment rather than an examination of the real alternatives.[14]

Key assumptions

Many of the micro assumptions used in the CIÉ evaluation were questioned by the consultants. They focused on a number of issues, namely the range of benefits to be included in the appraisal, traffic demand forecasts, the measurement of time savings and accident and vehicle operating cost savings. The CIÉ study calculated the benefits of the investment by estimating time savings for existing, diverted and generated rail passengers. Vehicle operating cost savings and accident cost savings were also included. Neither potential benefits to freight traffic nor environmental benefits arising from the switch from car to rail were assessed. Both of these effects are considered to be minor and their exclusion does not affect the overall result.

The evaluation assumed that fares remain constant. Thus, costs savings are reflected in lower deficits for the company rather than an increase in benefits to passengers. This improves the financial appraisal with no effect on the CBA.

Traffic demand forecasts

Forecasting passenger demand is a vital part of the evaluation. These are calculated by CIÉ using a model which takes account of consumer demand, the level of fares and various dummy variables. Modest growth in numbers is forecast. However, no traffic growth is assumed for the post 2002 period which is identified as a weakness of the CIÉ analysis.

Account is also taken of increases in traffic resulting from reductions in journey times on foot of the investment plans. These figures are estimated allowing for the responsiveness of demand to changes in journey times. The new traffic volumes estimated are considered to be conservative on the basis of UK evidence.

Time savings

According to the consultants, the estimate of time savings applied to the traffic volumes tend to over-estimate likely benefits for two reasons. Firstly, the value of time saved in the analysis is higher than the values recommended by the Transport guidelines. It is felt that for consistency all transport projects should use these values. Secondly, time savings are estimated assuming that passengers travel the full length of a line. In situations of few end-to-end journeys this will lead to a significant overstatement of benefits.

In relation to the cost of accidents the values used are higher than those recommended by the Commission guidelines. The vehicle operating cost savings data are, however, broadly comparable with the recommended figures.

The consultants conclude their review of the CIÉ evaluation stating that 'given the problems outlined, the estimated economic return to both the broad options and the line investments are subject to considerable error'.

Re-evaluation

Introduction

The re-evaluation sought to remedy the deficiencies of the CIÉ evaluation outlined above. It focused on five lines – Dublin to Sligo, Galway, Waterford and Rosslare in addition to Tralee-Mallow. The analysis was extended to cover flows on discrete sections of lines as well as end-to-end journeys, thus remedying a key deficiency of the CIÉ study.

This analysis is extremely detailed. The flaws in the original approach are tackled while there are a number of additional elements. We focus here on the main themes rather than a detailed examination of every issue.

Counterfactual

The level of proposed investment was evaluated by comparison with the investment likely to have occurred in the absence of external funding. This is different to the assumption in the CIÉ analysis which assessed the impact of bringing forward investment. To facilitate this approach the proposed investment was allocated across the different routes. This level of investment was subsequently compared with the do-minimum scenario in order to assess the incremental effects of the plan.

Value of time saving

The analysis of demand and time savings in the earlier evaluation is augmented in a number of ways. The characteristics of passengers are examined as an important determinant of the value of journey time savings to be assigned. The evaluation takes account of the proportion of business travellers on a route and the proportion owning/driving a car. A higher time-saving value is attributed to routes with a high proportion of work/business travellers while for routes with a high proportion of car owning passengers it is suggested that a switch to these routes will involve a similarly high proportion of car owners.

In essence, the average value of time savings per route was estimated with reference to the value put on working and non-working time and the proportion of travellers falling into each category. This is in line with accepted practice.

The impact of time savings on demand for the various routes is estimated using elasticities of demand. This approach is used to analyse the impact of the investment plan on passenger demand. Under the do-minimum strategy, increases in journey times are expected on each of the routes due to the need to impose speed restrictions arising from safety considerations. The investment programme proposed to reverse these increases and achieve net reductions by 1999 compared with the 1995 position on all routes except Dublin-Sligo. The journey time elasticity was applied to the net change over the initial journey time to estimate the impact on passenger demand. Improvements in journey times on the competing road network are not considered, except for the Sligo line in the subsequent sensitivity analysis.

Accident saving

The estimation of accident savings is dependent upon the number of car journeys diverted to rail. The proportion of diverted car users out of the total increase in passenger numbers was assumed to be equal to the proportion of rail travellers with cars on each route. The estimate of passenger kilometres was converted to car kilometres by the average car occupancy. On the basis of 0.39 accidents per million car kilometres, the reduction in accidents as a result of the diversion from car to rail is computed.

Overall results

The study provides a very clear distinction between economic and financial evaluation. It is noted that higher rail fares will improve the results of the financial appraisal but has the opposite effect on the economic evaluation through its effect on demand and total quantity of time savings.

These results suggest significant differences in the estimated IRR, NPV and cost-benefit ratios for the different routes. The returns on the Dublin-Sligo and Dublin-Galway routes are substantial with a moderate estimated return on the Dublin-Waterford route. However, the Dublin-Rosslare and Mallow-Tralee routes indicate unacceptably low rates of return. For the appraisals reviewed in this paper, these are the only examples of projects that failed to pass the standard criteria.

In the absence of a subsidy the financial results are poor with none of the routes having a positive IRR at the 5 per cent rate. A better return would require higher passenger numbers or a reduction in operating costs. The difference in the results of the economic and financial evaluations reflects the inclusion of time savings in the former. However, as the price elasticity for rail travel is less than unity, an increase in fares might close the gap between the two, although the elasticities might alter in response to large increases.

Conclusions

This evaluation report is very impressive. It provides a valid critique of the evaluation undertaken by CIÉ and seeks to correct the deficiencies identified. The re-specification of the co-minimum option compared to the proposed investment is a clear improvement, although it implies strong criticism of the original methodology. The report does not, however, include a comprehensive sensitivity analysis for all routes.

The report clearly distinguishes between the economic and financial appraisals. The costs and benefits of relevance to each are clearly stated. Moreover, the estimation of costs and benefits is very comprehensive and accords with generally accepted practice in this area.

This is particularly the case for the calculation of benefits. The methodology to estimate passenger demand seems reasonable. The impact on demand due to changes in journey times between the do-minimum and investment scenarios is estimated using derived elasticities. For the economic evaluation a value for time savings is applied to these estimates taking account of the characteristics of passengers on each of the routes.

No account is taken, however, of the impact modal competition might have on passenger demand. This is mentioned as a deficiency in the approach which needs to be tackled. Ideally, investments in competing transport modes should be jointly assessed. At the very minimum the assumptions used should be comparable.

The treatment of the shadow price of labour has been a recurring theme of this paper. We believe the consultant's criticisms of CIÉ's approach to this issue are well-founded. In general, using market prices provides a more reliable estimate of returns. This approach is adopted for all other inputs in addition to labour.

The estimates of accident savings are based on a clear methodology. The same could be said for the estimation of vehicle operating costs savings. It is noted, however, that accident savings are not included in the appraisal of road projects.

Section Eight: Conclusions and recommendations

It is clear that infrastructural projects in the CSF are not being appraised on a consistent or uniform basis. The diversity of projects and the complexity of some highlights the need for a flexible approach. Nonetheless evaluations should follow a consistent and logical structure. They should also contain the same basic elements. Our research has shown that the identification of costs and benefits varies by project. In deciding the components of a project's costs and benefits the available guidelines are often ignored.

Different discount rates are also used despite guidelines specifying the standard rate to be used. There may be circumstances where a different discount rate may be appropriate (e.g. riskier projects) but the rationale ought to be explained and justified. For appraisals examined which did not use the public sector norm the explanation was not convincing. There are also question marks regarding the time horizon over which the costs/benefits are discounted.

A positive feature of the appraisals reviewed is the extent of the sensitivity analyses undertaken. This important feature was included in most cases. There is a problem, however, concerning the choice of baseline against which the various scenarios are compared. There were examples where the baseline assumptions did not seem the most plausible. This is in part related to the definition and identification of project alternatives and the correct counterfactual. Improvements in this area could be made if the guidelines produced by the Commission were adhered to.

The valuation of external benefits is naturally an area of particular importance as minor changes to assumptions can have a large impact on a project's estimated return. There is a need for methodological improvements in this area. The estimation of indirect and spin-off effects of projects is somewhat arbitrary and inconsistent. There is confusion over which effects ought to be included while the use of employment and income multipliers varies considerably. The treatment of taxation gives rise to similar problems.

The treatment of employment is the most serious deficiency identified. The market wage rate is normally subject to significant adjustment to reflect the assumed low opportunity cost of labour due to high unemployment. With the exception of the transport area the shadow wage rate is set well below the market rate, increasing the estimated net value of the project. For projects where the output is sold mainly in the marketplace the principal social benefit is this gap between the shadow and market wage. As discussed in some detail we disagree with the valuation of the shadow wage used in most of the appraisals.

It is clear that in some instances the net present value of projects has been overstated. Innovative approaches have been adopted to estimating project benefits. As a consequence, project selection may not have been wholly consistent with the goal of maximising the returns from the CSF. This represents a potential waste of resources with implications for living standards and employment.

We recommend that detailed application rules and parameter values for the issues identified be developed. These would supplement rather than replace the guidelines already in existence and could be modelled on the work done by DKM in the transport area. The main objective would be to achieve a consistent approach to appraisal. This is obviously lacking at the moment and, as a consequence, the integrity of the cost-benefit approach is being compromised.

We recommend that such a study identify the costs and benefits that ought to be included, taking account of sectoral differences. There is also a need to review the use of income and employment multipliers, focusing on the methodological approach. The types of direct and indirect effects that should be included ought to be clarified. In addition there is a need to outline specific parameter values.

We recommend further research on the shadow price of labour, drawing on that already undertaken by the ESRI. This is the most important issue requiring methodological improvement. Clear guidelines for not using the market wage should be specified. A decision has to be reached on the appropriate value to use. This may vary depending on the circumstances but a range of values should be specified with an outline of the factors to be considered in determining the most appropriate value to use within the specified range.

We recommend that a section/agency within, or attached to, the Department of Finance be charged with responsibility for drawing up and implementing these guidelines. This would entail participation on committees established to select consultants. This section/agency would have a role in clarifying issues and generally advising on methodological issues. It might also have a role in expressing a view on the robustness and quality of evaluations. This quality assurance function might take place prior to the submission of project applications for funding to the Commission.

NOTES

1   For the Transport OP the Monitoring Committee has agreed additional guidelines for the selection of projects.
2   This section draws heavily on Fitzpatrick (1993), Gray (1995), ESRI (1995) and Layard and Glaister (1994).
3   This well-documented and standard methodology is discussed in section 6.
4   This is not the case, however, where market prices are not available.
5   For more details, see Honohan (1995).
6   It is assumed that the higher cost is reflected in lower profits for the ESB or a higher subsidy from the government.
7   As mentioned, NERA draw heavily on earlier work by Blackwell and Associates in considering the project's employment impact.
8   We are aware that the Commission queried aspects of this study which were subsequently addressed by the consultants. Our focus is on the CBA which forms the basis for the application for EU assistance. Accordingly, the additional analysis undertaken by the consultants after their final report was submitted has not been considered here.
9   For the remainder of the chapter data quoted refer to the RDS plan.
10 The discount rate and the time horizon over which the benefits are analysed seems reasonable. This is in contrast to the financial appraisal where the discounting was limited to 10 years.
11 This is equivalent to £12m-£20m adjusted for the fact that additional demand will require additional capital investment with an associated opportunity cost.
12 CBA Parameter Values and Application Rules for Transport Infrastructure Projects, February 1994.
13 Mid-term Evaluation of the Transport Operational Programme, DKM, February, 1997.
14 It is our understanding that this assumption is based on the fact that line closures were not seen as a viable option.

*

This article was first produced as a report by the Community Support Framework Evaluation Unit in 1997.

REFERENCES

Commission of the European Communities (1997). *Guide to Cost Benefit Analysis of Major Projects in the context of EC Regional Policies*, Brussels: Coordination of Evaluation Unit, DGXVI

Dept. of Finance (1994). *Guidelines for the Appraisal and Management of Capital Expenditure Proposals in the Public Sector*, Dublin: Government Publications and Sales Office

Ecotec Research and Consulting Ltd (1996). *Cost Benefit Study of the National Conference Centre in Dublin*, Dublin: Bord Fáilte

Fitzpatrick Associates (1993). *Economic Consultancy on Environmental Programmes: Water/Sanitary Services and ENVIREG*, Dublin: Dept. of Environment

Goodbody Economic Consultants (1996). *The Mainline Rail Investment Programme*, Dublin: Goodbody

Gray, A.W. (1995). *EU Structural Funds and Other Public Sector Investments – A Guide to Evaluation Methods*, Dublin: Gill & Macmillan

Honohan, P. et al (1995). *Appraisal for the Industrial Development Agencies*, Dublin: ESRI

Jonathan Blackwell and Associates (1993). *Appraisal of the Socio-Economic Impact of the New Peat-Fired Power Station in the East Midlands Region*, Dublin: Bord na Móna

Layard, R. and S. Glaister (eds) (1994). *Cost-Benefit Analysis*, Cambridge: CUP

National Economic Research Associates (1995). *Socio-Economic Cost Benefit Analysis of Investment in a Peat-Fired Power Station*, London: NERA

Tecnecon Ltd (1997). *Development of National Museum of Ireland*, Dublin: Department of Arts, Culture and the Gaeltacht

8

Evaluation of Applications for Grant-Aid: The Basic Formula*

PATRICK HONOHAN

Section One : An Introduction

Industrial policy incentives in Ireland

Industrial development policy in Ireland has long been characterised by its reliance on both discretionary and non-discretionary incentives. The former includes a range of grants for new investment or expansion projects in manufacturing and certain internationally traded service sectors. The latter features a low rate of corporation profits tax rate applicable (up to now) to essentially the same sectors (though the profits tax rate will soon be unified at a low rate for all sectors). Although, like its predecessor export sales relief, the regime does not discriminate between foreign-owned and indigenous firms, it was probably always envisaged chiefly as a mechanism for inducing an inflow of foreign direct investment. The low tax rate, combined with international tax treaties, is of great advantage to US and other firms with unsheltered foreign tax liabilities: the discretionary grants enable the Irish development agencies to compete with other possible destinations for internationally mobile investment projects. The success of the policy is evidenced by the remarkably high share of foreign-owned companies in manufacturing whether measured by employment (45 per cent) or output (70 per cent).

While the benefits of the tax and grant regime are thus evident, there have also been costs. Use of public funds for this policy imposes a tax burden on the rest of the economy which could be very damaging. It also potentially damages the rest of the economy by bidding-up the price of labour and other resources (Barry and Hannan, 1995). Indeed, unless supported by other policies, rapid industrial expansion can also entail a variety of external congestion costs which are only recently becoming evident. As the Culliton report (1992) argued, the discretionary element of the grants can encourage rent-seeking that may distract local entrepreneurs from productive activity.

Evaluation of applications for grant-aid

Taking as given both the discretionary policy and the existence of grants, the Irish industrial development agencies still need a system of *ex ante* evaluation of specific applications for grant assistance. The Economic and Social Research Institute recently carried out a review of the evaluation model which had been in use by the agencies since the late 1970s and which was based on economic cost-benefit methodology.[1] Although specifically tailored to the needs of the agencies, several key elements of our approach have a wider application, as they address some important though oft-neglected issues in cost-benefit work in Ireland more generally.

We started from the position that the evaluation model is essentially a management information system designed to improve decision-making in regard to grant approvals. As such, the model should be based on the policy-maker's understanding of the economic distortions to which policy is addressed, and employ a credible quantification of these distortions. It should, when employed, result in satisfactory policy decisions which are not them-selves distorting.

Interest in cost-benefit analysis was at its strongest in the 1970s, when economic policies perpetuated distortions, and when (in an era before privatisation) policy-makers looked extensively to semi-autonomous state agencies to target public funds to social goals. Chapter 4 of this volume reviews the fluctuating fortunes of cost-benefit, and provides a general introduction to the present application.

The major issues

This chapter isolates three main issues in cost-benefit that stand out from the study of industrial development grants as having a wider application and being of general interest. First is the need to take better account of system effects in arriving at the appropriate treatment of labour costs (shadow wage). Second is the importance of measuring and valuing the tax and government expenditure flows involved in such incentive schemes. Third, account needs to be taken of deadweight: the fact that (despite the best efforts of the agencies) some grants will be higher than necessary to secure the project. This chapter sets out the basic cost-benefit formula and shows precisely where the assumptions about shadow wage, about the net cost of tax revenue foregone and about the burden of deadweight enter.

There are other considerations one could bring into the analysis – environ-mental issues, congestion, technology spin-offs. But increasing elaboration into uncharted territory could weaken rather than strengthen the practical use-fulness of a formal evaluation scheme. When the decision-makers know which factors have been quantified, they can make their own allowance for the rest.

Shadow wage

Despite high unemployment in Ireland, a shadow wage as low as 15 per cent of market wage (i.e. ignoring 85 per cent of the project's wage costs in making the evaluation) cannot be defended. Employment creation policy is not as effective in reducing employment as is often believed. The well-documented rapid and substantial migration responses to changes in the difference between Irish and UK unemployment levels confirm this. The fact that unemployment is falling now reflects low unemployment in the UK as well as the strong job growth at home. It is primarily because of this linkage that we argue that the shadow wage used for this kind of job creation measure should be much higher than it has been. We recommend using a shadow wage of about 80 per cent.

Tax revenue and the shadow-price of public funds

While the treatment of tax revenues in appraisal can be controversial, the position here is clear. Indeed, in contrast to conventional project appraisal, where the major costs are in terms of economic resources, the question of industrial policy is centrally focused on grant and tax costs. Not only must tax revenue be included in the calculation, but account must be taken of the fact that making up for lost tax revenues or the cash cost of grants imposes costs on the economy more than pound-for-pound. The latter consideration is taken account of by applying a premium factor (called the shadow-price of public funds) to all government revenues and expenditures.[2] This factor is estimated to be about 1.5 in Ireland at present, down from over 2 in the mid-1980s (Honohan and Irvine, 1990). Because projects differ in their labour and tax intensity, including tax revenue in the calculation can alter the ranking of projects.

Deadweight in grant assistance

What about the investment that would have gone ahead anyway without the inducement of special taxes or grants? Some account must be taken of this deadweight. Of course the agencies do their best to strike a hard bargain, but so do the investors. Knowing that some grants will be unnecessarily generous, but not knowing which ones, implies that the cut-off for grants, the maximum that can be offered, should be lowered. This is quantitatively an important point, and it is not one for which the literature provides a ready answer. Our approach has been to develop a simple theory based on modern bargaining theory (Osborne and Rubinstein, 1990), together with empirical estimates[3] of the degree to which manufacturing activity in Ireland is grant-sensitive (the aggregate elasticity of manufacturing activity with respect to the rate of grant), to arrive at an estimate of the allowance that needs to be made for deadweight. Quantification here is somewhat tentative (we suggest 80 per cent deadweight), but the logic of the approach is clear and has a wider applicability.

Section Two: Evaluation of applications for grant-aid:
the basic

The formal cost-benefit appraisal system operated up to now by the industrial development agencies has been based on a standard criterion function which expresses the discounted present value of the project benefits as a multiple of the grant paid. Our modifications remain within this general framework.

Oversimplifying to convey the essential point, it may be said that the old model took the cost to be the grant outlay, and the benefit to be 85 per cent of the wages generated through jobs created.[4] This is equivalent to using a shadow wage rate of just 15 per cent, well below rates commonly reported in the literature. On the other hand, in order to be approved, projects had to satisfy a threshold benefit to cost ratio set arbitrarily at 4 to 1.

While retaining the general approach, we see a need to modify the formula in three major respects.[5]

First, the shadow wage rate needs to be increased to take better account of known general equilibrium effects. This also has a knock-on effect on the shadow prices of other inputs, since they are linked to the shadow wage through the estimated labour content of the inputs.

Second, there has to be a fuller treatment of taxation, including tax revenue as a benefit offsetting grant costs and also applying a weighting (the shadow prices of public funds) before adding revenue benefits to private benefits. There is no basis for ignoring (as the old method did) tax revenue, including income tax and expenditure taxes, generated by the project as an offset to the grant cost incurred.

Third, projected benefits must be reduced by a deadweight factor, designed to take account both of the response elasticity of projects and jobs to grant levels and the degree to which an increase in grants can be confined to those projects that are actually dependent on it.

Our modifications partly reflect a new emphasis in the cost-benefit literature on system effects and also the increased importance and higher rates of taxation. This new approach does result in some alternation of the ranking of projects, and introduces a completely new approach to the threshold, though not a drastic change in practice to the cut-off.

For any given grant-aid application, the following ratio of costs to benefits function is calculated on the basis of projected flows:

$$(1 - \theta)\{\Sigma_i x_i p_i \, [(1 - v_i)+ \phi \, \text{Ti}]+ \phi \, \tau_o \pi\}/(\phi g) \qquad (1)$$

using the following notation:

π is profits

p_i are the market prices of each input i

v_i are the ratios of shadow to market prices

x_i are the volumes of each input

τ_i are the tax rates on each input (inclusive of a standard allowance for saving on social welfare payments resulting from a fall in unemployment)

τ_0 is the tax rate on profits

θ is the deadweight factor – the allowance for the fact that some grants will have been unnecessarily large

ϕ is the shadow price of public funds

g is the grant cost.

All of these elements are calculated in present value terms. The changes from the old formula are the inclusion of the shadow price of public funds (this would previously have been unity) and in the deadweight factor (this would previously have been zero – but a threshold of 4 would have been imposed).

In words, the formula simply sums the value (at shadow prices adjusted for the shadow price of public funds) of all the inputs, adds the taxes on inputs and profits and reduces the total by the deadweight factor to get a figure of the 'benefits', before dividing by the grant cost.

It may be helpful to look at the formula step by step, beginning with the term immediately after the summation sign, which measures the net social benefit of one input *(i)* used in the project plus net tax revenue.[6]

$$x_i \, p_i \, \{(1 - v_i) + \phi \tau_i\} \qquad (2)$$

Here $x_i \, p_i$ is the total market cost of the use of input *i*. If the shadow price of that input is equal to the market price, *i* does not contribute net value to the project. That is the meaning of the term: $1 - v_i$. It maps the market cost of the use of input *i* to the net social value. The tax rate τ_i is multiplied by the marginal cost of social funds ϕ.

This term is summed over all the inputs,[7] and the tax revenue from profits – again multiplied by the marginal cost of social funds – is added to obtain the part between parentheses:

$$\Sigma_i \, x_i \, p_i \, [(1 - \nu_i) + \phi\tau_i] + \phi\tau_o\pi \qquad (3)$$

which represents the total 'benefits'.

Finally, this is all premultiplied by the adjustment for deadweight $(1 - \theta)$, before being divided by the grant 'cost' g, which is also multiplied by the marginal cost of social funds ϕ.

To anticipate the conclusions we can say here that, in contrast to the old procedure, we arrive at much higher figures for the ν's, especially for labour where we use 0.8 instead of 0.15. The suggested value of ϕ is 1.5 (previously, in effect it was 1) and for θ it is 0.8. Of course the other difference from the past is the inclusion of the tax revenues.

*

This article is an extract from Honohan, P., *Key Issues of Cost-Benefit Methodology for Irish Industrial Policy*, Dublin: Economic and Social Research Institute, 1998

NOTES

1　The review was carried out by the author and Eoin O'Malley, with a contribution by Philip O'Connell and the assistance of Jane Kelly, Siobhán Kenny and Alan Wall.

2　The fact that government can freely borrow on international capital markets does not alter this: the debt will ultimately have to be serviced out of tax revenue.

3　In practice we have inferred this from estimates of elasticity of demand for labour in manufacturing (Bradley, FitzGerald and Kearney, 1993).

4　Both directly in the project being grant-aided and indirectly from the project's sub-supply needs, cf. O'Malley (1995).

5　Several additional modifications are not discussed in the present paper.

6　In the case of labour, the tax element includes savings on social welfare. Thus we can think of these two elements as being essentially (i) the private benefit obtained by those individuals who are no longer involuntarily unemployed and (ii) the net additional cash flow to the Exchequer resulting from the additional employment and reduction in unemployment.

7　All outputs are assumed to have shadow price equal to market price, so they do not contribute any net social benefit.

REFERENCES

Barry, F. and A. Hannan (1995). 'Have Multinationals Crowded Out Indigenous Employment?', Presented at the Irish Economic Association Annual Conference, Ballyconnell, May

Bradley, J., J. Fitzgerald and I. Kearney (1993). 'Modelling Supply in an Open Economy Using a Restricted Cost Function', *Economic Modelling*, vol. 10, pp 11-21

Culliton Report (1992). *A Time for Change*, Report of the Industrial Policy Review Group, Dublin: Government Publications

Honohan, P., and I.J. Irvine (1990). 'Deadweight Loss Measurement with Generalised Gorman Polar Forms', *Public Finance*, vol. 45, pp 260-267

O'Malley, E. (1995). *An Analysis of Secondary Employment Associated with Manufacturing Industry,* General Research Series No. 167, Dublin: The Economic and Social Research Institute

Osborne, M.J., and A. Rubinstein (1990). *Bargaining and Markets,* San Diego, Ca.: Academic Press

9

Economic Evaluation in Health Care*

FERGAL LYNCH

Introduction

Health care markets are substantially different from those for many other commodities. They are not generally competitively organised; they are subject to highly imperfect information; demand on the part of individuals is unpredictable; and there is at least some scope for supplier-induced demand.

Since much health care is funded either by the state or through private insurance, neither the demanders nor suppliers may have a significant incentive to contain costs or to limit demand. According to traditional economic theory, this *third party* payment system results in demand beyond the level of both productive and allocative efficiency.1

Figure 9.1 contrasts the markets for 'ordinary' commodities, in which consumption will occur at the point where marginal benefits equal marginal cost (i.e. Q1), with the market for health care where, assuming full payment by a third party, consumption continues right up to the point where marginal benefits have been exhausted, i.e. Q2.

The *welfare loss* to society is illustrated by the shaded area abQ2, in which health care has been supplied well beyond the point where the marginal cost of its production exceeds the marginal benefits derived from it.

This is not to suggest that health care markets are entirely different from those for all other commodities. A number of other markets are also subject to imperfect information, monopoly power, uncertainty of demand and a substantial third party payment system. Nonetheless, health care has a higher incidence of these differentiating characteristics than most other markets.

Quite apart from the elements of health care that make it significantly different from any other markets, another marked characteristic is the apparently widening gap between expectations and supply. Thwaites (1987) illustrated the difference between the health care market's ability to provide services for the population and the resources available.

162

Figure 9.1: Contrasting usage of health care with other commodities

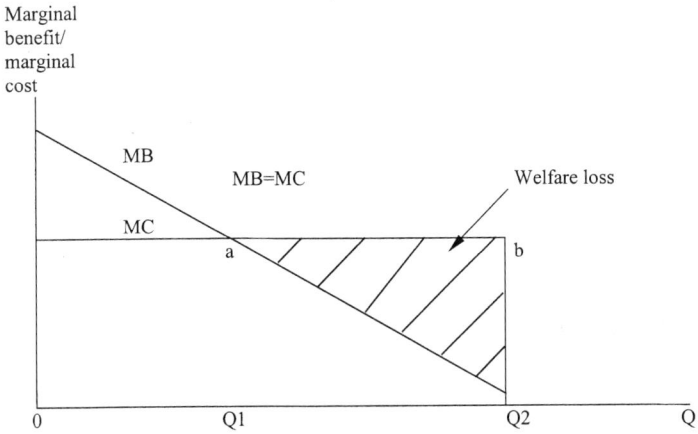

Figure 9.2: Widening gap between expectations and resources

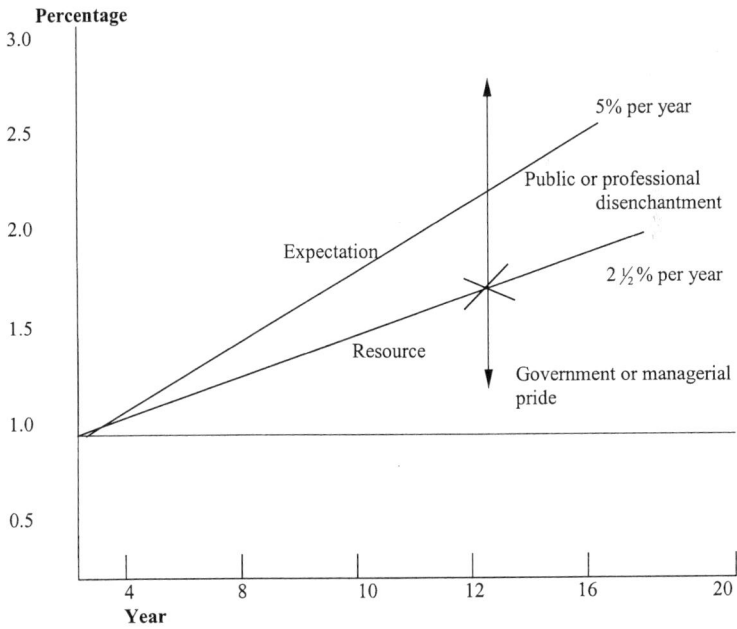

Source: *British Medical Journal*, adapted from Thwaites (1987)

Such a framework helps to underline the importance of establishing rational and (as far as possible) objective ways of determining priorities in health care. Economic evaluation offers an important tool to aid decision-making in health care. This article explores the main applications of economic evaluation to health care, discussing the main uses to which it can be put and the challenges involved in doing so.

As in all other areas of evaluation, the application of appraisal techniques to health care must be seen as an aid to, rather than as a substitute for, other forms of decision-making. It would be wholly misleading to suggest that economic appraisal can offer clear-cut or ready-made answers that immediately justify implementation. Instead, economic evaluation in health care helps decision-makers formulate a series of relevant questions and encourages judgements and assumptions, which would otherwise be made implicitly, to be made explicitly.

Perspective of the evaluation

It is important to be clear about the perspective from which an economic evaluation is to be carried out. In health care, a programme or a form of treatment could be analysed from the viewpoint of:

- the individual patient

- a definable group of clients (e.g. the elderly)

- the provider (hospital, doctor or another professional) or

- society as a whole.

The widest perspective is obviously that of society as a whole, and is often the preferred point of reference. Robinson (1993a) notes two implications of the societal approach:

- It usually involves placing a value on items not normally priced by the market.

- Some costs (or savings) must be excluded from the evaluation because they merely represent transfers of resources from one part of society to another. This might arise in the case of income maintenance payments to, say, the disabled. Although a cost to government, they are a transfer of money within society.

The main approaches to evaluation

There are four main approaches to economic evaluation in health care. Moving from the least to most complex, these are cost-minimisation analysis

(CMA), cost-effectiveness analysis (CEA), cost-utility analysis (CUA) and cost-benefit analysis (CBA).

Which of the four methods to use depends on the nature of the question being asked and the type of information available for analysis. To date, CMA and CEA have been the more popular methods in health care, but in recent times there has been a growing use of CUA. Practical and theoretical difficulties have hindered the extensive use of CBA, but notwithstanding this some of its main principles can be of substantial assistance in an economic evaluation.

CMA is generally applicable where the outcomes of alternative options are considered likely to be very similar. Then it is primarily a matter of identifying the best-cost option. CEA is required where outcomes between options are expected to differ and a quantification of those outcomes is therefore required.

CUA reflects a growing concern to evaluate the benefit (or utility) offered to patients by alternative treatments or programmes in health care. It attempts to take account of the quality improvements brought by health care interventions in a way that is not possible under CMA or CEA. Finally, CBA focuses on whether a programme of treatment offers a net benefit to society by measuring benefits and costs in a single unit of value, usually money. It differs from the three other methods by evaluating the overall gain to society as a whole.

Cost minimisation analysis (CMA)

In some cases it may be clear that the results produced by different options in health care, such as alternative treatments for a particular condition, are very similar. If so, the main question to answer in an economic evaluation is: which option can be implemented at least cost? A cost minimisation analysis is appropriate in these circumstances since the relative success of alternative options is assumed to be the same.

However, it is important to establish that outcomes will, in fact, be very similar. Otherwise a CMA based on an inaccurate assumption about results of alternative options will be misleading.

Drummond et al (1987) argue that 'a full economic evaluation through cost minimisation analysis requires some evidence on which to believe that outcome differences of the alternatives are nonexistent or unimportant'.

Ideally CMA studies should be performed alongside, or immediately after, supporting clinical trials which establish the close similarity of outcomes between alternative options. A practical difficulty may arise here, in terms of availability of data or ease with which an appropriate set of trials can be carried out. CMA may therefore have to rely on previously collected evidence, medical opinion or assumptions about results from earlier studies.

Applications of cost-minimisation analysis in health care are most often found in choosing between alternative medical treatments or sites of medical treatment. Examples include analysis of treatments for minor conditions such as hernia, haemorrhoids and varicose veins. Drummond et al describe studies in these areas, where the choice may be between day surgery and traditional in-patient care. There are many other potential uses of CMA in the area of treatment alternatives; the key prerequisite to its use is that the outcomes are expected to be very similar.

CMA need not be confined to decisions concerning alternative treatments. It can also be applied to questions of how best to achieve a given objective at least cost. If, for example, it is decided to make a 'meals-on-wheels' type service available to non-ambulant elderly people in their own homes, there may be different options for doing so. One is by grant-aiding an existing voluntary organisation for the elderly, while another is by utilising employees of the local health authority or board. A third option is to contract with a private catering firm to supply and serve the meals.

In each case the outcome (meals delivered directly to the homes of a selected dependent population) could be expected to be the same, but the cost of providing the service would probably vary between options. While most CMAs are directed towards decisions regarding the relative cost of alternative treatments, the meals example underlines that the scope of this type of analysis can be much wider.

CMA can be applied not only to potential new areas, but also to existing programmes. A CMA on alternative ways of providing a service can be applied to programmes already in operation. The analysis would scrutinise the way in which a service is currently being provided, compared with a number of alternative options.

It is in this area that economic evaluation is perhaps under-used in posing often awkward questions about the performance of existing programmes or services compared with different methods of achieving the same result. Appraisal techniques can therefore offer a valuable means of reviewing services already in operation. They need not be confined to new programmes or treatments.

Cost-effectiveness analysis (CEA)

Cost-effectiveness analysis is used when both the costs *and* results of alternative options are expected to vary. Thus it takes the appraisal a step further than CMA by quantifying changes in outcome as well as in cost. It is important, however, that the varying outcomes can be measured in common units; otherwise it is not possible to compare the results of different options.

CEA is a popular method for comparing alternative treatment regimes;

outcomes can be measured in terms of standard indicators that are present in all cases treated. For example, alternative treatments of renal failure can be compared in terms of life years gained, or for hypertension in terms of blood pressure. The costs – and marginal costs – can of course also be compared.

The value of CEA in these cases is that it can take account of differing results from alternative treatments, while at the same time comparing costs. Treatments for varicose veins may have varying outcomes in terms of side-effects, recuperation time and duration of improvement in condition, but these factors can be taken into account in a CEA. When a common unit of output has been established, such as

- life years gained from a renal treatment

- number of positive cases detected by a screening programme

- post-operative infection rate using alternative methods of surgery

- degree of mobility after a set period following orthopaedic surgery

- proportion of cases in which complications were avoided

then the resource implications of each alternative treatment can be expressed in terms of a *cost per unit output*.

A number of valuable studies have been carried out using CEA. Robinson (1993 b) notes a series of CEA studies in which useful conclusions were drawn regarding the relative performance of alternative treatments. Among these are Boyle et al's (1993) study of neonatal intensive care for very low birthweight babies, in which the author compared results prior to the introduction of neonatal intensive care with those after its introduction and measured costs in the context of additional lives saved.

Other uses of CEA, as reported by Robinson (1993b), include an evaluation of Pap tests (smears taken for the detection of cervical cancer) by Mendelblatt and Fahs (1988) and a study by Oster and Epstein (1987) of antihyperlipaemic therapy in the prevention of coronary heart disease. Both studies use an estimate of the cost per life saved as the unit of measurement. Robinson lists a number of other studies in which the unit of measurement varies from the number of pain-free days to the number of successful diagnoses (using alternative diagnostic strategies), to the number of episodes of fever cured and deaths prevented.

Many studies measure cost-effectiveness in terms of just one of the above indicators or criteria. However, a potential disadvantage arises in this approach. The single measure chosen may conceal or distort variations within the alternative options under review. For example, a study of different treatment regimes which focuses on a single measure of abatement in a condition, such as blood pressure, might miss another important outcome factor, such as patient discomfort during treatment.

With this in mind, some studies use a multi-dimensional approach, taking account of a greater number of outcome measures. Thus Percival and Setty's (1992) study of day surgery versus in-patient treatment for cataract surgery used a set of measures of effectiveness namely operative and post-operative infection; visual acuity after three to six days following surgery and again ten weeks to six months after surgery; and a survey of patient satisfaction.

The use of a set of cost-effectiveness measures is valuable where there is concern about how meaningful a single measure would be. However, it creates difficulties in assessing the overall cost-effectiveness of competing options where the results do not consistently favour one option. In Percival and Setty's study virtually all of the indicators pointed towards day surgery over the in-patient alternative, making the conclusions clear-cut. Nevertheless, studies which find the results produced by different options to be more finely balanced face a difficult task in reaching conclusions. They can still, however, advance the decision-making process by pointing to the differing results from the measures chosen. At the very least, judgements can then be made about the relative priority of each measure chosen, with the decision-making process being influenced accordingly.

To date, the discussion of CEA has been concerned mainly with its application to clinical trials and alternative treatments for a given condition. However, as in the case of CMA, its potential in health care extends well beyond decisions of this nature. CEA can be used to examine the relative cost-effectiveness of existing programmes or services compared to alternative options. It might, for example, be applied to evaluating the most cost-effective way of providing residential care for a group of elderly people in a specific catchment area. A CEA study might compare the relative performance, or the marginal cost, of existing homes for the elderly owned by a health board, with that of homes operated by voluntary organisations grant-aided by the health board. In each case, the measure of output might be judged in terms of, for example, client satisfaction.

Similarly a CEA approach could be used where a health board is allocated a pre-determined amount of money to reduce waiting times for a given speciality. Thus the question facing decision-makers would be to identify the most cost-effective means of spending €500,000 to reduce waiting times in the health board's catchment area for, say, orthopaedic procedures. The measure of output in this case is reduction in waiting times. The options for achieving this might include contracting with another health board with excess capacity, employing additional staff on a temporary basis in its own area, or switching the use of a ward and facilities from another speciality to orthopaedics. This is but one example of how the use of CEA can extend beyond individual treatment options or other medical-related decisions.

CEA provides another example of economic evaluation as a useful aid to decision-making. It can provide a rational and objective means of judging between alternatives but it should not be seen as the exclusive basis of making a decision.

An important consideration in all of the CEAs presented above is that they do not question the desirability of achieving specified objectives. Neither do they question the level of priority that should be attached to the objectives. For example, CEA does not determine whether it is appropriate to devote resources to reducing orthopaedic times; it is concerned only with identifying the most cost-effective means of doing so. Similarly, a CEA does not question whether the €500,000 allocated to orthopaedics might more appropriately have been devoted to a competing purpose, such as waiting times in another speciality, to rehabilitation services for the disabled, or to any other health care service.

This limitation is not a serious disadvantage. Instead it can be regarded as an important element of the framework within which CEA operates. Failure to take account of the fact that CEA does not question the underlying desirability of the objective under consideration will lead to invalid inferences about the evaluation's conclusions. Since CEA sets out only to determine the most cost-effective option of achieving a particular objective, it should not be taken as a validation of the priority of achieving that objective above all others.

Cost-utility analysis (CUA)

Background

We have seen that cost effectiveness analysis (CEA) is useful in clarifying choices by taking account of differing results from alternative options and estimating a cost per unit of output. However, if decisions have to be taken regarding the priority to be attached to alternative programmes or treatments, i.e. if a choice must be made between different service areas, then CEA is less helpful. This is because the units of output from the competing programmes are likely to differ. It would be difficult, using CEA, to choose between, say, a service for the elderly and a treatment protocol for premature babies, because the units of output being measured would differ greatly.

In the case of residential service for the elderly, the unit under examination might be client satisfaction, while in the case of premature births it could be specific mortality or morbidity indicators.

CEA is therefore less useful in setting priorities between competing programmes or interventions; its strength lies in identifying the most cost-effective means of achieving an objective after priorities have been set. An increasing emphasis in health care is on assessing the health and social gain,2 i.e. the added benefit brought about by the health services. Under this approach, it is not sufficient to establish that a programme is cost-effective, or that the money allocated to a service was devoted to the purpose for which it was intended. It is necessary, in addition, to examine the extra benefit or utility brought about by the intervention under review.

CUA and quality of life

Cost utility analysis (CUA) is a means of measuring the utility conferred by treatments on patients in terms of improved quality of life. This is a technically difficult and often controversial approach to economic evaluation, but it offers significant advantages in clarifying the implications of alternative options. It attempts to be explicit about valuations made implicitly in the absence of such appraisals; decisions about the relative priority of projects are made in any event. By estimating the improvements in quality of life brought about by a health care intervention, and the cost of that improved quality, CUA can inform decision-makers in the setting of priorities. As in the case of CEA and CMA, it is intended primarily as an aid to decision-making by clarifying the implications of choosing alternative options.

Application of CUA: the QALY

CUA uses measures of the utility placed on different states of health and on varying degrees of social functioning. A number of such measures has been devised, including the Nottingham Health Profile, the Rosser Index and the Oregon Demonstration Project described in Robinson (1993c). All are directed towards quantifying the value placed by individuals on varying indicators of quality of life. CUA takes these a step further by estimating the costs involved in programmes or treatments which improve that quality of life.

The Quality-Adjusted Life Year (QALY) is one of the most widely used measures of quality of life in CUA. It comprises both a qualitative measure of quality of life and a quantitative estimate of life years. It can then express treatments or other health care interventions in terms of a cost per QALY gained. The marginal cost per QALY can, of course, also be calculated. A fuller outline of QALYs is provided by Gudex and Kind (1988).

The Rosser Index has been used in the calculation of QALYs in the UK. The index describes states of health in terms of two dimensions – disability and distress. Eight levels of disability are described in increasing stages of deterioration from no disability to unconscious as shown in Table 9.1.

The eight levels of disability and four categories of distress are then combined to produce a matrix of 32 possible states of health. Rosser interviewed a selected set of doctors, nurses, patients and volunteers in good health to establish their views on the relative severity of each of the 32 states of health compared with each other. The results were expressed in an index ranging between 0 = dead and 1 = perfect health.

Table 9.1: Levels of disability

I	No disability
II	Slight social disability
III	Severe social disability and/or slight impairment of performance at work. Able to do housework except very heavy tasks
IV	Choice of work or performance at work very severely limited. Housewives and old people able to do light housework only but able to go out shopping
V	Unable to undertake any paid employment Unable to continue any education Old people confined to home except for escorted outings and short walks and unable to go shopping Housewives able to perform only a few simple tasks
VI	Confined to a chair or wheelchair or able to move around in the house only with support from an assistant
VII	Confined to bed
VIII	Unconscious

Source: Kind, P., R. Rosser and A. Williams (1982)

Four levels of distress are defined by Rosser:

Table 9.2: Levels of distress

A	No distress
B	Mild
C	Moderate
D	Severe

Source: Kind, P., R. Rosser and A. Williams (1982)

Using this approach it is possible to assign any disease or condition a quality of life score by placing it within one of the 32 health states devised by Rosser. While the actual index assigned to any state of health has been criticised, Robinson (1993c) notes Gudex and Kind's finding that:

a single training session on the approach was sufficient to obtain a high level of agreement between doctors on rating patients ... these descriptions could be used to categorise patients reliably, accurately and quickly.

Having established a method for expressing health status in a single score from 0-1, the next step was to continue it with a measure of the life years gained as a result of a particular treatment or intervention. One of the best known studies in this area is Williams' (1985) evaluation, using QALYs, of treatment options for angina patients. In it he asked three cardiologists to give their judgements about the life expectancy and relative states of health of angina patients, some of whom had received surgery for the condition (coronary artery bypass) and others of whom had not.

Williams was then able to estimate the number of quality-adjusted life years (QALYs) for patients with mild to severe angina, distinguishing between different types of the disease (e.g. left main vessel, triple vessel, etc). Comparisons of the quality and expected length of life could then be made between those undergoing surgery and those receiving medical management alone, i.e. without surgery.

Having calculated the QALYs gained from treatments, it is then possible to attach costs to them so that the cost per QALY of alternative treatments (or other health care interventions) can be estimated. A series of 'league tables' has been calculated in the UK, which draw attention to large variations in the cost per QALY of different interventions. An extract from one such league table is shown in Table 9.3. It demonstrates, for example, that the cost per QALY of cholesterol testing and treatment by diet was £220, compared with £1,180 for a hip replacement and £17,260 for home haemodialysis.

At the extreme, a nuerosurgical intervention for malignant intracranial tumours was estimated to cost over £100,000 per QALY.

The results from league tables of the type shown in Table 9.3 are not intended to suggest that resources should automatically be transferred to interventions with a lower cost per QALY. Instead they are meant to make decisions about allocating resources between alternative interventions more explicit. If however the intention is to achieve as much health gain and social gain as possible from health care programmes, then the cost per QALY of competing priorities cannot be ignored. The ultimate decision may be to channel resources towards interventions that produce the highest net benefits, but equally it may be that certain procedures with a relatively high cost per QALY should still be accorded a high priority. The advantage of this approach is that decision-makers have been made more fully aware of resource implications of the priorities that they have established.

Table 9.3 Sample QALY league table (Costs as in August 1990)

Treatment	Cost (£) per QALY
Cholesterol testing and treatment by diet (age 40-69)	220
Neurosurgical intervention for head injury	240
Pacemaker implantation	1,100
Hip replacement	1,180
Kidney transplantation	4,710
Breast cancer screening	5,780
Home haemodialysis	17,260
Neurosurgical intervention for malignant intracranial tumours	107,780

Source: Extracted from Mason J, M. Drummond, G. Torrance (1993)

Criticisms of the QALY approach

It is not surprising that the QALY approach, and its use in CUA, has been the subject of strong criticism. At a methodological level, the complaints centre on the means of assigning values to different states of health, through the use of interviews. McGuire, Henderson and Mooney (1988) note a number of these as follows:

- A person may respond in a markedly different way to a hypothetical question than to a real one. Preferences may alter as more information is acquired, or as the choice assumes greater practical significance.

- Most of the surveys for estimation of health status have assessed movements from a position of good health to poorer health than, for example, from a previously chronic condition to a better one. The law of diminishing marginal utility, if applied to health, would suggest that the results of movements from good to poor instead of poor to good health states may be significantly different.

Added to the methodological criticisms of QALYs and their calculation are several practical charges. These include the argument that, by focusing on the benefits that health care can bring and the cost of those benefits, they discriminate against the elderly. QALYs are also criticised for paying insufficient attention to equity; once again the focus on the cost of achieving a particular health gain, and the length of time for which it may be of practical value, is cited as an attack on fairness in decision-making.

Some of the critics of QALYs, such as Gafni et al (1993), argue in favour of alternative measures such as healthy year equivalents which estimate the number of years of good health that is equivalent to a longer lifetime of poor health, claiming that they are more in accordance with the principles of economics and therefore to QALYs for economic evaluation of health care interventions. However, other studies, such as Culyer and Wagstaff (1993), suggest that both measures produce identical rankings under most assumptions.

Appropriate use of CUA

Many of the criticisms of the QALY approach, and the use of CUA generally, can best be addressed by bearing in mind the early stage of development of CUA, and the qualifications attached to it by its advocates. The key elements to take into account are that it must be used appropriately, bearing in mind its limitations, and that its results should be judged in that light. Robinson (1993c) points out that CUA:

> is probably the most sophisticated form of economic evaluation available at present. However, sensible use of the technique and interpretation of research findings based on the approach should recognise that cost-utility analysis is at a fairly early development stage and treat it accordingly.

Drummond, Stoddart and Torrance (1987) provide guidelines on the appropriate use of CUA. They suggest it might be used in the following circumstances:

- when quality of life is *the* important outcome (as in the case of alternative programmes for treating arthritis)

- when quality of life is *an* important outcome (such as a life-saving treatment, where quality as well as survival is important)

- when a programme effects both morbidity and mortality and a common unit of outcome is required for combining both effects. (Drummond et al quote the example of oestrogen therapy for menopausal symptoms which improves quality of life by reducing discomfort, and which reduces mortality from hip fractures, but which increases mortality from certain complications such as uterine bleeding and gall bladder disease)

- when the programmes being compared have a wide range of different outcomes and a common unit of output is needed. (The advantage of CUA over CEA in this regard was noted earlier)

- when a programme is being compared with others that have already been the subject of CUA.

Drummond et al argue that CUA should not be used in the following circumstances:

- when only intermediate indicators of effectiveness can be obtained. (This means that final measures of outcome are not available, leaving no scope for conversion to QALYs for application to CUA)

- when other forms of analysis are sufficient. (If, for example, it is clear that the options are equally effective, a CMA may be all that is required)

- when indicators relating to quality of life can be captured in natural units. (Drummond et al quote the example of alternative treatments for leg fractures being compared to a single variable – reduction in days of restricted activity)

- when the extra cost involved in obtaining and applying measures of utility is itself not cost effective. (This might arise, for example, where CEA shows one alternative to be so superior to all others as to make a CUA unlikely to change the result).

These guidelines suggested by Drummond et al underline the importance of the appropriate use of CUA, and of avoiding CUA where the results would be misleading or more easily obtained by less complex methods.

Cost-benefit analysis (CBA)

A critical disadvantage of the three methods of economic evaluation in health care discussed to date is that they have no means of judging whether the options under review offer a net benefit to society. CMA, CEA and CUA can all offer important insights into the relative costliness of alternative options, and into their differing outcomes. However, they cannot in themselves measure whether the benefits of any option exceed the costs involved, i.e. whether there is a net gain for society. This is because they usually measure costs and benefits in different units.

By contrast, cost-benefit analysis (CBA) attempts to place a value (usually in monetary terms) on both the costs and benefits of health care. It is the most comprehensive form of economic appraisal, but is technically difficult to carry out. Attaching monetary values to costs and benefits that are often intangible raises practical and methodological problems. Because of these difficulties, CBA has had a relatively limited application in the health care market to date.

Since valuation of the more intangible benefits and costs presents a particular challenge in health care, it is important to set criteria at the outset for determining how far these valuations should be taken. Drummond et al suggest that the following questions should be asked in the valuation of health care programmes:

- Are the results of the study likely to be altered by gathering additional information on intangible items?
- Can the costs of gathering the information be afforded?
- Will the valuation of intangible outcomes lead to more informed decision-making? Drummond et al argue that this may depend on how decision-makers interpret and use the valuations offered.

Two of the most popular approaches to valuing benefits and costs are based on human capital and willingness-to-pay.

Human capital approach

In health care the early applications of CBA placed valuations on intangible benefits and costs using the human capital approach. This equated an individual's rate of pay, or other estimates of productive activity, with benefits achieved or costs incurred. Estimates were made on the basis that human beings, like capital equipment, could be regarded as having a flow of productive activity which could be discounted over time. Benefits of health status could therefore be measured by reference to the flow of income (or other monetary value) foregone as a result of ill health.

In an example of a possible CBA, Drummond et al (1987) deal with the case of a breast screening programme for cancer, in which the valuation of women's time taken up in mammographic screening tests is estimated using the human capital principle. Lost earnings for women in employment and imputed earnings for those not in paid employment are taken into account. However, the authors point to problems in using lost wages as an estimate of the true value of lost production. These include factors such as restrictive market practices and distortions in the labour market which may result in a gap between the value of production and the actual wage rates paid.

Another criticism of the human capital approach in health care is that it does not place a valuation on pain or discomfort of patients or on the distress of relatives. A further difficulty arises in wider economic terms because the human capital approach depends on external valuations of benefits (such as pay rates and wages foregone) rather than on individuals' judgements of cost and benefits to themselves. The approach thus runs contrary to the standard economic assumption that the consumer is best placed to judge his or her own welfare.

Willingness-to-pay approach

This approach uses observed behaviour or stated preferences (as measured by individuals' actions) to estimate the value of intangible costs and benefits. Observing behaviour is, according to Robinson (1993d), useful only in limited circumstances; acceptance of 'danger-money' for high-risk jobs or payments of premium prices for extra safety features in consumer goods are examples.

However, the willingness-to-pay approach can survey individuals directly to establish their readiness to meet the cost of avoiding illness, curing disease or reducing pain or discomfort. In the Drummond et al (1987) breast screening example quoted above, the valuations placed on reassurance of those being screened and on the life-years saved is put forward, in part, on the basis of willingness to pay.

A difficulty of this approach is its dependence on an individual's income; Robinson (1993d) points out that people's answers to questions of this type 'may reflect the value people attached to money itself as well as to their valuation of the benefits of health care'.

Various other methodological problems arise, including the need to cross-check for consistency of answers with related questions about willingness-to-pay and the need to take account of the fact that the questions, by their nature, are hypothetical.

However, some of the difficulties associated with willingness-to-pay valuation in health care can, according to Morrison and Gyldmark (1992), be addressed if the following criteria are observed:

- Questions regarding willingness-to-pay should be expressed in terms of how much an individual would pay in the form of an insurance premium. This would take account of the fact that a person's demand for health care is uncertain both in timing and volume.

- The likelihood of needing a treatment or service should be stated in terms of probability so that it can be expressed as a mathematical prospect.

- Care must be taken to survey representative samples of the population so as to establish the willingness-to-pay of the relevant population being studied.

Use of CBA

It is clear that the problems of valuation of costs, and particularly of benefits, lessen the applicability of CBA to the health sector. The difficulty of expressing those costs and benefits in terms of a single unit is especially significant in health care, as noted for example by Tolley and Rowland (1995) in relation to counselling services. However, there are some useful examples in which

CBA has been applied to health care, including Weisbrod et al's (1980) study of hospital-based versus community-based treatment in mental health. Robinson (1993d) notes that a number of studies of willingness-to-pay have also been made, including the cases of mobile coronary care units, treatment for rheumatoid arthritis, provision of pacemakers in the context of freedom from certain symptoms associated with heart disease, and continuing care accommodation for the elderly.

Strength of CBA

Despite its apparently limited application to health care, CBA offers a valuable tool of analysis. Its principal strength is in offering scope for comparison between a wide range of alternative programmes, both within and outside the health sector. The fact that it establishes the net benefit to society makes it superior to all other forms of economic evaluation since it examines not only the relative performance of options but whether their benefits actually exceed their costs. When it is possible to express costs and benefits in a common unit, CBA helps clarify greatly the implications of alternatives.

While it may not be possible to carry out a complete CBA for practical or methodological reasons, even an application of its main principles will be of considerable use in the health care studies. At the very least, it can help decision-makers to formulate the most relevant questions, and it is likely to do much more than that.

Treatment of costs and benefits in health care evaluation

Finally, two issues relating to the conduct of economic appraisals in health care may be noted. The first is of relevance to all forms of economic evaluation – the inclusion and exclusion of certain costs. The second is of particular concern to health projects because of disagreement regarding the correct approach, namely whether benefits as well as costs of health care projects should be discounted.

Costs

Identification and correct valuation of appropriate costs are critical to the validation of all forms of economic evaluation. So too is the exclusion of costs which would represent double-counting or which arise irrespective of whether the programme under review was to proceed.

In health care three main elements of cost arise: those relating to the health service itself (including treatment, staff time, drugs, medical supplies and 'hotel'-related items); costs incurred by patients and their relatives (including travel time and hours spent taking care of the patients, as well as indirect costs such as stress and loss of income); and costs incurred by society as a whole (including losses to the economy from absenteeism due to illness).

In each case we must ask: Who bears the cost (the health services, patients and their relatives or society in general)? It is also important to take account of marginal, as opposed to total, costs where appropriate. This arises particularly where the question being examined is concerned with how much of the programme of service should be provided, rather than whether it should be provided at all.

A distinction must also be drawn between marginal and average cost. There are numerous examples of where the marginal cost of additional production in health care has been shown to be substantially greater than the average cost involved. These include Oster and Epstein's (1987) study of the cost-effectiveness of antihyperlipaemic treatment in the prevention of heart disease, where the marginal cost per life saved greatly exceeded average costs as patients grew older. Another example is Neuhauser and Lewicki's (1975) study of sequential guaiac stool tests, where the sixth successive test was shown to have a marginal cost of $47.1 million compared with an average cost of just $2,451.

Discounting costs and benefits in health care

The same considerations in relation to discounting of costs apply to health care projects as to appraisals in other areas. Discounting relies on the principle that account must be taken of how soon the costs will arise. The later the cost is incurred, the more attractive, irrespective of inflation or interest charges.

Similar considerations normally arise in the case of benefits and it would at first seem logical to discount benefits over time in the same way as costs. However, in the health area, it is sometimes argued that benefits should not be subject to discounting. Typically, as in Drummond et al (1987), it is argued that:

- individuals cannot 'trade' their health in the same way as other resources

- individuals do not 'invest' in health status, unlike other goods

- there is no evidence that individuals necessarily place a higher value on future health states than present ones, making a discounting approach inadvisable

- it makes little sense to discount 'future' years of life gained at a higher rate than 'present' ones.

However, there are some practical reasons why discounting cost, but not benefits, would produce unrealistic results. The most obvious is that undiscounted benefits flowing over very long time periods (as perhaps, in the case of health promotion programmes) would eventually exceed time-discounted costs almost irrespective of the initial cost. Moreover, there may be some justification, as in Michael Grossman's (1972) model of demand for health care, to assume that people invest in their health in a similar way as in a capital good.

A common conclusion is that, while there may be strong theoretical arguments for using a zero discount rate for benefits in economic appraisals in health care, the present state of development in evaluations will not make this approach likely for some time to come.

Use of casemix measurement in economic evaluation

Casemix measurement techniques offer a valuable additional tool of analysis for the evaluation of health care projects.

Casemix measurement involves classifying hospital patients into defined categories, usually by reference to their clinical and economic characteristics. The most commonly used casemix measure for in-patients is the diagnosis related group (DRG). Other classification methods are used for day cases, such as day patient groups (DPGs) and ambulatory patient groups (APGs). DRGs classify in-patients in terms of the patient's diagnosis and the treatment provided (clinical characteristics) and the amount of hospital resources used (economic characteristics). DPGs and APGs classify day cases using similar principles, although the focus is on medical or surgical procedures provided rather than on diagnosis.

It is possible to classify the vast majority of in-patients into one of about 500 DRGs. Similarly day cases can be categorised into one of 60 DPGs or into a combination reflected from over 200 APGs. When classified in this way, the scope for meaningful comparison between groups of cases and between hospitals is substantial. For example, economic evaluations using CEA can use DRG or DPG data when studying the most cost effective treatment for a particular condition. Similarly, CUA can draw upon casemix data when reviewing changes in the quality of life of a defined set of patients following a particular surgical procedure.

Casemix data have been used since 1993 to influence the level of funding allocated to acute general hospitals in Ireland, but the role of casemix in assisting economic evaluations has yet to be developed. Casemix measurement is not a tool of evaluation in itself. Its value lies in classifying cases into comparable groups which can be analysed using a technique such as CEA or CUA in the knowledge that the data are accurate and have been categorised in a meaningful way. A fuller treatment of casemix measurement and its application in Ireland can be found in Fitzgerald and Lynch (1998).

Conclusion

Economic evaluation in health care is of growing importance. The use of cost minimisation analysis, cost-effectiveness analysis and increasingly, cost-utility analysis, can greatly assist decision-makers in clarifying options and in making the implications of alternative approaches all the more explicit.

While all approaches, including the more sophisticated cost-benefit analysis, encounter some disadvantages, their use in health care offers significant potential if properly applied. There is a growing emphasis on ensuring that health care evaluation studies meet certain minimum criteria in design and analysis and that the results between studies are comparable. In this example, the Panel on Cost Effectiveness in Health and Medicine, an independent multidisciplinary expert group established by the US public health service, has published a report edited by Gold et al (1996) aimed at providing guidance on the conduct of economic evaluations in health care, with particular reference to cost-effectiveness analysis. Guidance of this sort helps promote the validity and reliability of economic evaluation in health care.

*

This article was first published in Mulreany, M., (ed.) *Economic & Financial Evaluation: Measurement, Meaning and Management,* Dublin: Institute of Public Administration, 1999.

NOTES

1 Productive efficiency may be defined in terms of minimising inputs per unit of output, or of maximising output per unit of input. Allocative efficiency can be expressed in terms of an optimal mix of products, having regard to consumer preferences.

2 Health gain is defined in the Irish strategy for health as being 'concerned with health status, both in terms of increase in life expectancy and in terms of improvements in the quality of life through the cure or alleviation of an illness or disability or through any other general improvement in the health of the individual or the population at whom the service is directed'. Social gain is defined in the strategy as being 'concerned with broader aspects of the quality of life. It includes, for example, the quality added to the lives of dependent elderly people and their carers as a result of the provision of support services, or the benefits to a child of living in an environment free of physical and psychological abuse' Department of Health (1994).

REFERENCES

Acton, J. P. (1973). *Evaluating Public Programmes to Save Lives: the Case of Heart Attacks*, Santa Monica: Rand

Boyle, M. H., G. W. Torrance, J. C. Sinclair, A. Sargent, P. Horwood (1983). 'Economic Evaluation of Neonatal Intensive Care of Very-Low-Birth-Weight Infants', *New England Journal of Medicine*, vol 308, pp 1330-7

Culyer, A. J. and A. Wagstaff (1993). 'QALYs versus HYEs', *Journal of Health Economics*, vol 11, pp 311-323

Department of Health (1994). *Shaping a Healthier Future*, Dublin: Stationery Office

Drummond, M. F., Stoddart, G. L. and G. W. Torrance (1987). *Methods for the Economic Evaluation of Health Care Programmes*, Oxford: Oxford University Press

Fitzgerald, A and F. Lynch (1988). 'Casemix Measurement: Assessing the Impact in Irish Acute Hospitals', *Administration*, vol 46, no 1, pp 29-54

Gafni, A, S. Birch and A. Mehrez (1993). 'Economics, Health and Health Economics: HYEs versus QALYs', *Journal of Health Economics*, vol 11, pp 325-339

Gold M. R., J. E. Siegel, L. B. Russell and M. C. Weinstein (eds), (1996). *Cost-Effectiveness in Health and Medicine*, New York: Oxford University Press

Grossman, M. (1972). *The Demand for Health* , New York: National Bureau of Economics Research

Gudex, C. and P. Kind (1988). The QALY Toolkit, York: University of York, Discussion Paper No. 38

Hunt S., S. P. McKenna and J. McEwan (1986). *Measuring Health Status*, London: Croom Helm

Kind, P., R. Rosser and A. Williams (1982). 'Valuation of Quality of Life: Some Psychometric Evidence' in Jones-Lee, MW (ed) *The value of Life and Safety*, Amsterdam: North Holland

McGuire A., J. Henderson and G. Mooney (1988). 'The Economics of Health Care', *International Library of Economics*, London: Routledge and Kegan Paul

Mason, J., M. Drummond and G. Torrance (1993). 'Some Guidelines on the Use of Cost-Effectiveness League Tables', *British Medical Journal*, vol 306, pp 570-2

Mendelblatt, J and M. Fahs (1988). 'Cost Effectiveness of Cervical Screening for Low Income Elderly Women', *Journal of the American Medical Association*, vol 259, pp 2409-13

Morrison, G. C. and M. Gyldmark (1992). *Appraising the Use of Contingent Valuation in Health Economics*, vol 1, pp 233-243

Neuhauser, D, and A. M. Lewicki (1975). 'What do we Gain from the Sixth Stool Guaiac?', *New England Journal of Medicine*, vol 293, pp 226-228

Oster, G. and A. M. Epstein (1987). 'Cost-Effectiveness of Antihyperlipaemic Therapy in the Prevention of Coronary Disease: the Cost of Cholesthramine', *Journal of the American Medical Association*, vol 258, pp 2381-7

Percival S. P. B. and S. S. Setty (1992). 'Prospective Audit Comparing Ambulatory Day Surgery with In-Patients Surgery for Treating Cataracts', *Quality in Health Care*, vol 1, pp 38-42

Robinson, R. (1993a). 'Economic Evaluation & Health Care: What does it mean?', *British Medical Journal*, vol 307, pp 670-673

Robinson, R. (1993b)., 'Economic Evaluation & Health Care: Cost-effectiveness analysis', *British Medical Journal*, vol 307, pp 793-795

Robinson, R. (1993c). 'Economic Evaluation and Health Care: Cost utility analysis', *British Medical Journal*, vol 307, pp 859-862

Robinson, R. (1993d). 'Economic Evaluation and Health Care: Cost-benefit Analysis', *British Medical Journal*, vol 309, pp 924-926

Thwaites, B. (1987). *The NHS: the End of the Rainbow*, Southampton: Institute for Health Policy Studies

Tolley, H. and N. Rowland (1995). *Evaluating the Cost Effectiveness of Counselling in Health Care*, London: Routledge

Weisbrod, B.A., M.A. Test and L.L. Stein (1980). 'Alternatives to Mental Hospital Treatment', *Archives of General Psychiatry*, vol 37, pp 400-5

Williams, A. (1985). 'Economics of Coronary Artery By-Pass Grafting', *British Medical Journal*, vol 291, pp 326-329

10

Evaluation and The Environment*

J. PETER CLINCH, FRANK J. CONVERY

Introduction

We tend to judge the value of items or activities by the amount of money we pay to acquire or experience them. A loaf of bread or an evening at the theatre can be valued using the price we have to pay for them. The fact that we buy the loaf and pay for the theatre ticket indicates that, for us, the experience of eating and enjoying are worth at least the price we pay. However, much of what we enjoy is not directly mediated through markets. We fall in love without putting a price on it, we enjoy a joke with a friend without demanding payment, we walk in the uplands without having to pay a price for admission, we enjoy looking at an old building and having it 'anchor' our sense of place and time without paying the owner for the privilege.

In many situations, it is neither logical nor is there a need to place a value on such dimensions of our lives. Indeed, the very attempt to do so may undermine the value itself. Putting a 'price' on friendship, for example, may undermine it, in the same way that pre-nuptial agreements may induce a sense of the transient in a nominally perpetual commitment. But sometimes choices must be made when it would be useful to be able to provide some values where none are readily available. For example, if a choice has to be made between the planting of two woodland types, such as broadleaves or conifers, on a particular site, the market values for wood outputs can be assessed relatively easily, but the implications for carbon fixing and therefore global warming, for landscape quality, for biodiversity and for water quality are all unvalued in markets. If reasonably credible estimates of market-type values could be derived for what can be categorised as 'non-market' outputs it would help to clarify the implications of choices. Indeed, in a decision-making system where monetary value is perforce regarded as the prime performance indicator, unless there is such valuation there is a tendency for non-market outputs to be ignored in the decision-making process and this can lead to incorrect decisions.

This issue is of central concern in regard to environmental endowments. Environment can be defined as that part of our existence which we somehow share in common. However, that which belongs to all, in a sense belongs to no one. It is this common property characteristic of environmental assets which results in their destruction. In the absence of property rights, that which Garrett Hardin (1968) so brilliantly, if somewhat over simplistically, characterised as the 'tragedy of the commons' occurs. Everyone has free access and the system does not value conservation and so the incentives lead to destruction. The neoclassical economic paradigm says that the market has failed, resulting in a scarce and therefore valuable asset, the environmental endowment, being destroyed. This is because no market exists which can reflect the environment's scarcity value as a price and therefore this value is not reflected in the incentives which users and others face. The solution favoured by most economists is to create markets by some combination of the assignment of property rights, the imposition of charges and taxes which reflect scarcity value, and the encouragement of a market in tradeable permits. The market failure rationale is developed more formally later in this chapter. The point here is to recognise that the absence of values is inimical to good decision-making.

In this chapter, we show how economists are attempting to address this problem by firstly considering the problem of market failure in greater detail. We then provide a framework within which the economic value of environmental assets may be analysed. A number of techniques for assessing non-market values are then outlined. In addition, we address some other aspects which must be considered when evaluating the environment or projects or policies which affect the environment. These include whether the discount rate to be applied to environmental projects should be different from the market discount rate, how cost-benefit rules can be modified when evaluating a project which will cause the irreversible destruction of a natural asset, and the role of non-market valuation in the assessment of sustainability.

The values and market prices discussed below are a product in part of the existing income distribution. If the distribution of income changes, prices will change, and so will non-market values. In addition, the estimates of values are made at the margin. The plausibility of the techniques described depends in part on the fact that most things remain the same, with the implicit assumption that there is no paradigm shift in values, power, income and the like over the time period of assessment.

Market failure

The rationale for the consideration of environmental values in economic evaluation was formally recognised in 1936 when the US Flood Control Act introdu:ed welfare economics into public decision-making by deeming flood control projects to be desirable 'if the benefits to whomsoever they may accrue are in excess of the costs'. This distinguished financial appraisal where the only costs and benefits of a project considered are those faced by the private agent (such as an individual or firm), from cost-benefit analysis where the costs and benefits of a project are considered to be those faced by society as a whole. The divergence between these costs and benefits results from what is known as market failure.

As a result of market failure, certain adjustments must be made when evaluating the costs and benefits of a project to society. For instance, shadow prices are used in place of market prices where there are considered to be distortions within the economy which render certain prices invalid as indicators of social opportunity cost (Drèze and Stern, 1994). These distortions include monopoly power, indirect taxes and subsidies (unless they are correcting for some other form of market failure) and unemployment. However, in relation to the environment, the key manifestations of market failure are externalities and public goods.

Baumol and Oates (1988) provide the following formal definition for the existence of an externality: 'An externality is present whenever an agent's utility or production relationships contain real (non-monetary) variables whose values are chosen by other agents without attention to the effects on the first agent's utility.'

More simply, an external cost is a cost resulting from an activity which is not borne by the agent engaging in that activity and an external benefit is a benefit which results from an activity which is appropriated by someone other than the agent engaging in that activity. Examples of external costs can be found at local level such as fish kills from water pollution by farming, at regional level such as the damage to crops and buildings by acid rain resulting from sulphur emissions, and at global level such as the costs of global warming which result from the burning of fossil fuels. Examples of external benefits include the landscape benefits of a forest plantation and carbon sequestration and oxygen production from the world's forests. Most externalities feature 'non-rivalry' in consumption. For example, air pollution (an external cost) which is harmful to the population living in a town is likely to be equally harmful to each individual even if the population were to suddenly double.

A public good exhibits non-rivalry and non-excludability in consumption. For example, if a group of tourists stop to take a look at an attractive landscape, the value of that landscape will not be reduced should other tourists also view the same landscape but, in addition, it is not possible to exclude certain tourists from viewing the landscape; it is thus a public good. In some cases public goods can exhibit rivalry in consumption past a certain point. For example, a public park is usually thought of as a public good. However, as more people use it, congestion may set in after a certain point thus reducing the value of the experience to each user. This type of a good is known as an 'impure' public good. Since it is impossible to exclude individuals from consuming a public good, it is normally provided by the state or local government.

When an external cost results from some activity, there is a divergence between the cost to society (social cost) and the cost to the individual undertaking that activity (private cost), i.e.

$$\text{Social Cost} = \text{Private Cost} + \text{External Cost}$$

Similarly,

$$\text{Social Benefit} = \text{Private Benefit} + \text{External Benefit}$$

When an activity is appraised financially, external costs and benefits are excluded from the analysis. However, a proper cost benefit analysis should adjust for all forms of market failure including the existence of externalities and public goods. In the case of a public good this can be done using what is known as the total economic value framework. The evaluation challenge is to develop estimates of external benefits and costs which reflect as closely as possible the values which would have been yielded by market forces if the latter existed.

Why bother with environmental valuation?

There are two main reasons for engaging in environmental evaluation. Firstly, if we want to charge a polluter for emitting pollution or to compensate the victims of pollution, the existence of credible values facilitates a coherent debate regarding charges and compensation. Secondly, where projects and policies are being evaluated, and decisions must be made, if there is a significant component of the project which involves the imposition of external costs, or the generation of external benefits, then some estimate of the values of these 'non-market' aspects is an essential element in assessing whether the project is worthwhile from the point of view of society.

It is important to note the difference between environmental impact assessment (EIA) and 'non-market' valuation. EIA is a cluster of techniques for estimating the physical implications for the environment and the effect of environmental change on human well-being whereas 'non-market' valuation is a cluster of techniques which provides market values for these effects and thus allows the environmental effects to be compared with other costs and benefits. In other word 'non-market' valuation is a necessary component of cost-benefit analysis (CBA). A useful analytical tool in CBA is known as the total economic value (TEV) approach.

Total economic value

The TEV approach expands the traditional neoclassical concepts of value to include option value and existence value. An environmental asset has both 'use' and 'non-use' value. Use value can be broken down into actual use value and option value.

Use value

Actual use value is derived from the actual use of the asset, and is composed of direct use value such as timber from a forest and indirect use value such as the value that would be yielded to inhabitants downstream should the forest reduce flooding.

The notion of option value is more complex. Friedman (1962) had suggested that, if a national park closed down when run by a profit maximising entrepreneur because gate receipts would not cover operating costs, this is not a failure of the market. However, Weisbrod (1964) pointed out that this decision would ignore an option value, i.e. people would be 'willing to pay something for the option to consume the commodity in the future' since 'there is no practical mechanism by which the entrepreneur can charge non-users for this option'. Thus, 'user charges are an inadequate guide to the total value of the park'. In his seminal piece *Conservation Reconsidered*, Krutilla (1967) defined option demand as 'a willingness to pay for retaining an option to use an area or facility that would be difficult or impossible to replace and for which no close substitute is available. Moreover, such a demand may exist even though there is no current intention to use the area or facility in question and the option may never be exercised'. Option value[1] can be broken down into a number of components (Pearce and Turner, 1990): the value individuals place on the preservation of an asset so that they may have the option of using it in the future (value of future options for the individual), the value they attach to preserving the asset because it can be used by others[2] ('vicarious value'), and the value they attach to preserving the asset so that future generations have the option of using it ('bequest value'). Thus, total use value is defined as follows:

Total use value = Direct use value + Indirect use value + Option value

where

Option value = Value of future options for the individual
+ Vicarious value + Bequest value

Non-use values

Non-use values are 'existence' values. Existence values reflect the benefit to individuals of the existence of an environmental asset although those individuals do not actually use the asset. These values may exist due to sympathy for animals and plants and/or some human approximation of the intrinsic value of nature, i.e. this value reflects a sense of stewardship on the part of humans towards the environment. Evidence of these values is shown in the willingness of people to contribute to charities which preserve wildlife. While many of the donors are unlikely to ever see these animals in the flesh, they value the fact that they exist. Krutilla (*op. cit.*) first introduced the concept of existence value: 'there are many persons who obtain satisfaction from mere knowledge that part of wilderness North America remains even though they would be appalled by the prospect of being exposed to it'. There has been some disagreement regarding existence values. McConnell (1983) sees the concept as 'far fetched' and that 'existence value occurs only insofar as bequest or altruistic notions prevail', thus it is a use value. However, it is clear that individuals often contribute to animal charities not because they want animals to be preserved for others or for future generations but because they gain utility themselves from knowing that the animals are being preserved. Thus, following Krutilla's definition, existence value is classed as a non-use value such that total economic value is defined as follows:

$$TEV = \text{Actual use value} + \text{Option value} + \text{Existence value}$$

It is important to note that the TEV approach attempts to encapsulate all aspects of a resource which enter into the utility functions of a human, i.e. it is anthropomorphic. Thus, it does not attempt to find an intrinsic value for the environment where 'intrinsic' means the value that resides in something which is unrelated to human beings altogether (Pearce and Turner, *op. cit.*). However, it does attempt to include the intrinsic value which humans bestow on nature.

There is no agreement on the exact breakdown of the values in the TEV framework. However, the important issue in CBA is to account for all these values as best as possible.

A forestry example

Taking the example of an afforestation project, the TEV might be composed of the value of: the timber (T), the sequestering and storing of carbon, thereby reducing greenhouse gases in the atmosphere (G), restriction of water flow (W_f), water pollution resulting from the 'scavenging' and deposition of air pollutants by the tree and pollution from forestry practice (W_p), recreation (R), wildlife habitat (A), aesthetic/landscape value (L).

In this case, the benefit of afforestation is measured by:

$$B = T + G + W_f + W_p + R + A + L$$

Some of these components may be negative, i.e. external costs are included as negative benefits.

In order to assess the efficiency of an afforestation project using CBA, the costs of the inputs into afforestation would then be subtracted from these benefits.

Non-market valuation methods

Since externalities are not captured within markets, they do not have an obvious 'price' which can be included in a CBA. Thus, what are known as 'non-market' valuation methods must be used to calculate some of the components of TEV. We outline below a number of techniques for estimating these non-market values.

All of these techniques use consumer surplus measures to value non-market costs and benefits. This involves estimating the aggregate willingness to pay to capture benefits [Hicksian compensating variation (CV)] or to avoid costs [Hicksian equivalent variation (EV)] or aggregate willingness to accept compensation for costs (CV) or to forego the benefits (EV).

These methods include:

- *Production function approaches*, whereby we value a non-market output by the value of the loss of (or addition to) production as a result of that output

- *Hedonic pricing*, whereby the value of the non-market output is approximated by estimating the change in the market value of a traded good which is attributable to that output

- *Travel cost* whereby the value of a non-market asset (e.g. a forest park) is approximated by the willingness to pay of individuals for admission to the asset on the basis of the costs incurred in travelling

- *Contingent valuation*, whereby those actually or potentially affected by the provision of a non-market good are asked to place a value on it.

Production function approaches

Production function approaches are indirect methods of valuing externalities. Environmental goods often enter into firms' and households' production functions, e.g. a fishery combines water quality (q) with purchased inputs (x), labour (*l*) and capital (*k*). Where *F* is the output of fish, the production function would take the form:

$$F = f(l, k, x, q)$$

Thus, if a factory causes a deterioration in water quality, *F* will be reduced (assuming $\partial F/\partial q > 0$)[3]. This cost can be estimated in two ways:

- By the cost of the increase in other inputs which would be necessary to achieve the same level of output after the reduction in water quality as before (defensive expenditures/ avoided cost approach) or by the cost of restoring the damage done, e.g. restocking a river (replacement cost)

- By the value of productivity changes, i.e. the value of the lost output of fish (dose-response functions).

Avoided cost and replacement cost approaches

If there is a deterioration in water quality, defensive expenditures may be necessary to reduce the impact on productivity. These expenditures can be used as a proxy for the cost of the damage to the water supply. In most of the literature, this is expressed from another point of view, i.e. the benefits of an improvement in environmental quality can be measured by the defensive costs avoided, hence it is known as the avoided cost approach. If the productivity after defensive expenditures is equal to the productivity prior to the deterioration of the quality of the water, then the defensive expenditures give a reasonable approximation of the external cost imposed by the activity which causes the pollution. If productivity with defensive expenditures is less than the productivity prior to the deterioration in water quality then this approach underestimates the external cost. If the defensive expenditures result in benefits other than the maintenance of productivity, e.g. if for some reason they were to improve the quality of the fish, then this approach would overestimate the external cost. Hanley and Spash (1993) conclude that in most cases the avoided cost approach is likely to provide a lower bound on willingness to pay for environmental quality.

The replacement cost approach measures the cost imposed on society by the degradation of an environmental asset by the cost of replacing or restoring that asset. This approach tends to underestimate damage costs since it is usually impossible to restore something to exactly its original state. In the less usual case of an asset being replaced by a more valuable asset, e.g. a small building being burned down and a new larger building being erected in its place, then the replacement cost would overestimate the cost of the damage.

The replacement cost approach is often a poor proxy for externalities because there is no necessary linkage between the costs of restoration and the benefits lost. Take the case of a fish farm which is wiped out by siltation caused by deforestation upstream. The costs of restoring the fish farm may be several times the cost of relocating the business elsewhere. The latter cost is more relevant as an estimate of the external cost of deforestation.

Dose-response functions

Hanley and Spash (*op. cit.*), from which this explanation is adapted, provide a clear outline of dose-response method. These methods seek a relationship between environmental quality variables and the output level of a marketed commodity. They take natural science information and include it in an economic model. There are three approaches:

- *The traditional model.* Taking the example of an externality manifesting itself in damage to an agricultural crop, the traditional model multiplies yield changes based on current area in production by the current price of the crop. This assumes that resource use and prices (and therefore consumer surplus) remain constant. Therefore, for the answers to be legitimate, it is necessary to assume that any reduction in yield will leave prices unaltered.

- *Optimisation models.* Optimisation models consist of linear programming models and quadratic programming models. These are normative models which are specified as cost-minimising or profit-maximising models. In linear programming, changes in environmental quality can be simulated by using biological dose-response functions to alter the quantity of output produced from the set of inputs required for each production activity. The disadvantages of these models is that they require large data sets and it is not unusual for considerable discrepancies to exist between model solutions and the real world. This can be due to either mis-specification of the model or the inaccuracy of the assumption of optimality in the real world.

- *Econometric models.* Econometric models resolve some of the problems just mentioned since they rely upon historical data. However, the institutional setting is taken as given and the models cannot capture changes in technology that have not been captured in the data.

In conclusion, while the accuracy of the traditional approach relies on very strict assumptions, it is the most simple dose-response approach and it requires very little data. While optimisation and econometric models are more sophisticated, they require larger data sets and depending on the way in which responses are modelled, widely varying estimates emerge.

Hedonic pricing

The hedonic pricing method (HPM) developed by Griliches (1971) and Rosen (1974) is used to estimate the implicit prices of the characteristics which differentiate closely related products (Johansson, 1993). The value of an asset is measured by the stream of benefits which flow there from. This is best explained using an example. The value of a forest park will be partially reflected in the difference in price between a house beside the park and one further away from the park. However, in addition, the price of the house is likely to be a function of a number of other variables. The first stage is to estimate an equation of the form (Pearce and Turner, 1990):

property price = f (property variables, neighbourhood variables, accessibility variables, environmental variables)

The extent to which changes in the environmental variable (the forest park) 'explains' changes in the property price can be estimated by multiple regression. The willingness of people to pay for the environmental commodity can then be derived. Aggregate consumer surplus is calculated by summing across all households. Thus, the absence of prices for environmental assets can be overcome by disaggregating the market price of a private good; in this case, by disaggregating the house price function.

Travel cost

The travel cost method (TCM) uses costs of travel to an environmental asset as a proxy for the value of that asset. This was first proposed by Hotelling but first used by Clawson in 1959 (see Clawson and Knetsch, 1966). Using this method, demand for a recreation site can be measured by the costs of travel to that site. Take, for example, a single recreation site that can be reached by individuals in a certain area. The area can be divided into a number of zones according to distance from the site, zones A and B with B, for example, being further from the park. By surveying those attending the site from the zones in question, estimates are made of the number of trips per capita and the average cost of travel which includes the direct costs of people's travel to the site such as petrol, depreciation of their car etc. and the opportunity cost of the trip, i.e. time. Sets of observations like these can be used to estimate a 'distance decay curve' for trips which is negatively sloped such that the further away from the forest a community is situated, the higher the cost and the fewer the visits, all else being equal. Average consumer surplus from a visit to the recreation site from areas A and B is calculated from the curve, and total aggregate willingness to pay for the forest is given by total consumer surplus plus actual travel cost.

Contingent valuation (stated preference) method

The contingent valuation method (CVM) is the only direct non-market valuation approach. The CVM collects information on preferences by asking households how much they are willing to pay for some change in the provision of a public good, or the minimum compensation they would require if the change was not carried out (Johansson, 1993). The advantage of the CVM is that, unlike other methods, it can elicit option and existence values. In addition, it can measure Hicksian consumer surplus directly.[4] The CVM is the most controversial of all non-market valuation methods. Therefore, it is worth exploring the methodology and the controversies surrounding the method in some detail.

History of CVM

According to Hanemann (1992) the CVM was first suggested by S.V. Ciriacy-Wantrup in 1947 although its significance was not immediately appreciated. In 1958 the United States (US) National Park Service was the first to use the CVM when a survey of outdoor recreational activities was undertaken on their behalf which elicited the willingness to pay a site entry charge to publicly owned recreation areas. In 1961, Davis (1964) carried out the second contingent valuation (CV) study when he used a survey to value hunting in the Maine woods.[5] Up until the mid-1980s, the CVM did not stand out from other non-market valuation measures. Since then, however, this method has become the most widely used approach for valuing public goods and there has been an explosion in the number of CV studies (Mitchell and Carson, 1995).

CVM steps

A CV study consists of the careful selection of a representative sample of the population whose valuation of a public good is being elicited. The interview technique is then selected (face-to-face, telephone or mail) and a questionnaire is developed. This questionnaire contains (Mitchell and Carson, 1989) the following:

- A detailed description of the good being valued and the hypothetical circumstance under which it is made available to the respondent, i.e. the researcher constructs a hypothetical market which is communicated to the respondent in a realistic scenario including a plausible method of payment.

- Questions which elicit the respondent's willingness to pay for the good being valued. These are constructed to facilitate the valuation process.

- Questions about the respondent's characteristics (e.g. age and income), their preferences relevant to the good being valued (e.g. how concerned or interested is the person in the environment), and their use of the good. This information is used in a regression equation for the good. If these variables 'explain' the individual's valuations, as the theory would suggest, then this is a partial test of reliability.

The study is pre-tested using a pilot survey and then the full survey is carried out. The mean and median willingness to pay or accept can then be calculated and the results generalised to the population.

Appropriate welfare measures: willingness to pay vs. willingness to accept

There are two key problems in choosing an appropriate consumer surplus measure. Firstly, there is the theoretical observation that willingness to pay (WTP) and willingness to accept (WTA) can differ in size. Secondly, it has been observed that respondents to CV questionnaires react differently to each approach. Willig's classical work (1976) showed that the difference between WTP and WTA should be relatively small in most cases and while Willig's results were for price changes, Randall and Stoll (1980) extended these results to cover quantity changes where expenditures on the good were a small proportion of income. They suggested that, in CV experiments, the difference between WTP and WTA should not be more that 5 per cent. However, empirical studies still showed a large divergence between WTP and WTA measures. The following possible reasons as described by Mitchell and Carson (1989) may explain this divergence:

- *Rejection of WTA property right*. This occurs when respondents do not accept the property right implied by the question. For example, they may refuse to 'sell' the environmental asset at any price, regarding this as unethical. More frequently, individuals do not see the property right as plausible, e.g. they may be asked how much compensation they would accept for the deterioration of air quality in their area. However, if they have never been compensated for environmental damage in the past, they may see this as implausible. This tends to result in 'protests' and/or infinite bids.

- *The cautious consumer hypothesis*. Under conditions of uncertainty, risk-averse individuals will offer smaller WTP amounts and larger WTA amounts than they would under certainty.

- *Prospect theory*. According to prospect theory, the value function from a neutral position is steeper for losses than for gains, i.e. people value a loss more highly than a gain since the former is considered the loss of a 'right' and the latter is considered only as a 'bonus'.

Criticisms of the contingent valuation method

Up until the mid-1980s, the bulk of the research on the CVM had been carried out in agricultural economics departments in the 'state' universities in the US, where the fields of resource and environmental economics developed. However, the lack of interest on the part of 'mainstream' economists quickly disappeared in the aftermath of the Exxon Valdez oil spill in Alaska in 1989 when the state and federal governments decided to undertake a contingent valuation study to assess the magnitude of the damages. Whereas the government assembled a group of resource economists to carry out the CV, the Exxon Corporation hired a panel of economists, mainly from outside this discipline, in an attempt to prove that the CVM was an unreliable method for valuing natural resource damage (Mitchell and Carson, 1995). A book of the papers produced by the Exxon economists was published in 1993 (see Hausman, 1993 and also Diamond and Hausman, 1994). The main criticisms of the CVM relate to sources of bias.

Sources of bias:

- *Free-riding and strategic bias.* Samuelson (1954) suggested that the individual has an incentive to understate his or her WTP for a public good on the understanding that others will pay for it and therefore he or she will benefit from its provision in any case. On the other hand, the individual may engage in strategic behaviour to raise the mean bid by overstating his or her WTP on the basis that the level of provision is subject to the size of the mean bid. Brookshire *et al* (1976) test for, and reject, strategic bias while the results from Rowe *et al* (1980) suggest that WTP bids are a good reflection of true valuations. While experiments suggest free-riding does occur, it appears to be less prevalent than standard neoclassical theory would predict (Bateman and Turner, 1993).

- *Hypothetical bias.* Critics of the CVM suggest that the hypothetical nature of the market renders the answers invalid. Bishop and Herberlein (1979) showed a significant difference between hypothetical WTA for duck hunting licences and their true WTA when offered 'real' money. However, Mitchell and Carson (1989) show that the significance of the difference relied on the truncation decisions in the original analysis, i.e. the authors' assumptions regarding the length of the distribution of WTP/WTA. Further studies suggest that actual and hypothetical WTP differences are much smaller than in the case of WTA due largely to the rejection of the WTA property right as explained above. Duffield and Patterson (1991) show that hypothetical willingness to contribute to charitable organisations is higher than actual contributions. However, the authors suggest that the differences are small enough for CV to be used to estimate real WTP. Evidence produced from a study comparing hypothetical WTP for strawberries with actual purchases (Dickie. *et al*, 1987) was reinterpreted by Diamond *et al* (1993) as showing that the CV approach tends to systematically overestimate quantity demanded at each price. However, Arrow *et al* (1993) qualify the results in two ways: firstly, the quality of the survey was poor and secondly, it is going too far to conclude that systematic overestimation means that CV can tell us nothing about the demand for strawberries.

- Part-whole (mental account) bias. Some authors testify that results from CV studies are invalid as they are inconsistent with rational choice. Several authors have found that WTP does not increase with the size of the good. Kahneman (1986) found that there was no significant difference between WTP for the clean-up of lakes in a small area of a province and WTP for clean-up of all the lakes in the province. This 'embedding' effect was also shown by Kahneman and Knetsch (1992) by giving one sample group a more inclusive public good and the other sample group a less inclusive good. The results showed no significant difference between the mean WTP for each good. The authors proposed that this is due to a 'warm glow' whereby people are contributing because they feel good about improving the welfare of society. Thus, WTP does not measure their true valuation of the good. A number of other papers have also demonstrated this phenomenon (e.g. Desvousges *et al*, 1993 and Diamond *et al*, 1993). Smith (1992), Hanemann (1994) and Mitchell and Carson (1995) have argued that Kahneman and Knetsch's findings result from poor instrument design and poor information (see 'General responses to the critics' below).

- *Information bias*. One of the most controversial issues in CV relates to the quantity of information which is supplied to the respondent. It should go without saying that if individuals are given incorrect information, the use of their responses in making policy decisions is invalid. The more disputed claim is that the provision of more information elicits a higher WTP. Willingness to pay is likely to be a function of information but, if adequate information is provided, information bias should not be an overriding problem. Another criticism of CV surveys is that they often provide only vague descriptions of the good in question (this has also been a criticism of the CV studies carried out by economists wishing to demonstrate the flaws of the CVM).

- *Payment vehicle bias*. Choice of payment vehicle, e.g. an increase in taxes or a contribution to a 'fund', has been shown to influence WTP (see Desvousges *et al*, 1983 and Navrud, 1989). It is therefore suggested that controversial payment methods be avoided and that the payment vehicle should be that which is most likely to be used in reality. The method of payment should also be such that the respondent is aware of the substitutes for the public good in question. This is important due to the criticisms of opponents of the CVM who question the large mean WTP figures for environmental improvements that emerge from CV studies. They ask whether individuals would really be willing (or able) to pay similarly large amounts if asked to pay for all environmental improvements. In addition, there is a common criticism that respondents do not consider their budget constraints when stating their WTP if the payment vehicle is unrealistic. Arrow *et al* (1993) state that 'to date very few CV surveys have reminded respondents of the very real economic constraints within which spending decisions must be made'.

- *Bid level bias*. There are a number of ways of eliciting bids in CV studies (Hanley and Spash, 1993):

  - *As a bidding game*. The interviewer asks the individual whether he or she will pay a specified amount. If the respondent says 'no', the interviewer lowers the amount until he or she says 'yes'. If, in the first instance, the respondent says 'yes' then the amount is raised until he or she says 'no'. This approach often results in a large number of 'protests' since some respondents find this 'auctioning' of a public good either unethical or unrealistic. It also can suffer from what is known as 'starting point bias' whereby the initial bid suggested influences the WTP of the individual. Mitchell and Carson (1989) suggest that the provision of a starting point reduces the effort people put into making their choice of WTP.

  - *As an open-ended question*. Individuals are asked their maximum WTP with no value being suggested to them. Respondents tend to find it difficult to answer questions of this type when they have no experience of trading in the commodity in question. Open-ended CV studies are subject to 'free-rider' bias much more than the other approaches.

  - *As a payment card*. A range of values is presented on a card which helps respondents to calibrate their replies. This is less problematic than the bidding game. However, in some instances respondents also may find the approach rather unrealistic. This approach can produce 'anchoring bias' whereby the respondent assumes that the 'correct' valuation is one of the values on the card and therefore he or she is reluctant to go outside that range.

  - *As a closed-ended referendum*. This approach is also known as 'take-it-or-leave-it' or 'dichotomous choice'. The sample is split into sub-samples and a single payment is suggested to which the respondent must agree or disagree. A different amount is presented to each of the sub-samples. This is the most incentive-compatible approach. However, the analysis of binary responses requires more sophisticated econometric techniques and larger samples. Sometimes the question is followed up by a higher or lower offer depending on whether the answer to the first question is 'yes' or 'no'. This is called the double bounded dichotomous choice approach. The dichotomous choice approach may be subject to anchoring bias if the payment amounts chosen do not cover the full range of WTP. In addition it may be subject to 'yea-saying' whereby individuals may just say 'yes' in order to avoid having to think carefully.

- *Interviewer bias*: The interviewer may intentionally or unintentionally put pressure on the respondent to give particular answers to questions. This is most common in face-to-face surveys.

General responses to the critics

Hanemann (1994) criticises the papers referred to in Diamond and Hausman (1994) and Hausman (1993) for the weakness of the CV studies they use to back up their claims of the inappropriateness of the CVM. He states:

> None uses in-person interviews. Many are self-administered. Most use open-ended questions. None is cast as voting. Many ask questions with a remarkable lack of detail. Several seem designed to highlight the symbolic aspects of valuation at the expense of substance. The Exxon surveys were designed and fielded in great haste, with little pre-testing, just at a time when federal agencies were gearing up for natural resource damage regulations. The only way to justify this is to make the tacit assumption that, if contingent valuation is valid, details of its implementation should not matter. This is fundamentally wrong: measurement results are not invariant with respect to measurement practice in *any* science.

Mitchell and Carson (1995) explain two misconceptions about contingent valuation that arise in the debate regarding the validity of the CVM. Firstly, they reprimand the critics of the CVM for failing to realise that a CV question involves much more than just asking a respondent to express a WTP for some good. Asking respondents whether they are willing to pay €50 for cleaner air is an 'attitudinal' WTP question. Neither the payment vehicle nor the good are specified clearly. A CV question measures 'behavioural intention' by setting out the specific details of the good which is being sold to the respondent, how the good would be provided and how the good would be paid for. Mitchell and Carson (*op. cit.*) criticise Kahneman and Knetsch (1992) for presuming that an attitudinal WTP question is a sufficient basis upon which to test the reliability of CV. In one experiment Kahneman and Knetsch ask one sample of

Vancouver residents how much they would be willing to pay 'to improve sport fish stocks in British Columbia fresh water' and ask the other sample 'how much they would be willing to pay to improve sport fish stocks in Canada fresh water'. They do not explain the meaning of 'fish-stocks' and 'fresh water', the size of the improvement, how long the improvement would be maintained, who will provide the good, how it will be provided, when it will be provided, and how the respondents will pay for it. It is not surprising therefore that respondents give quick and not so meaningful answers. Studies that test the CVM using attitudinal as distinct from behavioural surveys are not a reasonable basis upon which to discount the CVM.

The second observation made by Mitchell and Carson is that all CV surveys are not equally reliable and that therefore it is not reasonable to choose surveys selectively in order to criticise the method. This amounts to asserting that CV results are averse to CV practice.

Guidelines for the contingent valuation method

With such conflicting views on the validity of the CVM, the US National Oceanic and Atmospheric Administration (NOAA) convened a blue ribbon panel of experts (known as the NOAA Panel) to deliberate on all the evidence produced and to answer the question: 'Is the contingent valuation method capable of providing estimates of lost non-use or existence values that are reliable enough to be used in natural resource damage assessments?' (Portney, 1994). This was chaired by Nobel prize winners Kenneth Arrow and Robert Solow and had four other members.[6] The panel reported its findings in 1993 (Arrow *et al*, 1993) and drew the overall conclusion that: 'CV studies can produce estimates reliable enough to be the starting point for a judicial or administrative determination of natural resource damages – including lost passive value.'

The report suggests that, so long as the study is well designed, the CVM is a reliable tool. In this regard they issued a comprehensive set of 'best practice' guidelines for the carrying out of such studies including details regarding sample size and type, non-response and protests, the interview method, reporting, pre-testing, the elicitation format, the payment method, the description of the programme or policy concerned, bid curve estimation and aggregation issues. The requirements are very detailed and rigid. However, it is important to bear in mind that the NOAA Panel's guidelines are for CV studies which are to be used in natural resource damage assessment. Mitchell and Carson (1995) note that these guidelines set a 'very high' and 'very costly' standard. They suggest that the extent to which the guidelines must be adhered to will depend on the importance of the policy question being examined.

Other stated preference methods

Other stated preference methods include contingent ranking and choice experiments. A choice experiment values a good as a function of the attributes of that good. These experiments can be used to place an economic value on individual attributes of which they are a part. Limitations of scope preclude further consideration of such stated preference methods in this chapter.

Discounting and the environment

In undertaking economic evaluation, account must be taken of the fact that costs and benefits arise at different time periods. Thus future costs and benefits must be discounted so that they can be compared with present costs and benefits (B). Having calculated the costs (C) and benefits of a project, it is necessary to compare them in present value terms. Where r is the discount rate, the net present value of the investment is the sum of benefits less costs across all time periods (from $t = 0$ to T) i.e.

$$NPV = \sum_{t=0}^{T} \frac{(B_i - C_i)}{(1 + r)^t}$$

The project is accepted if and only if,

$$NPV > 0$$

Problems with discounting

There have been a number of controversies surrounding the choice of discount rate. There are some general arguments regarding the measurement of the discount rate and the difference between the market rate of discount and the social rate of discount (the rate at which society as a whole would wish to discount the environment) which are beyond the scope of this chapter.[7] However, in relation to the environment, discounting tends to be controversial in the eyes of many environmentalists because it rules out certain projects they would see as desirable and encourages certain activities they would see as undesirable. For example, it encourages more rapid exploitation of resources, but discourages certain long-term projects such as the planting of broadleaved forests, which would reduce the costs of potential damage in the long run as a consequence of global warming.

Worrell (1991) summarises three schools of thought concerning the use of discounting:

- Provided externalities are included in the CBA, and the preferences of future generations are accounted for by sustainability constraints, discounting provides an accurate picture of consumer behaviour. Sustainability criteria would maintain a constant stock of natural capital or provide compensation for environmental damage either by implementing other environmental (shadow) projects or by replacing natural capital with man-made capital (see 'sustainability' below).[8]

- Alternatives to straight-forward discounting should be used. One such method, known as the modified discounting method, allows new individuals in new generations to discount costs and benefits from the start of their lives and this effectively reduces the discount rate.[9] Another approach is to disaggregate the determinants of the discount rate (time preference, diminishing marginal utility of income, etc.) and explicitly include their individual effects separately in analyses.

- Discounting is unacceptable and counter to sustainable resource use and therefore a zero discount rate should be used.

The choice of discount rate is most important. However, since economists have been unable to provide a definitive figure for the social rate of discount let alone resolve the issues which arise in relation to the environment, it has become something to be chosen rather than something that is measured (Heal, 1981) and as Leslie (1989) states, 'all views on discount rates are opinions'. In reality, the discount rate used to assess government projects is chosen via the political system.

Irreversibility and sustainability

Krutilla-Fisher algorithm

In their seminal work, *The Economics of Natural Environments*, John Krutilla and Anthony Fisher (1985) consider the example of the economic evaluation of a proposed hydro-electric dam to be built on a wilderness area which has value in its natural state. They considered the necessary changes in project investment rules where a project would result in an irreversible change, i.e. where damage could not be rectified. Pearce and Turner (1990), from which this discussion is adapted, provide a succinct summary of the analysis of Krutilla and Fisher. In carrying out a cost benefit analysis of the development of the site, it is necessary to consider the present value of the development benefits of the site [PV(BD)], the development costs [PV(CD)] and the net opportunity cost of development, i.e. the present value of the benefits of preservation [PV(BP)] and the direct cost of preservation [PV(CP)]. The traditional cost-benefit rule approves the development if,

$$[PV(B_D)\text{-}PV(C_D)] > [PV(B_P)\text{-}PV(C_P)]$$

However, this rule does not distinguish between a decision which is reversible and a decision which would result in the irreversible destruction of an environmental asset. The Krutilla-Fisher algorithm adjusts the rule to reflect irreversibility by treating the benefits foregone as part of the costs of development, by assuming preservation benefits increase over time at a rate g as the natural environment becomes more scarce, and by including an offsetting discount factor k which represents technological decay such that the development benefits are likely to be reduced over time (Pearce and Turner, *op. cit.*).

Supposing the costs of development are €1 and arise in the current time period and the development benefits amount to €D per annum, then where r is the discount rate, the present value of development is,

$$PV(D) = -1 + \int_0^\infty De^{-rt}\, dt = -1 + \frac{D}{r}$$

The opportunity cost of development is the present value of per annum preservation benefits (P), i.e.

$$PV(P) = \int_0^\infty Pe^{-rt}\, dt = \frac{P}{r}$$

and thus the net present value of development is,

$$NPV(D) = -1 + \frac{D}{r} - \frac{P}{r}$$

According to the traditional cost-benefit rule, $NPV(D)$ must be positive for the project to be worthwhile so the project goes ahead if,

$$(D - P) > r$$

Introducing a discount factor k which represents technological decay reduces development benefits over time such that development benefits at time t are given by

$$D_t = D_0\, e^{-kt}$$

and including the growth rate g in the 'price' of the natural asset (over and above inflation) which reflects the increasing scarcity of environmental assets such that the preservation benefit at time t is given by

$$P_t = P_0\, e^{gt}$$

gives a new expression for the net present value of development,

$$NPV(D) = -1 + \int_0^\infty De^{-(r+k)t}\, dt - \int_0^\infty Pe^{-(r+k)t}\, dt = -1 + \frac{D}{r+k} - \frac{P}{r-g}$$

For $NPV(D)$ to be positive and for the project to be accepted under this modified rule, the following expression must hold,

$$\sqrt{D} > (\sqrt{P} + \sqrt{k+g})$$

and thus the higher is the discount rate r, the lower are the development benefits, all else being equal. The lower is r, the stronger is g in making preservation benefits more attractive, all else being equal. This modified cost-benefit rule allows for a greater weighting of the benefits of preservation when a decision to destroy an environmental asset is irreversible. For example, if P is 0.4 and $k = g = 0.02$, then, from the above expression, $D = 0.5989$ such that the ratio of D to P is 1.50. Thus, for the project to pass the modified cost-benefit test, development benefits must be 50 per cent higher than preservation benefits.

Uncertainty can be built directly into the decision-making rule (as opposed to indirectly by using sensitivity analysis) by requiring the net present value of development to be greater than some positive number.

Sustainability

Valuation of non-market effects has become of considerable importance in the assessment of sustainability. There is an emerging consensus that traditional measures of economic performance such as gross domestic product (GDP) and gross national product (GNP) are not adequate measures of well-being. They do not measure at all, or they measure only very obliquely, much that is of central importance to well-being, such as safety, literacy, health and environmental gains or losses, and though they value an annual flow of goods and services produced, they give no indication about what is happening to stocks. Thus a country can seem relatively prosperous as it harvests its natural forests; large annual flows of goods and services being produced and valued in markets, but the stock on which the flow is predicated is being depleted. This depreciation of the stock is not captured in the traditional measures of economic performance.

Pearce and Atkinson (1995) have developed an interesting means of categorising countries to indicate whether or not they are on sustainable development paths. They make a distinction between 'weak sustainability', the constant capital rule, whereby an aggregate capital stock no smaller than the present one is passed onto the next generation, and 'strong sustainability', whereby, in addition to conserving the aggregate capital stock, that component of the aggregate capital stock characterised as 'natural' is not diminished.

They apply the weak sustainability rule to a number of countries as follows: for each country analysed, they take estimates of the rate of depreciation of natural capital (sometimes called resource rent) and of 'made' capital, and compare these with the rate of savings. If the rate of depreciation of natural and 'made' capital drawn down exceeds the rate of savings, then the country is not re-investing sufficient to 'replace' the natural and 'made' capital drawn down, and fails the 'weak sustainability' test. If a country has a higher savings rate than the rate of depreciation of natural and 'made' capital, then it passes this test. The results for a few countries are shown below.

Table 10.1: Weak sustainability test results for selected countries

Country	Rate of saving (i)	Rate of depreciation of made capital (ii)	Rate of depreciation of natural capital (iii)	Net saving rate (i) – [(ii) + (iii)]
Japan	33	14	2	17
Poland	30	11	3	16
Costa Rica	26	3	8	15
Netherlands	25	10	1	14
USA	18	12	3	3
Mexico	24	12	12	0
UK	18	12	6	0
Malawi	8	7	4	–3
Nigeria	15	3	17	–5
Ethiopia	3	1	9	–7
Burkina Faso	2	1	10	–9
Madagascar	8	1	16	–9
Mali	–4	4	6	–14

Source: Pearce and Atkinson, 1993

In order to estimate the rate of depreciation of natural capital, they had to estimate the value of as much as possible of the non-market outputs provided by such capital. Valuation of non-market outputs is therefore a necessary concomitant towards identifying whether we are on a sustainable path.[10]

Conclusions

Much that sustains us physically, socially and spiritually is not mediated through markets. In particular, environmental endowments, being defined as assets held somehow in common, are not readily integrated into markets. Increasingly, however, markets are being viewed as the arbiters in the allocation of resources and in the measurement of well-being. If something does not have a price, a perception can emerge that it does not exist and/or is not important. To help ensure that non-market goods and services in general, and environmental goods and services in particular, can command the requisite degree of attention and resources, a wide range of techniques has been developed to generate non-market values. In this chapter we have attempted to provide the reader with a sense of the rationale for including these values in the evaluation process, the techniques for so doing and some of the other issues which should be considered when undertaking a cost benefit analysis. While the techniques require a degree of sophistication in derivation and application and a certain leap of faith that the proxy measures do indeed adequately mimic markets, they can make an important contribution to ensuring that we do not neglect to see the true value of the environment.

*

This article was first published in Mulreany, M., (ed.) *Economic & Financial Evaluation: Measurement, Meaning and Management,* Dublin: Institute of Public Administration, 1999

NOTES

1   The reader is referred to an excellent exposition on option value by Bishop (1982).
2   In the late eighteenth century, Adam Smith in his *Theory of Moral Sentiments* (1790) drew attention to this 'sympathy principle' (Kriström, 1990).
3   $\partial F/\partial q$ is a calculus convention meaning a change in F with respect to a change in q.
4   Thus, actual willingness to pay and willingness to accept is measured.
5   Some authors suggest that this was the first CV study.
6   Edward Leamer, Paul Portney, Roy Radner and Howard Schuman were the other members of the panel.
7   Interested readers may wish to consult Lind *et al*, 1982.
8   See Pearce *et al*, 1989 and Markandya and Pearce, 1988 for further details.
9   See Kula, 1988a, 1988b, 1989, Bateman, 1989, Rigby, 1989 and Hutchinson, 1989 for further details.
10 Readers interested in this area may wish to consult an excellent paper by Pezzey (1992).

REFERENCES

Arrow, K., R. Solow, P. R. Portney, E. E. Leamer, R. Radner and H. Schman (1993). 'Advance Notice of Proposed Rulemaking, Extension of Comment Period and Release of Contingent Valuation Methodology Report,' *Federal Register*, vol. 58, pp 4601-14

Bateman, I. (1989). 'Modified Discounting Method: Some Comments-1,' *Project Appraisal*, vol. 4, no. 2, pp 104-06

Bateman, I. J. and R. K. Turner (1993). 'Valuation of the Environment, Methods and Techniques': The Contingent Valuation Method, in R. K. Turner (ed.), *Sustainable Environmental Economics and Management*, London: Belhaven Press

Baumol, W. J. and W. E. Oates (1988). *The Theory of Environmental Policy*, 2nd edn., Cambridge: Cambridge University Press

Bishop and Herberlein (1979). 'Measuring Values of Extra-Market Goods: Are Indirect Measures Biased?', *American Journal of Agricultural Economics*, vol. 61, pp 926-30

Bishop, R.C. (1982). Option Value: An Exposition and Extension, *Land Economics*, Vol. 58, no.1, pp 1-15

Brookshire, D.S., B.C. Ives and W.C. Schulze (1976). 'The Valuation of Aesthetic Preferences', *Journal of Environmental Economics and Management*, vol. 3, pp 325-46

Clawson, M and J. Knetsch (1966). *Economics of Outdoor Recreation*, Baltimore: Johns Hopkins University Press

Davis, R.K. (1964). 'The Value of Big Game Hunting in a Private Forest', in *Transactions of the Twenty-ninth North American Wildlife Conference*, Washington D.C.: Wildlife Management Institute

Desvousges, W. H., F. R. Johnson, R. W. Dunford, K. J. Boyle, S. P. Hudson and K. N. Wilson (1993). 'Measuring Natural Resource Damages With Contingent Valuation: Tests of Validity and Reliability', in J.A. Hausman (ed.), *Contingent Valuation: A Critical Assessment*, Contributions to Economic Analysis 220, Amsterdam: North Holland

Desvousges, W.H., V.K. Smith and M.P. McGivney (1983). *A Comparison of Alternative Approaches for Estimating Recreation and Related Benefits of Water Quality Improvements*, Report no. 30-05-83-001, US Environmental Protection Agency, Washington D.C

Diamond, P.A. and J.A. Hausman (1994). 'Contingent Valuation: Is Some Number Better than No Number?' *Journal of Economic Perspectives*, vol. 8, no. 4, pp 3-17

Diamond, P.A., J.A. Hausman, G. K. Leonard and M. A. Denning (1993). 'Does Contingent Valuation Measure Preferences? Experimental Evidence', in J.A. Hausman (ed.), *Contingent Valuation: A Critical Assessment*, Contributions to Economic Analysis 220, Amsterdam: North Holland

Dickie, M.A. Fisher and S. Gerking (1987). 'Market Transactions and Hypothetical Demand Data: A Comparative Study', *Journal of the American Statistical Association*, vol. 82, pp 69-75

Drèze, J., and N. Stern (1994). 'Shadow Prices and Markets: Policy Reform', in R. Layard and S. Glaister (eds.) *Cost-Benefit Analysis*, 2nd edn., Cambridge: Cambridge University Press

Duffield, J.W. and D.A. Patterson (1991). 'Field Testing Existence Values: An Instream Flow Trust Fund for Montana Rivers', Paper presented at annual meeting of American Economic Association, New Orleans, January, 1991

Friedman, M. (1962). *Capitalism and Freedom*, Chicago: University of Chicago Press

Griliches, Z. (1971). *Price Indexes and Quality Change*, Cambridge: Harvard University Press

Hanemann, W. M. (1992). Preface, in S. Navrud (ed.), *Pricing the European Environment*, Oslo: Scandinavian University Press

Hanemann, W. M. (1994). 'Valuing the Environment Through Contingent Valuation', *Journal of Economic Perspectives*, vol. 8, no. 4, pp 3-17

Hanley, N. and C. Spash (1993). *Cost-Benefit Analysis and the Environment*, Aldershot: Edward Elgar

Hardin, G. (1968). 'The Tragedy of the Commons', *Science*, vol. 168

Hausman, J. A. (ed.) (1993). *Contingent Valuation: A Critical Assessment*, Contributions to Economic Analysis 220, Amsterdam: North Holland

Heal, G. M. (1981). 'Economics and Resources', in R. Butlin (ed.), *Economics of Environmental and Natural Resource Policy*, Boulder: Westview Press

Hutchinson, R. W. (1989). 'Modified Discounting Method: Some Comments-3', *Project Appraisal*, vol. 4, no. 2, pp 108-09

Johansson, P.-O. (1993). *Cost-Benefit Analysis of Environmental Change*, Cambridge: Cambridge University Press

Kahneman, D. (1986). 'Comments', in R.G. Cummings, D.S. Brookshire and W.D. Schulze (eds), *Valuing Environmental Goods*, Totwa: Rowman and Allenhead

Kahneman, D. and J. L. Knetsch (1992). 'Valuing Public Goods: The Purchase of Moral Satisfaction', *Journal of Environmental Economics and Management*, vol. 22, pp 90-4

Kriström, B. (1990). *Valuing Environmental Benefits using the Contingent Valuation Method – An Econometric Analysis*, Umeå Economic Studies No. 219, Umeå: University of Umeå

Krutilla, J.V. (1967). 'Conservation Reconsidered', *American Economic Review*, vol. LVII, no. 4, pp 777-86

Krutilla, J.V. and A.C. Fisher (1985), *The Economics of Natural Environments*, Second Edition, Washington D.C.: Resources for the Future

Kula, E. (1988a). 'Future Generations: The Modified Discounting Method', *Project Appraisal*, vol. 3, no. 2, pp 85-88

Kula, E. (1988b). *The Economics of Forestry: Modern Theory and Practice*, London: Croom Helm

Kula, E. (1989). 'Modified Discounting Method: Rejoinder', *Project Appraisal*, vol. 4, no. 2, pp 110-12

Leslie, A.J. (1989). 'On the Economic Prospects for Natural Management in Temperate Hardwoods' *Forestry*, vol. 62, pp 147-66

Lind, R.C., K.J. Arrow, G.R. Corey, P. Dasgupta, A.K. Sen, T. Stauffer, J.E. Stiglitz, J.A. Stockfisch and R. Wilson (1982). *Discounting for Time and Risk in Energy Policy*, Washington D.C.: Resources for the Future

Markandya, A. and D. Pearce (1988). 'Natural Environments and the Social Rate of Discount', *Project Appraisal*, vol. 3, no. 1, pp 2-12

McConnell, K.E. (1983). 'Existence and Bequest Value', in R. D. Rowe and L. G. Chestnut (eds.), *Managing Air Quality and Scenic Resources at National Parks and Wilderness Areas*, Boulder: Westview Press

Mitchell R.C. and R.T. Carson (1995). 'Current Issues in the Design, Administration and Analysis of Contingent Valuation Surveys', in P.-O. Johansson, B. Kriström and K-G. Mäler (eds.), *Current Issues in Environmental Economics*, Manchester: Manchester University Press

Mitchell, R.C. and R.T. Carson (1989). *Using Surveys to Value Public Goods: The Contingent Valuation Method*, Washington D.C.: Resources for the Future.

Navrud, S. (1989). *The Use of Benefits Estimates in Environmental Decision Making: Case Study on Norway*, Paris: OECD

Pearce, D. and G. Atkinson (1995). 'Measuring Sustainable Development', in D. Bromley (ed.), *Handbook of Environmental Economics*, London: Basil Blackwell

Pearce, D.W. and C. Nash (1981). *The Social Appraisal of Projects*, London: Macmillan Press

Pearce, D.W. and R.K. Turner (1990). *Economics of Natural Resources and the Environment*, Hemel Hempstead: Harvester Wheatsheaf

Pearce, D., A. Markandya and E.B. Barbier. (1989). *Blueprint for a Green Economy*. London: Earthscan

Pezzey, J. (1992). *Sustainable Development Concepts: An Economic Analysis*, World Bank Environment Paper No. 2, Washington D.C.: World Bank

Portney, P.R. (1994). 'The Contingent Valuation Debate: Why Economists Should Care', *Journal of Economic Perspectives*, vol. 8, no. 4, pp 3-17

Randall, A. and J. R. Stoll (1980). 'Consumer's Surplus in Commodity Space', *American Economic Review*, vol. 70, no. 3, pp 449-55

Rigby, M.W. (1989). 'Modified Discounting Method: Some Comments-2', *Project Appraisal*, vol. 4, no. 2, pp 107-08

Rosen, S. (1974). 'Hedonic Prices and Implicit Markets: Product Differentiation in Pure Competition', *Journal of Political Economy*, vol. 82, pp 34-55

Rowe, R., R. d'Arge, and D. Brookshire (1980). 'An Experiment on the Economic Value of Visibility', *Journal of Environmental Economics and Management*, vol. 7, pp 1-19 Samuelson, P. (1954). 'The Pure Theory of Public Expenditure', *Review of Economics and Statistics*, vol. 36, pp 387-89

Smith, V.K. (1992). 'Arbitrary Values, Good Causes and Premature Verdicts', *Journal of Environmental Economics and Management*, vol. 22, pp 71-89

Weisbrod, B.A. (1964). 'Collective-Consumption Services of Individual-Consumption Goods', *Quarterly Journal of Economics*, vol. 78, pp 471-77

Willig, R.D. (1976). 'Consumer's Surplus Without Apology', *American Economic Review*, vol. 66, no. 4, pp 587-97

Worrell, R. (1991). *Trees and the Treasury: Valuing Forests for Society*, Godalming: World Wide Fund for Nature

11

The Evaluation of Transport Projects*

OWEN P. KEEGAN[1]

Introduction

The need has long been recognised for an acceptable appraisal framework for evaluating public investment programmes and for promoting efficient choices in the allocation of scarce public resources between competing programmes and projects. An appraisal framework is essential for the optimal allocation of public expenditure including expenditure on transportation. While progress has been made in evaluating major transport investment programmes and in developing techniques for selecting between competing projects, significant work remains to be done.

In Ireland, the transportation sector has been to the fore in the development and application of public expenditure evaluation/appraisal techniques. As far back as 1961, O'Keeffe proposed the application of cost-benefit analysis (CBA) in the allocation of road expenditure in Ireland (O'Keeffe, 1961). By 1966, the then Department of Local Government had partly accepted this approach and was advocating a change from the then system of allocating funding for roads on the basis of historic provision towards a system based on traffic volumes (Department of Local Government, 1966). In 1971, the Dublin Transportation Study contained a CBA of its proposals (An Foras Forbartha, 1971). Through the 1970s and 1980s, while there was no systematic policy of appraising transport projects, some major road and rail projects were subjected to CBA. More recently, the major transport investment proposals contained in the report of the Dublin Transportation Initiative have also been subjected to detailed evaluation including CBA (Steer, Davies, Gleave, 1994).[2]

In recent years there has been an increasing recognition that a special approach is required for the appraisal of public sector transport projects. This is because of the key role of the transportation sector in economic and social development and the special nature of the arrangements that exist for the delivery of transport services including a number of different modes, different operators (both public and private), different levels of competition, complex subsidy regimes and so forth. Given the very significant costs involved in the provision of transport infrastructure and the demand for new investment there has always been a need to develop a basis for allocating scarce resources between competing projects.

The dominant role of the state and more recently of the EU in financing transportation projects has increased the pressure for better project evaluation and appraisal. Finally, the fact that time savings which constitute the major benefit of transport projects can be more readily measured and valued than the benefits of most other major public investment projects has also assisted the development and application of evaluation techniques to transport projects.

The evaluation of any transport project generally involves a number of different assessments. A detailed technical assessment dealing with the engineering/design approach to the project is usually required, together with an assessment of the project's environmental impact. In addition, depending on the nature of the project, a detailed financial appraisal and/or an economic appraisal will usually be required. A financial appraisal assesses the cost of the project and how it is to be financed, the revenue stream it will produce and the return that will be achieved on the capital invested. It also considers the impact of the project on the cash flow, the profit and loss account and the balance sheet of the enterprise. An economic appraisal identifies and attempts to measure the economic costs and benefits of the project. In the case of most road infrastructure projects and increasingly in the case of rail infrastructure projects, the emphasis in project evaluation is on the economic appraisal of the project using CBA.

This chapter focuses on a number of key issues that arise in the application of CBA to transportation projects in Ireland. These are:

- *Methodological issues:* the derivation of parameter values for the value of time, for accident cost savings and for vehicle operating cost savings; the choice of discount rate and the problems associated with forecasting traffic.

- *Environmental issues:* the treatment of environmental impacts in CBA studies.

Given the increasing reliance on CBA in the evaluation of transportation projects it is important that there should be a broader understanding of the issues that arise in deriving parameter values and in choosing a discount rate. Since traffic forecasts play a critical role in the calculation of benefits associated with transportation projects some understanding of the issues that arise in this area is also important.

A major criticism of most CBA studies is their failure to take explicit account of environmental impacts. The growing interest in measuring and valuing the environmental impacts of transport investments has been driven by the belief that if scarce resources are to be allocated efficiently and equitably, then it is essential that environmental effects be explicitly considered along with other costs and benefits. This chapter outlines both the progress that has been made in this area and the considerable obstacles that remain to be overcome.

To dispel any suggestion that the application of CBA to transport projects is purely a mechanical or technical process the chapter finishes with a consideration of suggested CBA application rules derived on the basis of the author's personal experience in undertaking and reviewing CBA studies of transport projects in Ireland.

Before addressing these issues it is necessary to consider the CBA approach to project appraisal and to explain why it is appropriate for some but not necessarily all transport projects. CBA is essentially a set of techniques designed to ensure efficiency, from an economic welfare perspective, in the allocation of scarce public investment resources. An investment is considered desirable where the economic benefits exceed the economic costs and the potential therefore exists for beneficiaries from the investment to fully compensate losers and still be better off. CBA requires costs and benefits to be assessed from the perspective of the economy as a whole. The profit maximising enterprise which is usually concerned only with private costs and benefits will choose the project which contributes most to total profits at the margin. However, for public infrastructure projects the objective is the maximisation of social/economic welfare which requires the interests of society as a whole to be taken into account. This in turn requires estimation of positive and negative externalities generated by the project, in addition to its direct benefits and costs. Compared with financial appraisal, CBA substitutes social benefit for the revenue of the enterprise and social or opportunity cost for the cost to the enterprise.

Some indication of the scale of the external costs of transport is given in a European Commission Green Paper (EU Commission, 1995).

> Although there is a large uncertainty surrounding cost estimates of individual externalities and costs vary significantly across and within modes, time and place of use, the order of magnitude of the total costs – which is broadly comparable to the total direct contribution of the inland transport modes to GDP – is so large that policy action is definitely warranted.

The EU Commission indicated rough estimates of the external costs of transport as a percentage of GDP as follows – air pollution (excluding global warning): 0.4 per cent, noise: 0.2 per cent, accidents: 1.5 per cent and congestion: 2.0 per cent. The Commission also indicated that over 90 per cent of these costs relate to road transport.

While major road investments may yield modest savings in road maintenance costs they do not generate income streams and cannot therefore be appraised on financial grounds. Even in cases where a toll is imposed on a road, financial appraisal is considered inappropriate for the following reasons:

- CBA measures the benefit to consumers in terms of the increase in 'consumer surplus' (i.e. the maximum amount a consumer would be willing to pay for a given quantity of a good less the amount he or she actually pays). However, to capture these benefits in the form of toll revenue on a road project would require the imposition of a toll on each user equivalent to the maximum amount he or she would be willing to pay which in turn would reflect the value of the time savings to each user. In practice, of course, a uniform toll is imposed on all users in a particular category (e.g. private cars). Thus toll revenue will always be less than the increase in 'consumer surplus' that results from a new road facility.

- The provision of a new road facility will usually result in a diversion of traffic from other parts of the road network resulting in benefits (e.g. reduced travel time, fewer accidents etc.) to other users of the network who do not pay any toll.

- Toll revenue will not reflect the full economic effects of accident savings and beneficial environmental impacts.

CBA is also applied in the case of other transport projects (e.g. investment in rail, port and airport projects) where it usually supplements more traditional financial appraisal. Since investments in these areas generate income in the form of additional revenue from user charges it is sometimes argued that financial appraisal on its own should be sufficient. However, just as in the case of toll roads, there are arguments in favour of the application of CBA to these projects. The primary advantage of the general application of CBA to all transport infrastructure projects is that this approach should ensure consistency in project selection between projects involving different modes. This is important if scarce public resources available for investment in transport are to be allocated efficiently and overall economic welfare maximised.

At the same time there are arguments for preserving a strong commercial focus in the evaluation of certain transport infrastructure projects especially where competitive markets now exist. One consequence of the effective deregulation of road haulage, inter-urban bus services and air and sea transportation services in Ireland is that competitive markets now operate in areas which were previously characterised by monopoly or near monopoly conditions. Special care is required in the application of CBA where competitive markets exist and where grant aid is being sought for a project. Such grants could lead to distortionary impacts on competition.

Similar considerations arise in the case of investment in ports because of the increasingly commercial and competitive nature of the port sector. It is not at all clear that investments in additional port capacity or in improved handling facilities generate benefits that cannot be captured in the form of additional revenue or cost savings by port operators. Because of doubts about the existence and scale of externalities associated with port projects and the need to avoid interfering in competitive markets, the evaluation of port projects should be based primarily on financial appraisal.

It is worth noting that in the UK there has been a reluctance to embrace CBA of rail projects unreservedly. It is argued that comparisons of cost between public road and public rail projects are distorted because rail costs include the maintenance cost of the permanent way whereas road costs do not include road maintenance. While the case for subsidising rail transportation is strong given the net positive externalities it generates, there is the drawback that subsidisation often leads to inefficiencies, to services that are not matched to demand, to a lack of innovation and to poor cost control. Objectives for appraisal of rail investment in the UK, set out below, reflect these competing pressures:

- There is a requirement that service improvements as a consequence of major investments should be funded out of additional fare revenue and operating cost savings. An exception is made in the case of urban rail and light rail schemes where it is argued that the benefits of major investments exceed the additional fare revenue likely to be generated.

- Subsidies are payable in respect of new schemes which reflect the value of external benefits (e.g. less road congestion).

- There is a presumption in favour of maintaining existing non-commercial services.

These policy objectives have resulted in a range of appraisal techniques from commercial appraisal to CBA to a combination of both approaches being applied to rail projects in the UK.

Parameter values, the discount rate and traffic forecasts

The main costs and benefits associated with transport investment projects which are valued in CBA are set out in the Table 11.1

Table 11.1: Summary of major costs and benefits associated with transport investment projects

Costs	Benefits
Capital cost	Time savings (e.g. business, commercial and leisure)
Delays during construction	Reduction in the number and severity of accidents
	Reduction in vehicle operating costs
	Net savings in maintenance costs

The value of time savings

Most transport infrastructure investments reduce travel times and increase the reliability of transport services. In the UK studies indicate that on average time savings account for over 75 per cent of the quantified benefits of major road improvement schemes. Valuing time savings is a critical element in CBA analysis of all transport infrastructure projects.

The cost of travel time can be regarded as having two distinct elements – an opportunity cost reflecting the value of the activity which would otherwise be engaged in, and a disutility element reflecting the characteristics of the journey itself as experienced by the traveller and including discomfort, waiting time, walking etc. The value of time savings to drivers/passengers depends therefore on how the opportunities made possible by the saving in time are used (e.g. whether for the purpose of increased production or for leisure).

Studies of the value of time generally distinguish between travel for business and working purposes on the one hand and travel for non-working purposes on the other. Various categories of non-working time savings such as commuting time, personal business time and pure leisure time are sometimes identified separately. Since many factors are known to influence the value of time including the purpose of the trip, its length, the amount of time saved, the mode of travel, characteristics of the traveller (e.g. age, income), whether time is saved in vehicle or in waiting, the certainty of the time saving, the time of day and whether the traveller has the opportunity to work in the course of the journey, it may not be appropriate to have a single value of time.

The normal approach in seeking to take account of all these factors that influence the value of time is to estimate a standard value of in-vehicle working time and to derive a series of modifiers which reflect consumer preferences in respect of the most significant influencing factors (e.g. travelling conditions, uncertainty and the activity value of waiting time). However, it is clearly not feasible to take account of all the personal factors surrounding an individual trip. The calculations must deal, as it were, with the average, or representative, user.

'In-work' time is a resource, the opportunity cost of which is the value of the other activities for which the time would be used. 'In-work' time savings are normally valued at the average wage rate for the workers whose time is saved, plus an allowance to cover the cost to the employer of hiring labour (i.e. overheads and employment taxes). It is important to appreciate that this approach is subject to a number of qualifications as follows:

- Individual employees will not behave as if they personally accepted this valuation of time. Thus the application of an average estimated value of 'in-work' time may result in either an overt or under-estimation of the value of time savings.

- Imperfections in the labour market may mean that the value in other uses of travel time saved may be less than the average wage rate. In an economy characterised by high and persistent unemployment, the wage rate may not reflect the economic cost of labour because of labour market inflexibilities which prop up wages. In these circumstances it might be argued that a more appropriate measure of savings in working time would be the opportunity cost of labour.

- The approach also assumes that resources released due to travel time savings will be converted into increased output. However, monopolistic labour market practices, limited possibilities for substitution between labour and capital, and divergences from the profit maximising assumption of the behaviour of firms may prevent this happening.

- Travel time is treated as a disutility, although in some cases travel time may be used productively (especially on a train or plane journey). In addition, the value the employee may place on journey time is not considered.

- Time saved in the transport of freight may be more valuable than the wage cost of the driver. Faster and more reliable delivery leads to other savings including reduced spoilage, reduced inventory costs, and more efficiency which employers may value at a higher rate than the wage of the driver.

Traditionally a single value of time has been applied for savings in 'in-work' time although, where different groups can be clearly identified, account is sometimes taken of variations in wage rates. For example, business travellers' time is more expensive than that of the average of the working population and if the higher salaries of business travellers represent a greater contribution to the output of the community as a whole then there may be a case for valuing the 'resource cost' element of business travellers' time savings at a higher rate. In some countries mode-specific values of 'in-work' time savings are derived reflecting the average earnings of travellers on the various transport modes.

There is no economic argument for excluding freight time savings from CBA studies although there is a question whether time saved in the transport of freight is necessarily more valuable that the wage cost of the driver. The main difficulty lies in valuing freight time savings. The MVA Consultancy (1987) quotes one study which examined the practices of transport operators using the Humber Bridge in England and concluded that the operators' valuation of travel time was of the order of the wage rate. This is an area where more research work would be very valuable.

Non 'in-work' time savings are the property of the traveller and it is, therefore, his or her own valuation of the combined opportunity cost and disutility which gives the basic value for this time. Values for the various categories of non-working time were traditionally derived from the 'observed preferences' revealed in people's actual travel choices. The main advantage of observed or 'revealed preference' information is that it shows actual behaviour whereas even the most carefully designed social survey data can only show hypothetical choices. However, the revealed preference approach can only be used where there are real trade-offs between time and money for alternative modes or routes. It cannot be used for potential trade-offs and this has proved a constraining factor.

More recently values of non-working time have been derived from 'stated preference' social surveys designed to elicit preferences for expenditure on various forms of travel compared to other potential expenditures within and outside the transport sector. One advantage of the stated preference approach is that it is easier to investigate the influence of different factors (e.g. age, household income, inherent characteristics of the various transport modes etc.) which affect the value of time.

A major study of travel time savings was undertaken for the Department of Transport in the UK using a combination of revealed and stated preference surveys (MVA Consultancy, 1987). As part of this project six major surveys of travellers were undertaken. Information was obtained from respondents on journey purpose, household income, household size and composition, employment status and age. The surveys were analysed to reveal the effect of these personal and household characteristics on the value of time. The major conclusions of the study were as follows:

• Household income was the most important single influence on people's valuation of time. Values of time increased with income, reflecting both a greater ability as well as willingness to pay for time savings at higher incomes.

- The study provided support for the notion of variations in the value of time by transport mode. The estimated values of time were higher for modes which were faster and more expensive and the influence of income on value of time became stronger with faster modes. The consultants recommended that mode specific estimates of the value of time be used.

- Retired people tended to have lower values of time than people in the working age groups (16-60 years) in the same household and income bands, and some studies showed that students also had slightly lower values, which may be income related. No significant differences were found in the values of time for men and women.

- In general, employment status had little effect on people's value of time after allowance had been made for the influence of income. The effect of unemployment on people's value of time showed up through lower incomes and not as a direct effect of their having more spare time available.

- *A priori* it seems reasonable that commuting should be distinguished from other non-work travelling and that the value of commuting time should be higher for a number of reasons, including greater time constraints on journeys to work, the fact that the conditions in which commuting trips are made are usually worse in terms of comfort, congestion etc. and the fact that for some people journeys to work may reduce the amount of time spent working. While one or two of the surveys identified some differences in the values of time for different non-work trip purposes, most surveys indicated little effect. In general, higher values of time were found to be associated with a need to keep appointments or make connections with other transport services and with journeys made more frequently.

- The evidence from the various surveys of the impact of car occupancy on drivers' valuation of time was conflicting. Some surveys indicated significantly higher values of time when there were passengers in cars and others revealed no significant effects of occupancy.

- The stated preference surveys of car drivers suggested that values of time were higher for congested road conditions compared with free flow (25 per cent to 40 per cent higher values were found), although this effect was not confirmed by the revealed preference studies. These higher values might reflect driver stress or indicate a reaction to uncertainty of journey times in heavy traffic. The stated preference surveys of the other modes generally identified a sensitivity to uncertainty of arrival time.

- A whole range of other factors such as time of day, day of week, possession of a company car, variability of working hours, and length of journey only made a small contribution towards explaining the variations in values of time in some of the studies.

- Urban bus surveys suggested that people valued walking time at about twice that of time spent in vehicles. This may reflect both a disutility associated with walking and the cost of walking time. Time spent waiting for public transport, and unscheduled time delays resulting from late running of public transport, were both valued more highly than scheduled in-vehicle time.

Revealed preference and stated preference estimates of the value of time reflect 'behavioural' values of time (i.e. the money that an individual would be prepared to pay to save a unit of time for himself or herself). In CBA studies the appropriate value of time to be used is the amount of money that the state would be willing to pay to save a unit of time for the individual. This is likely to differ from behavioural values of time because of misperceptions by the individual, the impact of taxation and subsidies which cause the cost affecting the individual to diverge from the true resource cost, a difference in time horizons between the individual and the state and a concern by the state for income distribution effects. It is appropriate that the state should modify behavioural values of time, especially given the state's concern with income distribution issues.

A departure from the 'equity' principle in the valuation of non-work time saving could result in investment measures which would increase the relative wealth of the better-off members of society by valuing their time savings more highly. A further argument for the application of 'equity' values for non-work time savings is that studies have shown that, in terms of utility, extra travelling time is as inconvenient to low income people as to high income people; it is merely that the latter are more able to afford the cost of avoiding such inconvenience. For similar reasons it is generally the practice to use a single standard value for project appraisal and not to make allowance for variations in the value of time for different income groups and modes.

The approach currently being adopted for valuing time savings in the appraisal of transport investments in the UK can be summarised as follows:

- Separate in-work and non-working time savings are estimated.

- The same value for all non-working time journeys (commuting, shopping, holidays, educational etc.) is used.

- Non-working time values are up-dated in line with changes in real GDP per head.

- Where time is spent waiting for a transport connection the value of time savings is increased (usually doubled).

- Where transport changes will have an impact on the time spent walking then these walking time savings are valued at twice the in-vehicle time savings. Walking time values are applied to all pedestrian journeys whether part of a wider journey by public transport or not. Walking time values are also assumed to apply to cyclists where their journey times and convenience are likely to be affected.

- Small and large time savings and the cost of journey time increases, where they occur, are valued at the same rate.

- The same values of time are used for urban and rural areas.

In Ireland, the usual approach has been to estimate values for working time savings based on average earnings and national income and expenditure data. Non-working time savings are usually valued at a fixed proportion of the wage element of the working time rate with an adjustment for the proportion of indirect taxes (net of subsidies) in consumers' expenditure.

The value of accident savings

Transport investments can be expected to contribute to savings in accidents in a number of ways including the following:

- by encouraging transfers to a safer mode

- by providing new and safer infrastructure, e.g. through the provision of motorways

- by removing hazards on existing infrastructure

- by reducing the level of exposure, e.g. by reducing the actual kilometres travelled.

Typically, in appraisals of road improvement schemes, accident savings account for up to 20 per cent of the total quantified benefits.

The central problem in valuing transport safety involves placing a monetary value on a human life and on human suffering. There can be an understandable reluctance on both moral and ethical grounds, to do this. However, if appropriate weighting is to be given to safety considerations in resource allocation between different transport projects and if the optimal trade-offs between safety and financial costs and other advantages and disadvantages of projects are to be made, then safety effects must be explicitly weighted and evaluated along with other costs and benefits. While the moral or ethical reluctance to place a monetary value on a human life is understandable, any decision to ignore benefits in this area would penalise projects which might save life or limb relative to ones which would not.

It is important to remind ourselves that we are not required to place a value on a specific life which could or could not be saved through a transport investment – a kidnapped millionaire may well be willing to pay to the limit of his/her wealth when facing a death threat. What is involved in a transport investment is the reduction in the statistical risk of a fatality or an injury. It is perfectly rational to ask what value is to be placed on reducing the risk of an event which is undesirable. At a practical level, this value cannot logically be either zero or infinity.

The traditional approach to evaluating personal accident costs was to estimate the value of the 'lost production' of the accident victim due to death or injury. An estimate of economic effects such as medical and police costs and vehicle damage was usually added and sometimes a subjective assessment for pain, grief and suffering of the victim and relatives was also included. The major objection to the foregoing 'gross output' approach is that it values safety on the basis of current and future levels of income and output whereas most individuals probably value safety on the basis of their aversion to the prospect of their own and others' death and injury *per se*. More recently there has been a change towards valuing transport safety on the basis of 'willingness to pay' with revealed and stated preference data being used to collect information on the value of a reduction in accident risk.

Under the willingness-to-pay approach to the valuation of safety, the amounts that those affected would individually be willing to pay for (typically small) improvements in their own and others' safety are determined. These amounts are then added to derive an overall value for the safety improvement concerned – a reflection of what the safety improvement is 'worth' to the affected group, relative to the alternative ways in which each individual might have spent his or her limited income. The adoption of this approach goes some way towards recognising that an individual is not a mere factor of production.

One consequence of the move towards the willingness-to-pay approach based on revealed and stated preference data is that there have been significant increases in the estimated value of a statistical life. However, there are methodological and practical difficulties in implementing this approach. The 'irrational' behaviour of car drivers in relation to safety (e.g. when not wearing seat belts) appears to conflict with revealed preference valuations on safety.

Jones-Lee (1990) reported the results of a series of studies which valued a 'statistical life' for transport risks and noted other studies which derived values of statistical life from observed wage premia for risk in labour markets. These studies generally involved the use of multiple regression analysis to control for the variety of other factors, besides job risk, that can be expected to influence equilibrium wage rates in labour markets. In broad terms the estimates of the value of a statistical life produced in these studies were consistent with the findings of the transport risk studies.

Accident rate reductions can often be anticipated and included in the calculation of benefits. However, there are severe practical difficulties in applying CBA methodology to accident cost savings in practical situations. For example, historical records of accident rates on particular segments of the road network may only be available in a rough categorisation of accident severity. Typically, the records will distinguish fatalities, injuries, and material damage. Fatalities are rare, and most network segments would never have had a fatality. But since measures of the severity of the other accident categories are not really feasible, two segments with the same apparent accident rate may in truth have very different safety characteristics.

The proper allowance to be made for accident reduction will depend on engineering judgement in many instances – a bend may be a dangerous bend even if the historical data are not capable of demonstrating high accident frequency and severity. High accident rates may also be due to driver behaviour, ambient conditions, or other factors which are not amenable to rectification through physical road improvements.

In some transport modes, historical records provide no guidance whatever. Most airports in the world, including airports which are quite busy, have never had an accident on takeoff or landing. Such accidents as do occur may be due to pilot error, equipment failure or other factors unrelated to infrastructure investment. Thus improvements which enhance safety may have to be evaluated from a probabilistic perspective: the likelihood of an accident is reduced by an improvement, even where the historical records show that no accident has ever occurred.

Vehicle operating cost savings

For road investments, there are well-established procedures for reckoning the savings in vehicle operating costs which may be expected to arise from network improvements. Some schemes will shorten journey times, either by shortening the distance to be travelled or by enhancing level of service. All relevant links in the network need to be considered – a by-pass will improve journey times for those using the 'old' route, for example. The main items of savings will include fuel, oil, tyres, maintenance and depreciation. Standing charges, which do not vary with the volume of usage, should be ignored. They include road tax, insurance, and the opportunity cost of the capital used to buy the vehicle. Some improvements can yield economies in fleet size which should be taken into account. For example, predicted passenger loads for an inter-urban bus or road freight operator might require a smaller fleet consequent on a major network upgrading.

Indirect taxation is a major element in vehicle operating costs, especially for road transport, where tax is as much as 60 per cent of the retail price of petrol in some European countries. Taxes are a transfer of resources between sections of society as a whole, and should be ignored in a social cost-benefit analysis. Direct taxation is treated differently to indirect taxation – gross pay is the measure of output foregone to society through lost working-time. But a gallon of petrol is really worth less than the price actually paid by the motorist.

The traffic engineering literature contains a range of empirical studies of the impact of road improvements on vehicle operating costs, allowing for savings due to such factors as better road surfaces and gradients. In non-road modes, similar considerations apply. An improved railway line will cut journey times and may lead to fleet economies also. In the case of sea and airports, the point-to-point journey times of vehicles are not, of course, directly affected by port improvements, but turnaround times may be reduced. Thus the probability of a ship having to wait for a berth is cut when an additional berth is constructed. Equally, when an airport widens a runway, the incidence of bad weather diversions for certain aircraft types should fall, and the probabilities can be calculated from meteorological and operating data. Improvements in air traffic control and in the technology of both airports and aircraft which increase the ability to operate safely in adverse conditions will have the same type of impact.

The discount rate

Discounting procedures are needed to compare costs and benefits over time, in a way which reflects the preferences of consumers and taxpayers for enjoying benefits earlier and incurring costs later. In private market transactions the justification for discounting reflects two factors – the productivity of capital and the time preference of individuals. Because of the former, a borrower who invests in a capital asset can expect to end up with more in value than he or she started with and will be in a position to pay interest to anyone who lent the resources in the first place. On the consumer side it is clear that consumers would prefer to consume a unit today than to defer consumption for a year. Many public sector decisions incorporate a judgement, implicit or explicit, about the importance of the more distant future relative to the present or near future. There are good reasons to presume some preference, by those affected by a public sector activity, for benefits to be sooner rather than later and for costs to be later rather than sooner.

Some measure of people's preferences is given by the real return which they are willing to accept on government bonds. Over the past twenty years the real yield on long-term Irish government debt has averaged approximately 3 per cent. The Department of Finance recommends a real discount rate of 5 per cent for use in public sector project evaluation (Department of Finance, 1994). Some observations on this rate are as follows:

- Five per cent is a low rate in absolute terms. It is a rate which is appropriate for a liquid, government-backed security, rather than for project finance.

- Investing in an index-linked government security is just about the lowest-risk project which can be imagined.

- The application of a uniform rate to all projects regardless of risk may not be appropriate unless the riskiness of projects is taken into account explicitly in the appraisal.

There are reasons for viewing bond yields as the lower limit rather than a mean estimate of the time preference of individuals. Not all individuals are net savers. Some are net borrowers and personal borrowing rates are generally above the long-term bond yield. There are also uncertainties about future returns to individuals. Some individuals will be dead or too infirm to enjoy extra income as much as they would today and their time preference will exceed the 'risk free' yield on long bonds.

Apart from a very general risk of some catastrophe such that the longer-term benefits (and costs) of any investment made now might not materialise, there are ordinary risks associated with all public projects (e.g. implementation risk and risks about future demand levels) which suggest that the discount factor should exceed the 'risk free' yield on long bonds. However, there are also arguments why the social rate of discount should be below the market rate. Reliance on individuals' time preference could result in society allocating too little to investment if the discount rate is too high. In addition, too high a discount rate may also have undesirable environmental implications since the future exploitation and consumption of natural resources, both renewable and non-renewable, will be assigned a low value. A high discount rate reduces the importance given to resource depletion and environmental damage in the future. In public projects financed out of taxes the risk is spread over a much larger population and this has led to suggestions that for these projects the risk premium should be excluded from the discount rate. There is another objection to including a premium in the discount rate to take account of risk: with a higher discount rate a greater weight is given to costs and benefits closer to the present and a lower weight to costs and benefits in the distant future; this procedure may (but does not necessarily) favour low risk projects and penalise high risk ones.

Overall the discount rate recommended by the Department of Finance is probably reasonable (if somewhat low) for use in the case of transport projects so long as risk is dealt with explicitly in the appraisal process, by modelling a range of possible outcomes based on different cost and traffic volume forecasts.

Traffic forecasts

Traffic forecasts play a key role in CBA studies. The evaluation of economic costs and benefits and the appraisal of environmental impacts depend on forecasts of the amount and pattern of traffic using the new network compared to the existing one. For the purpose of estimating the benefits of a transport project, future traffic should be divided into three basic types as follows:

- *Normal traffic*. This is the traffic that would have occurred without the investment. It benefits from the full reduction in operating costs and from the full time savings.

- *Diverted traffic*. This is traffic diverted to the new or improved facility from other facilities of the same mode or from other modes. The benefit to this traffic is the difference between future transport costs on the old route/facility and the new one. Traffic diversion depends not on relative economic costs but on actual financial costs including non-transport charges.

- *Generated or induced traffic*. The third type of traffic is that which did not previously exist and is generated as a consequence of the lowering of transport costs. It is not appropriate to apply the full reduction in costs to this traffic since the traffic would not have materialised without the reduction in costs.

It is important that a robust and acceptable methodology is used to derive forecasts of overall traffic, broken down into the different components. Where models are used to forecast traffic they should be subject to appropriate validation.

There has been considerable debate in the UK over the existence and scale of induced traffic associated with major road improvement schemes. Road traffic forecasts have traditionally been estimated on the basis of expected trends in economic growth, the costs of car ownership and the costs of car use. Account was generally taken of induced traffic only in particular cases (e.g. estuary crossings). However, it has been argued that the provision of additional road capacity itself encourages travellers to travel more or further.

An expert report by the Standing Advisory Committee on Trunk Road Assessment (1994) which examined this issue concluded that induced traffic does occur, probably quite extensively, although its size and significance is likely to vary widely in different circumstances. The report noted that induced traffic is likely to be of greatest consequence in cases where a network is operating at or close to capacity, where traveller responsiveness to changes in travel time or costs is high (e.g. where trips are suppressed by congestion and then released when the network is improved) and where the implementation of a scheme can cause significant changes in travel costs. The Committee recommended that the appraisal of road schemes should be carried out within the context of economic and environmental appraisal at a strategic area-wide level and that account be taken of induced traffic through variable demand methods which recognise congestion constraints. The issue of induced traffic is relevant in Dublin where planned transport investments may facilitate increased private car usage with negative environmental impacts.

The treatment of environmental impacts
A major criticism of CBA is its failure to take explicit account of environmental impacts. Transport infrastructure projects can have positive or negative environmental impacts. Positive impacts occur, for example, when road and rail projects take traffic away from congested town centres. Negative impacts include noise associated with a new airport development, or with a new urban motorway. This section considers specific issues which apply to transportation and the environment.

The main environmental impacts associated with investments in inter-urban transport infrastructure in Ireland are as shown in Table 11.2.

Environmental impacts are externalities since they do not usually affect the users of the new facility to any great extent. Other externalities are associated with the use of land and water resources and the production of solid waste as part of the construction and abandonment of roads, rail lines etc. Another type of environmental externality is the visual intrusion created by transport infrastructure. This affects residents or landowners rather than transport system users. Road schemes may pass through environmentally sensitive areas, and may be visually intrusive. Electric rail projects involve unsightly overhead gantries. These 'disbenefits' are notoriously difficult to quantify but are nonetheless real.

Table 11.2: Main environmental impacts of transport infrastructure projects

Noise	Associated with road traffic and to a lesser extent with rail and air traffic.
Air Pollution	Associated with all transport modes to different degrees.
Impact on neighbourhoods and on farmland and wildlife habitats	Associated with road investments and to a lesser extent with other transport investments.

In recent years there has been increasing recognition that the transport sector generates environmental externalities which impose costs on society as a whole and that transportation investments often magnify the incidence of these externalities. For example, in developed economies it has been estimated that the transport sector accounts for approximately 75 per cent of carbon monoxide emissions, for between 40 per cent and 50 per cent of emissions of nitrogen oxides and hydrocarbons and for significant proportions of the emissions of particulates and sulphur oxides. Given the sheer size of the transport sector in developed economies it is hardly surprising that it has a significant impact on the environment. In addition, since travel is highly income elastic, the size of the transport sector is likely to increase as incomes rise, and this has implications for the scale of associated environmental impacts in the future.

Significant progress has been made in recent years in environmental benefit estimation/damage assessment using revealed and stated preference studies of people's willingness to pay. Benefit estimation describes the process whereby monetary values are placed on the advantages that accrue to society from improvements in the natural and built environment. Damage assessment describes the obverse: placing monetary values on losses to society from environmental deterioration.

The main techniques used in valuing noise and air pollution impacts and other environmental externalities involve the use of hedonic property price indices. This approach to benefit estimation assumes that if different locations have different environmental attributes there will be observed differences in property prices. The methodology involves examining the revealed preferences of people in the housing market when they trade-off the noise/air pollution attributes of different properties against their prices. Statistical techniques are available to identify how much of an observed property price differential is due to a particular environmental difference and to infer from this how much people are willing to pay for an improvement in environmental quality. However, as might be expected the approach is fraught with methodological difficulties. It ignores the considerable transaction costs in the housing market and the infrequent turnover in the housing stock due to this and other factors. In addition, there are doubts about the capacity to allow for changes in all other factors that influence house prices.

An alternative approach is contingent valuation which asks individuals directly what they would be willing to pay for an environmental benefit or what/how much they would be willing to accept to tolerate an environmental cost. The aim is to elicit valuations which are close to those that would be revealed if an actual market existed. However, there are doubts about the accuracy of the contingent valuation approach because of the biases that can arise.

Evidence from the USA quoted by Button (1990) on the value of traffic noise nuisance using hedonic techniques, suggests a decline of between 0.08

per cent and 0.88 per cent of the house price per unit change in Leq (a measure of continuous sound levels) in a number of American cities. Somewhat higher values were found in Canada and Switzerland. Similar ranges of values were found in the context of aircraft nuisance. However, a UK study showed that while properties in areas affected by the noise of aircraft using Manchester International Airport had lower market values than those in other parts, the whole of the difference could be attributed to neighbourhood and other characteristics of the properties (Pennington, Topham and Ward, 1990). There is evidence from US studies that for seven large North American cities the percentage fall in property values for a 1 per cent rise in air pollution is in the range of 0.01 per cent to 0.22 per cent with part of the variation explained by the nature of the pollution.

The conclusion reached by the OECD is worth quoting (Pearce, Markandya, 1989):

> Overall we take the view that environmental pollution in the form of air pollution, noise nuisance and water quality deterioration has significant effects on the property values on which they impinge. The overwhelming evidence of the empirical studies supports this conclusion. The accuracy with which we can quantify such effects is however, much more debatable. There are many reasons for thinking the numbers can only be orders of magnitude ... It is also our opinion that this matter of fuzziness is not one that will be resolved by better measurement or better statistical techniques: it is inherent to the problem being considered.

And again:

> Also there has been considerable improvement over the last ten years in the quality of the data used and in the analytical techniques used. These improvements have resulted in a greater awareness of the accuracy of the estimates. It has now become clear that, even with the best techniques at our disposal, this accuracy remains quite low and that estimated costs ... could be out by a substantial margin in either direction.

The impact of transport developments on property values can be double edged. The noise and air pollution are a nuisance, but there may be an offsetting locational premium in being near the transport facility. Some people find it convenient to be near an airport, and studies of property values near airports have found both positive and negative effects. It is generally accepted that residential properties along the DART route in Dublin command a premium price.

The impact of noise, or air pollution, will depend on the location of any project. There will normally be a presumption that environmental impacts from noise, noxious odours and the like will be most significant in urban areas where substantial numbers of people will be affected. In rural areas, there will simply be fewer people to be adversely affected. But rural projects can have significant impacts on visual amenity, which might not be a concern in some urban areas.

In the UK, in appraisals of transport infrastructure projects, environmental considerations are not generally given monetary values. However, they are taken into account in the appraisal process. The factors considered are traffic noise, visual impact, community severance, agriculture, heritage and conservation areas, ecology, disruption due to construction, pedestrian amenity, the view from the road, and driver stress. In the case of some factors the effects are quantified. For example, in the case of noise, estimates are made of the number of properties that will experience at least a 3 decibel change compared with existing noise levels. The assessment also identifies who actually experiences the adverse environmental impact (e.g. travellers, property owners etc.) so that distributional effects can be considered. It is especially important in assessing emissions to include the upstream emissions in the production of the fuel source (e.g. in oil refineries or power stations).

The valuation of environmental externalities involves greater quantification difficulties than the other main elements in transport project appraisal. Given existing knowledge in this area we must accept that it is not feasible to value the environmental impacts of transport infrastructure projects with a view to incorporating these impacts into the CBA process. Clearly, however, environmental impacts cannot be ignored. Environmental Impact Statements are required for certain larger projects, and should be considered alongside the factors quantified by the cost-benefit analysis. In other cases the principal environmental aspects should be identified and their significance assessed.

CBA application rules

While the bulk of this chapter has concentrated on technical aspects of the application of CBA to transport projects, the fact that CBA is more than a technical process cannot be overemphasised. Adler (1987) remarks as follows: 'The appraisal of a project is not a mechanical process; a high degree of analytical ability and a broad imagination are required.'

The following application rules deal with some of the critical issues that arise in applying CBA to transport projects. They are intended to assist in preparing, reviewing and interpreting CBA studies.

The definition of a project for analysis purposes

Considerable care needs to be taken in the application of CBA to transport infrastructure projects, to ensure that the project is a meaningful unit for evaluation purposes and that it is properly defined. In particular, the unit of analysis (i.e. the project) should be specified so as to distinguish projects from programmes. All ancillary sub-projects which are essential to the achievement of the benefits of the main project should be included. Unfortunately this is frequently not the case in Ireland.

In the transportation area, developed countries will tend to be permanently engaged in programmes of investment in the various modes of travel. It is possible to evaluate these programmes, as a whole, and to conduct CBA evaluation of the entire investment package. But this can be highly misleading, to the extent that the programme consists of individual, stand-alone elements, which may not be equally desirable, or may not be equally urgent. It is best to break the programmes down into a series of self-contained projects, and to conduct CBA at the level of the project. To construct a motorway from Dublin to Galway is not a project; it is a programme. We know that traffic volumes along the route vary enormously, and that, while extra motorway capacity may be needed soon on certain sections, it will not be needed for decades, if ever, on other sections. Thus it makes sense, in evaluating road investments, to reduce the unit of analysis to a length of road that has uniform traffic volumes, or to a town by-pass, and this is the standard practice in Ireland. A good example is the Naas Bypass study (Barrett and Mooney, 1984).

However, it is likely that the improvement to one section of a road will, by simulating new traffic, affect other sections and account should be taken of these network impacts. For example, the opening of a new stretch of motorway will result in reduced transit times on that section. However, part of these savings may be dissipated by increased congestion on other sections of the route. This should be taken into account.

Even in the case of a route with uniform traffic it may be appropriate to split the project. For example, a route could go through some easy terrain and then through some difficult terrain. It might be appropriate to split the project into two projects, because the costs will differ, even where we expect the benefits to be uniform. The time-savings may justify the cost in easy terrain, but may not do so in difficult terrain.

Sometimes the true project may be bigger, rather than smaller, than it seems. If a new suburban rail or light rail facility cannot realise the benefits of traffic growth without extra car-parking (e.g. a 'park and ride' facility) or a feeder bus service, then the cost of the car park and/or the feeder bus service is part of the rail or light rail project. Similarly a port access road might be required to capture the full benefits of a major port project. Again the cost of a project involving the development of quality bus corridors should include the cost of the additional enforcement that will be required to ensure their effectiveness. The test should be that a project's costs must include everything needed to realise the benefits of the project, regardless of who meets these costs. Most CBA studies of transport projects in Ireland can be criticised on the ground of poor project definition.

Timing of a project

It is important to experiment with alternative starting dates in applying CBA to transport infrastructure projects. Even if a project shows an adequate return if commenced immediately, it may still not be a priority for inclusion in the programme of immediate works. There may be other projects which show a higher immediate return, and delay may not worsen the return on some projects at all, or may even improve it. The premature provision of transport infrastructure capacity in advance of traffic growth will always tend to put a project in this category. It is therefore always worthwhile to experiment with a range of future years as alternative starting points for any particular project. Unfortunately, it is the exception rather than the rule in CBA studies of transport projects in Ireland that consideration is given to alternative starting dates.

Alternatives to a project

Probably the most critical element of the application of CBA to transport infrastructure projects is the definition and analysis of alternatives to the project under consideration. Adler (1987) comments as follows: 'The most serious mistakes in project appraisal do not arise from the application of erroneous statistical techniques but from inadequate analysis of alternatives and results.'

The options of closing a route, of discontinuing a transport service, of developing an alternative mode, of using a cheaper technology (e.g. diesel instead of electricity powered suburban rail), or of simply doing nothing, should always be amongst the options considered in evaluating transport investments. However, even 'doing nothing' needs to be articulated carefully. In developed countries, and in the context of ongoing traffic growth, doing nothing may well mean deferral for, say, five or ten years. This deferral can itself be evaluated by considering the differential stream of costs and benefits that it implies.

The alternative could be to discontinue, either forthwith or at some future point, a particular service or route. The option of discontinuation is not normally considered in the case of certain transportation investments, where there is no feasible alternative method of catering for the traffic volumes. But this is not universally the case. It is feasible to discontinue regional air services, or off-peak bus services, or to close lightly-patronised rail lines. It may or may not be desirable, but that is a matter for CBA to establish. Whenever proposals for upgrading arise in these cases, the option of discontinuation should be regarded as the base case scenario.

Consideration of alternatives is especially important in transport investment because of the existence and extent of competition within and between modes.

For example, the proposal to build a new regional airport has an alternative, namely to do nothing, which would see the relevant traffic volumes catered for by other airports or by bus, rail, or car. In considering the costs and benefits of a new airport, or extensions or improvements to an existing one, the impact on other facilities and modes needs to be explicitly taken into account. Where freight, or public transport passengers need to be moved between A and B, a full CBA of a proposed investment in any mode must consider the relative merits of all modes for carrying the anticipated traffic, including bus, rail, air, truck or inland waterway as appropriate.

It is common in CBA studies in Ireland for alternatives to be selected by the project promoters or their consultants which are so implausible that one can only assume they were selected for the sole purpose of making the preferred project appear attractive by comparison. CBA studies prepared by or on behalf of project promoters most often fail because inadequate attention is given to alternatives or because appropriate alternatives are not considered.

Technology choice and frequency in public transport

Private transport modes, such as car or truck, have the advantage of continuous departure times at the option of the user. The only transport modes used by the public which offer continuous departures are taxis and hired vehicles or craft. Users of public transport, in planning their journeys must accordingly rely on timetables of published departure schedules. The only exception is in urban systems where frequency is so high that customers do not feel the need for timetables –DART approaches these frequencies as also do certain bus routes.

In Ireland, rail services between the principal cities and towns offer frequencies of 3 or 4 departures a day in many cases. Even frequencies up to 10 or 12 a day, which are not found in Ireland, mean that people will rely on timetables. There is evidence from many studies that improvements in frequency in these circumstances will help to generate increased patronage. So will shorter transit times, of course. The potential frequency on any route will depend on the choice of mode and on the choice of technology. Thus the bus mode offers the prospect of greatest frequency, but at some cost in terms of transit time, while within the rail mode, large, locomotive-based technologies will offer lower frequency than lighter, smaller railcars. The impact of these choices, through frequency, on passenger demand, needs to be taken into account in projecting patronage.

The time horizon and residual values

It is common in transport projects, to use time horizons of 25 or 30 years, perhaps with some ascription of residual value to the project's capital stock in the terminal year. At discount rates as low as 5 per cent (real) however, the present value of €1 of benefits or costs in year 25 is still 30c, and, particularly where benefit streams are expected to grow rapidly, there may be a case for using a longer time horizon.

Residual values, after a 30 year lifetime, will tend to be low or zero for many kinds of transport infrastructure, depending of course on volumes of planned maintenance spending. But where rolling stock or other equipment has to be acquired through the life of the project, the residual values will be more significant. There is a case for developing a common approach to both the time horizon and the determination of residual values for use in all CBA studies of transport projects.

The avoidance of double-counting

When user benefits have been fully accounted for, care should be taken to avoid double-counting through the inclusion of other projected occurrences which are induced by these user benefits.

It is sometimes argued that transport investments can have a sufficiently large impact on the available transport links as to alter the spatial pattern of economic development in a region or country. Examples are rare in developed countries, where transport investment programmes are ongoing and incremental in nature. But there are exceptions such as the Channel Tunnel.

In Ireland, some projects have been mooted from time to time which, it is claimed, would have such a large impact as to promote regional development objectives. In the late 1980s, there was some discussion of a motorway route linking the South West to the North West as a tool for stimulating the economic development of the West. Similar considerations have been raised in connection with the upgraded Dublin-Belfast rail link, and with some regional airport schemes. In evaluating such schemes, it is important not to double-count benefits, for example by ascribing value to the time-savings of users, and then ascribing a further and separate value to developmental stimuli which these savings are believed likely to induce.

An additional consideration is that transport links between, say, metropolitan areas and remote regions will not always have a uni-directional impact on the pattern of development. There are examples in the literature of such links facilitating greater, rather than less, concentration of economic activity. These may be exceptions, but the issue is complex, and intuitive notions can mislead.

Another frequent problem with CBA studies is that items are sometimes included erroneously as benefits, particularly when the CBA is too heavily influenced by project promoters. For example, the wage bill during construction is sometimes mentioned as a positive feature of the project, even though it is a cost rather than a benefit! Indirect economic benefits of a macroeconomic character are also sometimes attributed to transportation projects. Thus a new road which links into a less developed region may be said to yield benefits in terms of a higher rate of economic development for that region. However, these effects may be fully captured by the calculation of direct user benefits and their inclusion separately will almost always involve double counting.

Capital investment as a substitute for other policy interventions

One direct consequence of the availability of EU assistance in Ireland in recent years has been the increased emphasis on investment projects in the transportation area and the consequential expansion in the scale of transport investment programmes.

There is a danger that because of the availability of additional funding, investment projects will be seen as the only method of achieving desired benefits. This is especially likely to be the case where service provision is in the hands of state-owned monopolies. It is important to ensure that the potential contribution of more effective management and market deregulation as substitutes for capital investment are not ignored.

The impact of grant-aid

Because of the availability of EU assistance for transportation projects it is sometimes argued that only the domestically-financed portion of the capital costs of a grant-aided project should be evaluated, on the basis that the EU finance is somehow 'free'. By extension it is occasionally argued that given the availability of 'free' money a less rigorous approach to project evaluation will suffice. Even if this is not explicitly argued it is often implicit in the approach to the CBA study.

However, since the opportunity cost of EU funding is the return that could be obtained by investing the finance in another project there is no basis for making allowances for the source of finance and certainly no basis for adopting a less rigorous approach in the case of EU financed projects.

Parameter values

In the absence of any government guidelines, it is usually left to consultants undertaking CBA studies to prepare their own estimates of the parameter values to be used to define the project, to determine what alternatives will be examined, to prepare a time horizon for the analysis and to determine the treatment of residual values. It would be preferable if an external agency (e.g. the Department of Finance) were to specify the parameter values to be used in

CBA studies of all projects involving public expenditure, just as they specify the discount rate to be applied. Consideration might also be given by the Department to commissioning research studies of the value of time and of accident and vehicle operating costs in order to derive better parameter value estimates. Finally, guidelines on the approach to be adopted in forecasting traffic are required to ensure greater consistency in approach in CBA studies.

In conclusion, one must emphasise the need for exercising caution and judgement in preparing, reviewing and interpreting CBA studies. This need is all the greater in Ireland where CBA evaluations are usually prepared directly by the project promoter or by consultants acting on the promoter's behalf and where the government does not require compliance with detailed guidelines. There is significant scope for the misuse of CBA. In these circumstances it is hardly surprising that many CBA studies of transport projects in Ireland give the impression of having been carried out retrospectively to justify the promoters' preferred project rather than as part of an objective project selection process.

*

This article was first published in Mulreany, M., (ed.) *Economic & Financial Evaluation: Measurement, Meaning and Management*, Dublin: Institute of Public Administration, 1999

NOTES

1 This chapter draws on an earlier paper by Keegan and McCarthy (1994).
2 An overview of developments in the application of appraisal techniques to road projects in Ireland is contained in a report by Casey (Casey, 1986).

REFERENCES

Adler, H. (1987). *Economic Appraisal of Transport Projects*, Baltmore: Johns Hopkins
An Foras Forbartha (1971) *Dublin Transportation Study*, Dublin: An Foras Forbartha.
Barrett, S. D. and D. Mooney (1984). 'The Naas Motorway Bypass – A Cost Benefit Analysis,' Article in ESRI *Quarterly Economic Commentary*, January, pp 21-34
Button, K. J. (1990). 'Environmental Externalities and Transport Policy,' *Oxford Review of Economic Policy*, vol 6 no 2, pp 61-75
Casey, J. J. (1986). 'A Review of the Value of Time and Car Ownership Forecasts,' Unpublished Paper, (RT 326), Dublin: An Foras Forbartha
Department of Finance (1994). *Guidelines for the Appraisal and Management of Capital Expenditure Proposals in the Public Sector*, Dublin: Department of Finance
Department of Local Government Dublin (1966). *Arterial Roads Needs Study*, Dublin: Department of Local Government
EU Commission (1995) *Towards Fair and Efficient Pricing in Transport*, Green Paper Luxembourg: COM (95) 691 Final

Jones-Lee, M.W. (1990). 'The Value of Transport Safety,' *Oxford Review of Economic Policy*, vol 6, no 2, pp 39-60

Keegan, O. and C. McCarthy (1994). 'CBA Parameter Values and Application Rules,' Paper Prepared under the Technical Assistance Programme of the Operational Programme on Peripherality, Dublin: DKM Economic Consultants

MVA Consultants; Institute for Transport Studies, University of Leeds; Transport Studies Unit, University of Oxford (1987). *The Value of Travel Time Savings*, Newbury, Berkshire: Policy Journals

O'Keeffe, P. (1961). Economic Aspects of Road Improvement in Ireland,' Paper Presented to the Institute of Civil Engineers of Ireland, Dublin: Institute of Civil Engineers

Pearce, D.W. and A. Markandya (1989). *Environmental Policy Benefit : Monetary Valuation*, Paris: OECD

Pennington, G.N. Topham and R. Ward (1990). 'Aircraft Noise and Residential Property Values Adjacent to Manchester International Airport,' *Journal of Transport Economics and Policy*, vol 24, no. 1, pp 49-59

Standing Advisory Committee on Trunk Road Assessment (1994). *Trunk Roads and the Generation of Traffic*, London: HMSO

Steer, Davies, Gleave, in association with McHugh Consultants (1994). *Dublin Transportation Initiative: Final Report*, Dublin: Stationery Office

12

Developing an Economic Evaluation Procedure for Road Investments*

BERNARD FEENEY, JOHN DEVLIN

Introduction

In 1985, investment in roads amounted to some £130 millions, which represents, in real terms, a more than doubling of expenditure in six years. The impetus for this upsurge in investment was the Road Development Plan for the 1980s (Department of the Environment, 1978), which also had the effect of redirecting resources from maintenance expenditures and small-scale improvements to major improvements on National Routes. The Plan set out a list of such projects and a projected time scale for their implementation. The choice and timing of projects was based partly on an analysis of deficiencies in the National Primary Network, which had been undertaken some years previously (Devlin *et al*, 1974). This analysis was *needs based*, in that the capacity of each section of the network to carry predicted traffic at desired levels of service, as determined by operating speed, was assessed and deficient sections were identified. While the incremental economic rate of return on the investment which would be required to achieve successively higher levels of service, was determined on a global basis (Barrett, 1975), the economic return from improvements to particular sections of road or from specific improvement projects was not identified.

This chapter outlines the computerised project evaluation procedure subsequently developed by the Department of the Environment and An Foras Forbartha in order to help reassess priorities for projects within the Road Development Plan. A more detailed account of the procedure may be obtained from three complementary reports (Feeney, 1984 and 1987 and Department of the Environment, 1984).

General principles

Unlike private sector investments, the return on road improvements cannot be measured directly in financial terms, for the simple reason that there are no revenues which can be set against road construction costs. Cost-benefit analysis (CBA) is a technique widely used in such circumstances to estimate the economic return on public sector investments. The principal feature of CBA is the imputation of money values to the benefits arising from an investment and the comparison of these benefits with the construction and maintenance costs of the project. The procedure outlined below measures the benefits to road improvements by comparing the road user costs which arise in the absence of the investment to those which would occur when the investment is in place. User costs comprise the time, vehicle operating costs and accident costs facing road users. Figure 12.1 depicts this process. Road investments also give rise to environmental costs and benefits. These are more difficult to value and have not, as yet, been included in the procedure.

As roads are relatively long-lived assets, the benefits arising from them will accrue over a long period. The level of user costs in any year is related to traffic volumes and this implies that traffic forecasts are required for each year of the evaluation period, which, in this case, was taken to be thirty years. Section 3 outlines the traffic forecasting procedure used. As benefits are measured over a thirty-year period, there is a need to express benefits (and, indeed, costs) which occur at different times in equivalent terms. The evaluation procedure permits two approaches to this problem: in the first, a rate of return is calculated which equates benefits and costs, and projects with higher rates of return are preferred: in the second approach both benefits and costs in each future year are discounted to present values using a pre-set discount rate, and the sum of discounted benefits are divided by the sum of discounted costs to arrive at a benefit-cost ratio. The procedure permits testing of the sensitivity of the benefit-cost ratio to a range of discount rates, including the minimum 5 per cent level laid down by government.

Traffic Forecasts

The traffic forecasting methodology employed in the project evaluation procedure has been described in detail elsewhere (Feeney, 1985). Traffic forecasts were built up from separate forecasts of cars and goods vehicles which represent 74 per cent and 18 per cent of total road traffic respectively (Devlin, 1982).

Car traffic forecasts were obtained by combining forecasts of the national population, cars per person, and average car use as outlined in Figure 12.2. Forecasts of cars per person were based on a time series analysis using a

Figure 12.1: The cost-benefit procedure

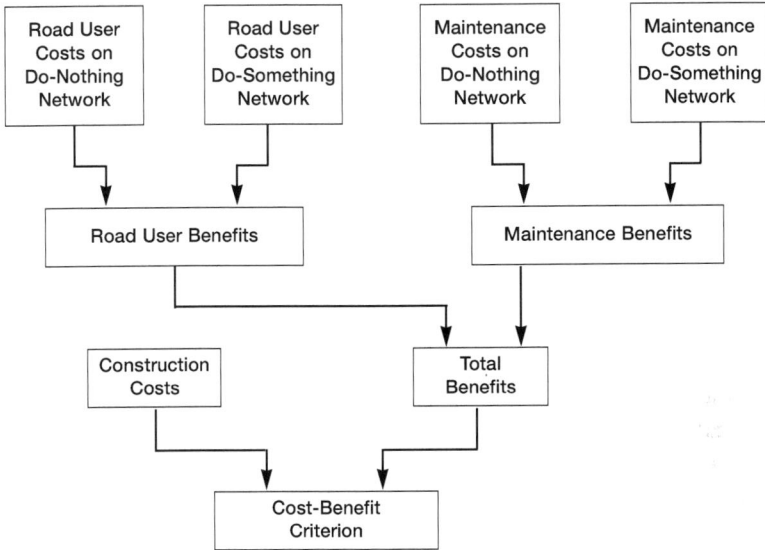

Figure 12.2: The car traffic forecasting process.

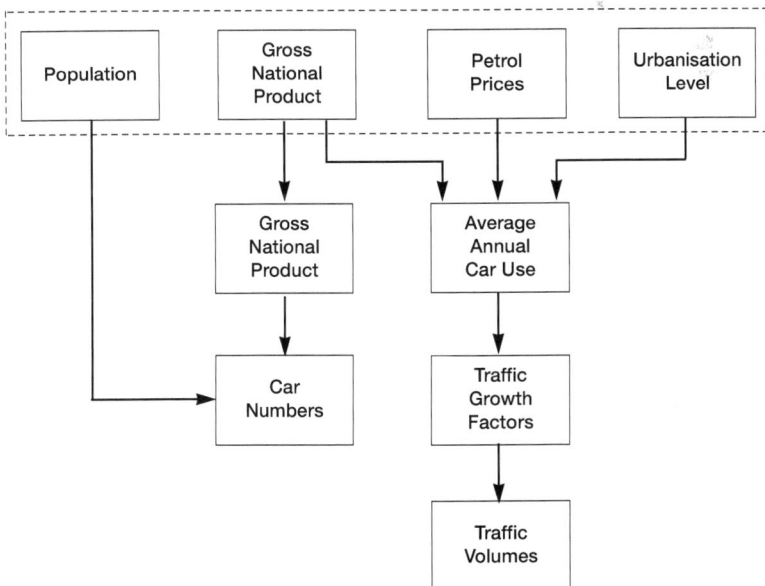

logistic function which related car ownership to per capita gross national product, under the assumption of an ultimate saturation level of 0.4 cars per person. Car ownership was forecast to rise from 0.216 cars per person in 1980 to 0.360 by the year 2005. When the projected population growth is applied to these figures a doubling of car numbers over a twenty-five year period is envisaged.[1] However, because average car use is expected to decline from the current high level of 10,500 miles per annum, car traffic is not expected to grow in line with the increase in car numbers. Research has established that average car use is positively related to GNP, and negatively related to car ownership levels, petrol prices and the degree of urbanisation of the population. On the basis of upward trends in the latter variables, a 16 per cent reduction in car use is forecast. Figure 12.3 summarises the forecasts for car traffic.

Turning to goods vehicles, a more simple forecasting methodology is employed. This was based on two features of goods vehicle use, namely, the trend towards heavier vehicles and the reduction in the utilisation rate within each vehicle weight category. The first step in the forecasting process was the projection of the proportion of vehicles in each weight category in line with trends in the weight distribution of *new* vehicles. The demand for fleet-carrying capacity was then projected on the basis of assumed GNP growth rates, and the fleet size structure predictions were used to derive the number of vehicles required to satisfy that demand.

Goods vehicle numbers were predicted to grow faster than car travel. However, this trend was offset by declining utilisation rates so that goods vehicle travel was predicted to grow in line with car travel. Thus, total traffic volumes were predicted to grow at a compound annual growth rate of 2.3 per cent over the period 1980-2005, as compared with 6.0 per cent in the period 1964-80.

Figure 12.3: Forecasts of car travel.

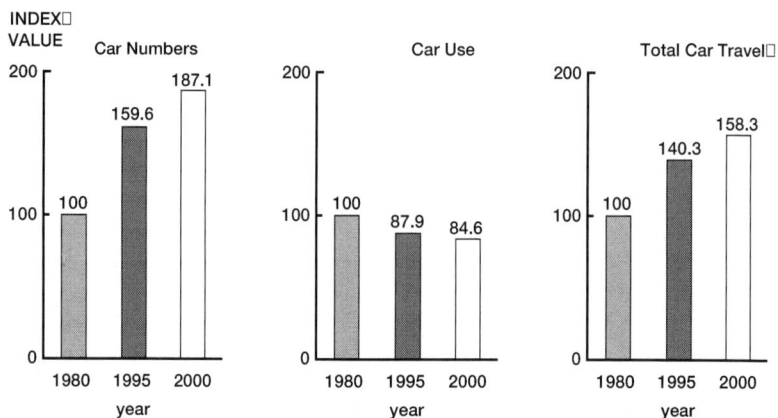

Valuing the benefits and costs of road improvements

The economic evaluation procedure adopted was based on the cost-benefit principle. This states that if investment in roads creates benefits which can be characterised as potential Pareto improvements, and if these benefits exceed investment costs, then such investments are desirable (see Mishan, 1971 for a fuller treatment of this issue). This implies that road investment projects are acceptable if the gainers from the investment are in a position to compensate the losers and yet be better off themselves. The tool normally employed for measuring such welfare gains and losses is the consumers' surplus, which is defined as the maximum a consumer is willing to pay for a given quantity of a good less the amount he actually pays. Figure 12.4 depicts the ordinary demand curve for travel between two points. If the market price of travel is P^0, then the demand curve indicates that Q^0 road users will travel between these points. For the marginal road user, the benefits of travel are sufficient to compensate him for the price P^0. Intra-marginal users, however, would be prepared to pay a higher price than this as measured by the demand curve between points A and B. The consumers' surplus can, therefore, be measured by the area P^0AB. If, as a result of investment in roads, the market price of travel falls to P^1, then Q^1 road users will travel and their consumers' surplus is measured by P^1AC.

The benefit to road users can then be measured by the change in consumers' surplus – P^0BCP^1. As roads are not directly priced, it is necessary to impute travel prices. A convenient way of doing this is through the notion of generalised costs, which imputes a money value to travel time and adds this to the vehicle operating cost, to derive the total user cost facing the trip-maker. In theory, the value placed on time should reflect the total non-money disutility of travel including the accident risk facing the user. In reality, however, the valuation of time is not sufficiently advanced to do this, so that the effect of accident risk must be assessed separately.

The evaluation procedure was simplified substantially by assuming that the investment projects would generate no additional traffic, that is, that traffic volumes would remain at Q^0. In this case, the change in consumers' surplus is measured as $P0BEP^1$ and the benefits can be characterised as road user *savings* – time-savings, vehicle operating cost savings, and accident cost savings.[2] This means that the procedure tends to underestimate benefits where significant additional traffic is generated.

Two types of time saving were distinguishable – savings of working time and savings of non-working time. Working time was valued as the output lost to the employer as a result of the time spent travelling by the worker. On the supposition that the value of the output lost must at least equal the cost of hiring labour for that time, the value of working time was measured by the

Figure 12.4: Consumers' surplus and the demand for travel

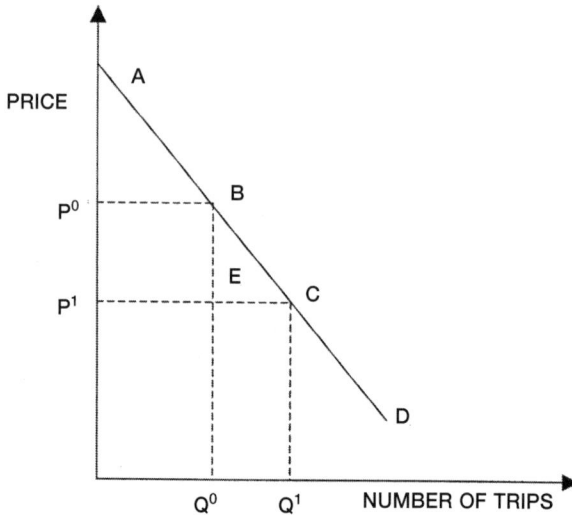

sum of wage and labour overhead costs. In the Irish context, this was measured at IR£4.85 per hour (1984 prices). The value of non-working time, i.e. time spent travelling to or from work, or on shopping, social or recreational visits cannot be valued directly. Instead, non-working travel time is valued by observing how people trade off time and money in making transport choices. Numerous studies of this nature were undertaken during the 1960s and 1970s, usually aimed at discovering the relative values commuters put on time and money when choosing travel modes.[3] While there is considerable variability in the results, these studies suggest that people value non-working time spent in vehicles at about 25 per cent of their gross wage rate or earned income. On this basis, non-working in-vehicle time was valued at IR£0.97 per hour (1984 prices).[4]

Valuing vehicle operating costs is more straightforward as these are priced in the market place. However, the market prices of fuel, oil, tyres and vehicle repair and maintenance were adjusted to remove the tax element, as this represents a transfer of resource between members of the community rather than consumption of resources.

The willingness of the community to pay for reduced accident risk is not easy to value. An alternative approach was used which seeks to place a value on a 'statistical death'. This was done by measuring the gross output lost as a result of a typical fatality. This is a measure of economic loss and does not include a valuation of the human misery and suffering caused by death.

Table 12.1 presents values for different accident types for 1984. They are inclusive of costs of medical treatment, damage to vehicles and other property and the administrative costs of police and insurance. As these values undoubtedly fall short of the community's willingness to pay for reduced risk, they must be regarded as minima. An alternative approach would be to forego putting a value on accident risk, leaving it open to the decision-maker to apply his own value.

Table 12.1: Costs per Accident on National Routes (£1984)

Accident Type	£
Fatal	101,00
Serious Injury	5,100
Minor Injury	1,500
All Injury	14,150

Construction costs are valued by assuming that the market prices for inputs reflect correctly their value to the community, once the taxation element is removed. All construction costs and benefits were valued at 1984 prices.

Inputs to the evaluation procedure

In order to measure benefits, the values placed on time savings, vehicle operating costs and accidents must be combined with physical measures of such savings – hours of travel time, litres of fuel, numbers of accidents. Quantification of these savings requires consideration of a series of inputs relating to the road network, the traffic flows on it (both current and predicted), the effect of road capacity, junction design and traffic flows on vehicle speed, the effect of road capacity on accident rates, and the effect of vehicle speed on vehicle operating costs. The money benefits, thus measured, must then be compared with the construction costs of the project and the change in maintenance costs arising. The sensitivity of the results to alternative traffic forecasts and parameter values can then be tested.

The road network

Two networks are described in the evaluation procedure. A 'do-nothing' network which normally describes what the road network currently looks like and a 'do-something' network which includes both the existing network and the proposed investment. The size of these networks depends on the area over which the proposed project is likely to have an effect. As traffic speeds may be expected to vary by location each network is subdivided into links, which are relatively homogeneous with regard to geometric characteristics. Each link is then categorised according to the level of capacity it provides, as this determines speeds on that link. Similarly, each link is assigned a traffic type category describing whether the traffic using that link is primarily commuting, inter-urban or tourist traffic. This is important because the distribution of traffic throughout the day and year is related to journey purpose. The networks also contain the major junctions, which are categorised as uncontrolled junctions, roundabouts, fixed time signalised and vehicle-actuated signalised. Each junction is also assigned a traffic type.

Traffic data

The basic information required for the calculation of vehicle speeds is the hourly traffic flow. In most cases, site-specific data of this type are not available. However, data relating to estimated Annual Average Daily Traffic (AADT) are available (Devlin, 1982 B) and together with typical hourly flow distributions for different traffic types, may be used to indicate the number of hours in the year during which hourly flows, representable as various percentages of AADT, occur (see Figure 12.5). Where the investment project under consideration envisages the construction of a new road link, e.g. a town by-pass, then the proportion of traffic which will divert to the new facility needs to be measured. This can be ascertained, by quantifying the proportion of existing traffic which stops in the town, through a number-plate-matching survey; or by origin and destination information obtained by roadside interview. A computerised origin-destination survey and analysis procedure, compatible with the needs of economic evaluation, is available (Borland, 1985).

Figure 12.5: The distribution of annual hourly traffic flows for rural road sections

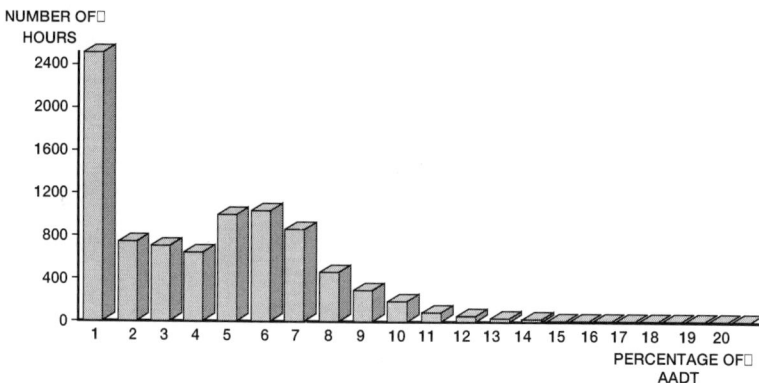

The final element of traffic data required is an estimate of the number of occupants in each type of vehicle (car, van, heavy goods vehicle or bus) and the journey purposes of occupants. Again, site-specific information requires a special roadside interview survey, although considerable information is available from a nationwide sample survey (Department of the Environment, 1979).

The effect of road capacity and traffic flows on vehicle speeds

The major benefit of road improvement is usually reduced journey time or higher traffic speeds. Although existing traffic speeds can be measured, these are of little use for the purposes of evaluation. This is, firstly, because even for the do-nothing network the vehicle speeds which may be expected to occur in the future need to be determined and these are related to predicted traffic flow levels. Secondly, the hypothetical do-something network contains links with increased capacity and this implies higher speeds. In practice, a distinction is made between speed-flow relationships for links and delay-flow relationships for junctions. Figure 12.6 describes the set of speed-flow relationships used for links of different capacities. These relationships, which are based on UK data (Department of the Environment, U.K. 1981), are combined with the hourly flow data described above to measure predicted speeds on both the do-nothing and do-something networks for each hour in the year.

Figure 12.6: Speed-flow relationship for rural roads.

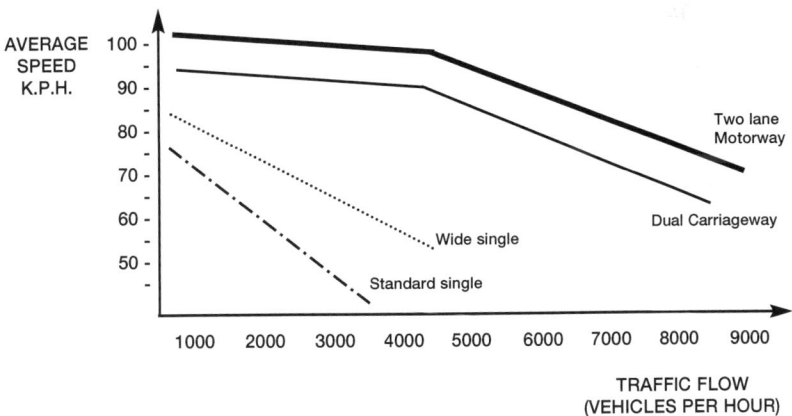

The effect of road capacity and alignment on accident rates

The realignment of existing roads can reduce accident rates by improving passing-sight distance and reducing the number of roadside developments and accesses. Research on accident rates on rural roads (Hearne, 1976) has shown that on standard 7.3 metre-wide roads with desirable features such as hard shoulders and absence of roadwide developments, there are 0.40 fatal and injury accidents per million vehicle kilometres. Roads 10 metres wide tend to have slightly higher accident rates at 0.47 accidents, possibly due to the higher speeds attainable. In contrast, the limited data available on dual carriageways indicate that they are considerably safer – 0.21 accidents per million vehicle kilometres. Existing unimproved roads have considerably higher accident rates. In the case of urban roads, for example, significantly higher accident rates have been determined (Hearne, 1980). For such roads with less than 2,000 vehicles per day (AADT), there are 1.2 accidents per million vehicle kilometres, declining to 0.5 for roads in excess of 8,000 AADT. Thus, the safety improvements resulting from by-passes can be determined by comparing the predicted accident rates on the by-pass route, which will have good geometric characteristics, with the existing accident rate for the through town route.

The effect of vehicle speed and road geometry on vehicle operating costs

Vehicle operating costs comprise fuel, oil, tyres, vehicle maintenance and repair and vehicle depreciation. With the exception of fuel, these are presumed to be unaffected by vehicle speed. Savings in these costs occur only if there is a diminution in distance travelled, as a result of construction of a shorter route. However, fuel consumption, which is the largest single item of vehicle operating cost, does vary with speed and with road geometry. There is no Irish body of research into the determinants of vehicular fuel consumption. However, as the characteristics of road surfaces are similar to those prevailing in the United Kingdom and the USA, research results from these countries can be used, if due allowance is made for the smaller size of the typical Irish vehicle. Figure 12.7 shows the relationships used for the typical Irish car (1250cc). Similar data were developed for vans and trucks.

Road improvements and maintenance costs

Reduced road maintenance costs can arise from road improvements, through the provision of stronger pavements and better construction. New alignments which lead to shorter road lengths reduce road maintenance costs, while longer road lengths, particularly through the construction of town bypasses, can have the opposite effects. At present, it is possible to estimate only those maintenance changes which are linked to changes in road length. This is done by using standard maintenance costs – £2,700, £3,000 and £5,400 per kilometre per year for standard two lane, wide two lane and dual carriageways respectively.

Figure 12.7: The effect of speed and road gradient on car fuel consumption

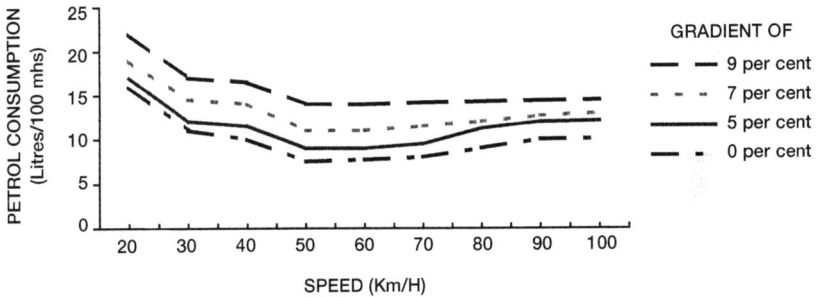

Results and further development

The procedures outlined above have been applied to thirty-nine road projects to date. These comprise major route realignments, town bypasses and urban inner relief roads. The benefits (B) and costs (C) of each of these projects were assessed over a thirty-year period and compared using two cost-benefit criteria. Table 12.2 summarises the results using the economic internal rate of return criterion (i), obtained by solving the following equation:

$$\sum_{t=0}^{30} \frac{Bt - Ct}{(1 + i)t} = 0$$

Table 12.2: The estimated internal rate of return on road projects

Rate of return per cent	Number of projects	Percentage of projects
<5	7	18
≥5 <10	12	31
≥10 <15	12	31
≥15 <20	6	15
≥20	2	5
Total	39	100

More than four out of five projects analysed achieved an economic rate of return of at least 5 per cent, which is the minimum acceptable to government. The simple average rate of return on all thirty-nine projects was 10.4 per cent. On those which reached the minimum 5 per cent, the figure was 12.1 per cent.[5] The rates of return calculated ranged from 0 to 29 per cent. The most successful projects were those which had high traffic volumes and reduced road lengths, and where construction costs were not inflated by poor terrain or the need to bridge a river crossing. These results are being used by the Department of the Environment to help determine the priority and optimum timing of projects.

As may be deduced, nearly all aspects of the evaluation procedure would benefit from further research and refinement. From the point of view of their importance in benefit and cost estimation, the following appear to be most in need of further work: the value of time, the speed-flow and delay-flow relationships, construction cost estimation, and, to a lesser extent, accident risk and valuation. In a wider context, the procedure suffers by the omission of environmental effects. Here, an interim solution might be the provision of a standard method of quantifying (rather than valuing) environmental effects.

At present, the road user savings approach which is used for benefit estimation, limits the application of the procedure to rural road realignments and small town bypasses. Its use in the urban context or for strategic road investment plans is not advisable because, in such situations, traffic levels may be expected to increase as a result of the investment. For example, in the urban context, road investments may cause existing road users to change their journey destinations and may induce additional trip-making which was previously suppressed by road congestion. In the context of individual project evaluation, the extension of the procedure to urban areas requires the development of small-area traffic planning models.

*

This article was first published in Irish Journal of Environmental Science, Vol. 4, No. 2, pp 1-9, 1987.

NOTES

1   forecasts have recently been reviewed (Casey, 1986) and no recommendations for change resulted. However, if a sustained period of poor economic growth is encountered in the short to medium term then some downward adjustment in the forecast for the year 2005 may be required.

2   In contrast, if Q^1 exceeds Q^0 total user costs could increase and no user cost savings would be evident. A different approach to benefit estimation is then required.

3   One such study has been conducted in Ireland (O'Farrell and Markham, 1975).

4   Values for both working and non-working time have been recently reviewed (Casey, 1986A) and an upward revision in the values of 15 per cent respectively has been recommended.
5   The equivalent figures when the projects were weighted by their construction costs were 7.9 per cent and 10.8 per cent respectively. The lower weighted rate of return is not surprising as low returns may be often caused by high construction costs resulting from, for example, poor terrain.

REFERENCES

Barrett, S. (1975). *An Application of Cost Benefit Analysis to the Improvement of the National Primary Route Network*. An Foras Forbartha Report RT. 151
Borland, D. (1985). *An Origin Destination Survey Method for Small Town Bypasses*. An Foras Forbartha Report RT. 303
Casey, J. (1987). *A Review of Car Ownership Forecasts*. An Foras Forbartha Report RT 326(A)
Casey, J. (1987a). *A Review of the Value of Time*. An Foras Forbartha Report RT. 326(B)
Department of the Environment (1978). *Road Development Plan for the 1980s*. Stationery Office, Dublin
Department of the Environment (1979). *Origin Destination Survey*
Department of the Environment (1984) *Economic Evaluation of Road Improvement Schemes*
Department of the Environment, UK (1981) COBA 9
Devlin, J. (1982). *Vehicle Kilometres of Travel 1980*. An Foras Forbartha Report RT. 257
Devlin, J. (1982 a). *National Roads and Traffic Flows 1980*. An Foras Forbartha Report RT 260
Devlin, J., C. McCarthy, P. McGuinness (1974). *A Roads Needs Study. The National Primary Routes*. An Foras Forbartha Report RT. 126
Feeney, B.P. (1984). *Economic Evaluation of Small Town Bypasses*. An Foras Forbartha Report RT. 275
Feeney, B.P. (1985). *The Demand for Road Travel – Recent Trends and Future Prospects*. The Engineer's Journal, March
Feeney, B.P. (1987). *General Principles and Parameter Valuation for the Economic Evaluation of Road Investments*. An Foras Forbartha Report RT. 333 (unpublished)
Hearne, R. (1976). *Selected Geometric Elements and Accident Densities on the National Network*. An Foras Forbartha Report RS. 167
Hearne, R. (1980). *Accidents in Irish Towns 1968-1978*. An Foras Forbartha Report RS. 244
Mishan, E.J. (1971). *Cost Benefit Analysis*. London: Allen and Unwin
O'Farrell, P.N. and J. Markham (1978). The Journey to Work: A Behavioural Analysis. *Progress in Planning* Vol. 3, Part 3. London: Pergamon Press.

=========== 13 ===========

Economic Evaluation of Small Town Bypasses*

BERNARD FEENEY

General

In the context of road planning, economic evaluation is concerned with assessing the merits of alternative schemes or designs from the point of view of society. If the social benefits of a scheme exceed the social costs, then the project may be deemed acceptable. The most acceptable scheme or design is that for which the return of benefits in relation to costs is the greatest. This chapter outlines a methodology for the economic evaluation of small town bypasses and presents a worked example.

The methodology employed compares the construction costs of a proposed bypass to the sum of the travel time (T), operating (O), accident (A) and maintenance (M) cost savings resulting from it. Travel time and operating cost savings will accrue not only to traffic diverted to the bypass, but also for traffic which continues to use the existing route. Accident cost savings usually arise from the transfer of through traffic to the safer bypass route. Maintenance cost savings are often negative, because if the investment takes place there is an additional bypass road to be maintained.

It may be noted that there are other relevant costs and benefits, e.g. environmental benefits associated with noise and air pollution, which are more difficult to evaluate, but which should be considered before a proposed improvement project is accepted.

Time, operating, accident and maintenance costs are measured for the existing road network under the assumption that no investment takes place, that is, for the do-nothing case. The same costs are then measured for the proposed road network, incorporating the new bypass route, and the benefits arising from the investment are obtained by subtraction.

The estimation of benefits by this method is valid for the evaluation of bypasses for small towns only.

Where the level of internal, as opposed to through, traffic is great, a more comprehensive approach involving computer modelling is required, so that the effect of the bypass on a more extensive road network may be gauged.

In comparing costs and benefits, it is not necessary to use the prices prevailing in the year in which the economic evaluation is carried out. However, the same price level should be used throughout the analysis. In the example which follows, all calculations are made in terms of 1977 prices.

As roads are relatively long-lived assets which produce benefits over a lengthy period of time, it is essential to forecast and evaluate future costs and benefits. The forecast and evaluation period adopted here is twenty-five years. Benefits are forecast for the first year of operation of the improvement project and for the years 1985, 1995 and 2005.

The remaining sections of this chapter outline the principal steps in the economic evaluation. These are the definition of the existing and proposed road networks, the estimation of present and future traffic volumes, the calculation of the project benefits and costs and, finally, the comparison of these benefits and costs.

Defining the road network

In the economic evaluation, the existing or do-nothing network is compared to an improved network containing a bypass. It is important that both networks have common terminal points so that like may be compared with like.

As traffic speeds vary over the length of a network, it is essential to subdivide the networks into sections which are relatively homogeneous with regard to geometric characteristics. No section should comprise road lengths which are subject to different speed limitations.

In Figure 13.1 a simple small town bypass is depicted. The do-nothing network is simply the existing road through the town centre. This is subdivided into three sections A, B and C. Section B is within the built-up area and is subject to a speed limitation of 30 m.p.h. The proposed network comprises the new bypass D together with the existing road A-B-C, which will continue to cater for traffic terminating in the town centre.

The lengths of each road section are set out in column 3 of Worksheet 1in the appendix to this article.

Figure 13.1: Do-nothing and improved networks

Do-nothing

Improved

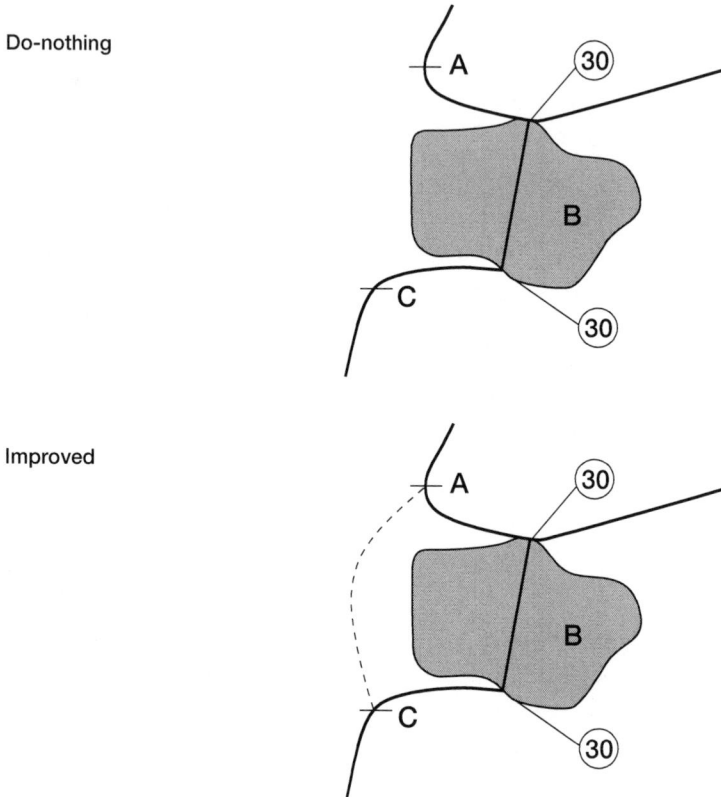

Traffic volumes

In order to calculate T + O + A + M costs, it is necessary to determine current and future traffic volumes for each section of the do-nothing and proposed networks. In particular, the Annual Average Daily Traffic (AADT) and the Annual Vehicle Mileage (AVM) must be calculated.

A best estimate of current AADT on existing sections of the National Route System is available from An Foras Forbartha.[1] Alternatively, the local authority may arrange a special sample traffic count, from which AADT may be derived using established factors.[2] AADT figures for each road section are set out in column 4 of Worksheet 1.

For bypass projects, it is necessary to calculate the proportion of traffic on the existing route which would divert to the new bypass. A simple assumption is that all non-stopping traffic would use the bypass. For small towns a registration number survey enables a reasonably accurate estimate of non-stopping traffic to be made. In the worked example, it is assumed that 75 per cent of the traffic, currently using section A, will divert to the bypass section D. AADT values for each section of the improved network may then be calculated.

Annual Vehicle Mileage (AVM) for each section may be obtained by multiplying the section length (L) by the total yearly traffic volume, i.e.

$$\text{AVM} = 365 \times \text{AADT} \times \text{L} \qquad (1)$$

For the purpose of estimating accident levels, the vehicle mileage of through-traffic must be calculated. This is done by applying the above formula 1 to the AADT of through-traffic.

Factors for forecasting traffic volumes on a nationwide basis are available as follows: 3

Year	1978	1985	1995	2005
Factor	1.0	1.4	2.0	2.6

If these factors are multiplied by the current traffic volumes, forecasts of AADT and AVM may be obtained. For the purpose of calculating project benefits it is unnecessary to derive traffic volume forecasts for each future year. It is suggested that traffic volume forecasts be made (by interpolation, if necessary) for the first year of operation and the years 1985, 1995 and 2005.

Calculating project benefits

Vehicle speeds

Travel time and operating cost savings are directly related to average vehicle speeds (S). The latter are determined by road capacity and traffic volumes. As traffic volumes vary considerably from hour to hour, it is necessary to select a typical hourly traffic volume (HTV) which will give substantially the same results as would a more detailed calculation using several hourly flow groups. This has been estimated at 6 per cent of AADT[4] i.e.

$$\text{HTV} = 0.06 \, \text{AADT} \qquad (2)$$

In order to calculate vehicle speeds (S), the HTV must be expressed in terms of passenger car units (PCU).

Currently, the breakdown of traffic flow by vehicle type for all National Primary Routes is as follows:

Vehicle Type	per cent
Private Car	73
Light Goods	7
Heavy Commercial	19
Other	1
	100

Assigning PCU values of unity to private cars and light goods vehicles, three to heavy commercial vehicles and zero to all others produces a figure of 1.36 as the conversion factor of traffic volume to PCU, i.e.

$$\text{HTV (PCU)} = 1.36 \text{ HTV} \qquad\qquad (3)$$

THV values for each section are given in column 7 of Worksheet 1.

Typical vehicle speeds are estimated using speed volume relationships. Figure 13.2 depicts the relationship between average vehicle speed and the ratio of hourly traffic volume (in PCU) and hourly capacity (in PCU). Once the capacity of existing road sections is known, this relationship may be used to estimate the average speed prevailing on existing roads for the typical hourly volume. Column 8 of Worksheet 1 gives the capacity of existing road sections.

The average vehicle speed on new road sections, i.e. the bypass section(s), may be determined from Figures 13.3, 13.4 and 13.5, which depict the relationship between traffic volume (in PCU) and average speed for roads of different standards.

In Column 9 of Worksheet 1 average speeds are presented for each section of the do-nothing and improved networks for the first year of operation of the improved network and the years 1985, 1995 and 2005.

Over the time period under analysis, traffic volumes are expected to grow substantially. This may result in extremely low predicted average speeds, especially on the do-nothing network. In practice, these speeds may not occur as some diversion and redistribution of traffic will take place. In order not to overstate the advantages of bypass construction, it should be assumed that the minimum average speed per section does not drop below 10 mph.

All road sections are currently restricted to certain speeds. The maximum average speed should be assumed to be 80 per cent of the speed limit.

Travel time and operating costs

The quantity of travel time expended per vehicle is inversely related to speed and can therefore be determined by using the average speeds derived from the speed-volume relationships.

Travel time costs per vehicle mile may be estimated by multiplying the quantity of time by the value of time.

The operating costs per vehicle mile also vary with vehicle speed. This arises primarily because the relationship between fuel consumption and speed is U-shaped with high levels of consumption at both low and high speeds. Other costs such as maintenance, depreciation, types and oil are not viewed as speed related.

Table 13.1 presents the sum of travel time and operating costs at various speeds. The 1977 figures were calculated using a value of time of 205 pence per vehicle hour, while the operating costs are measured at 1977 prices net of tax. The values for other years are obtained by assuming that the real value of time increases at a rate of 3.5 per cent per annum and fuel and oil prices at 5 per cent per annum.

Column 10 of Worksheet 1 sets out the sum of time and operating costs per vehicle mile appropriate to the predicted vehicle speeds on each section. Time and operating costs per road section per annum are obtained by multiplication by AVM. The results are given in Column 11 of Worksheet 1.

Accident costs

Accident cost savings are measured by determining the number of accidents attributable to through-traffic on the do-nothing network and on the bypass, multiplying by the respective costs per accident, and subtracting. A common problem with the calculation of accident numbers is that only a small proportion of total accidents is reported. The accident rates quoted below are obtained by multiplying reported fatal and injury accidents by a factor of 6.

Accident rates on the do-nothing network are likely to vary as between built-up and rural road sections.

Research conducted in An Foras Forbartha indicates that the accident rate attributable to through-traffic in built-up areas is of the order of 7.8 accidents per million vehicle miles.

Data on accident rates for through traffic outside built-up areas are obtainable from An Foras Forbartha report RS. 223. The personal injury accident data are in the form of three-year totals for each road section. Division by 3 and multiplication by 6 yields the total annual accidents per section. Division by the AVM gives the accident rate per million vehicle miles.

Figure 13.2

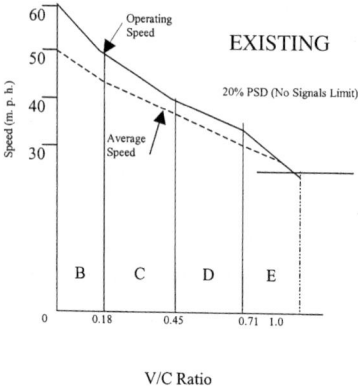

EXISTING

V/C Ratio

Figure 13.3

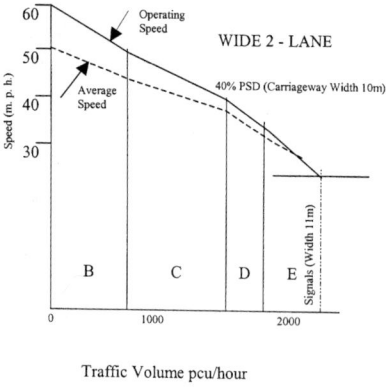

SINGLE

Traffic Volume pcu/hour

Figure 13.4

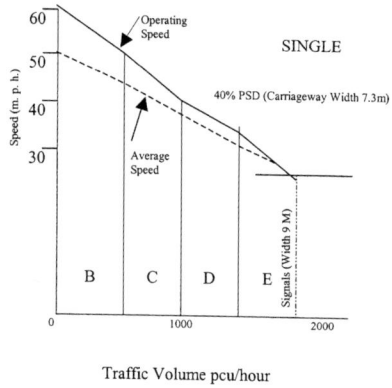

WIDE 2 - LANE

Traffic Volume pcu/hour

Figure 13.5

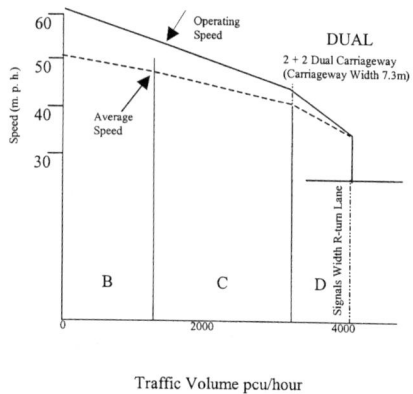

DUAL

Traffic Volume pcu/hour

Table 13.1: Average travel time and operating costs in pence per vehicle mile for various vehicle speeds

Speed	YEAR							
	1977	1981	1982	1983	1984	1985	1995	2005
10	29.00	32.40	33.40	34.40	35.60	36.80	50.90	71.50
11	27.50	30.70	31.60	32.55	33.70	34.80	48.05	67.40
12	25.95	28.95	29.80	30.70	31.75	32.80	45.20	63.35
13	24.45	27.25	28.00	28.90	29.85	30.80	42.40	59.25
14	22.90	25.50	26.20	27.05	27.90	28.80	39.55	55.20
15	21.40	23.80	24.40	25.20	26.00	26.30	36.70	51.10
16	20.65	22.90	23.50	24.25	25.00	25.80	35.20	49.00
17	19.90	22.05	22.60	23.30	24.05	24.75	33.75	46.90
18	19.10	21.15	21.70	22.40	23.05	23.75	32.25	44.80
19	18.35	20.30	20.80	21.45	22.08	22.70	30.80	42.70
20	17.60	19.40	19.90	20.50	21.10	21.70	29.30	40.60
21	17.15	18.90	19.40	20.00	20.55	21.15	28.50	39.45
22	16.70	18.40	18.85	19.45	20.00	20.60	27.70	38.30
23	16.30	17.90	18.35	18.95	19.40	20.20	26.90	37.10
24	15.85	17.40	17.80	18.40	18.85	19.45	26.10	35.95
25	15.40	16.90	17.30	17.90	18.30	18.90	25.30	34.80
26	15.05	16.50	16.90	17.50	17.90	18.45	24.65	33.85
27	14.70	16.15	16.55	17.05	17.45	18.00	24.00	32.90
28	14.40	15.75	16.15	16.65	17.05	17.50	23.30	31.90
29	14.05	15.40	15.80	16.22	16.60	17.05	22.65	30.95
30	13.70	15.00	15.40	15.80	16.20	16.60	22.00	30.00
31	13.50	14.80	15.20	15.60	15.95	16.35	21.70	29.55
32	13.35	14.60	14.95	15.35	15.70	16.10	21.35	29.10
33	13.15	14.40	14.75	15.15	15.50	15.90	21.05	28.60
34	13.00	14.20	14.53	14.90	15.25	15.65	20.70	28.15
35	12.80	14.00	14.30	14.70	15.00	15.40	20.40	27.70
36	12.65	13.80	14.10	14.50	14.80	15.20	20.10	27.30
37	12.50	13.65	13.95	14.30	14.60	15.00	19.80	26.90
38	12.30	13.45	13.75	14.10	14.40	14.80	19.50	26.50
39	12.15	13.30	13.60	13.90	14.20	14.60	19.20	26.10
40	12.00	13.10	13.40	13.70	14.00	14.40	18.90	25.70
41	11.95	13.00	13.30	13.60	13.95	14.30	18.80	25.55
42	11.90	12.95	13.25	13.55	13.90	14.25	18.65	25.40
43	11.80	12.85	13.15	13.45	13.80	14.15	18.55	25.30
44	11.75	12.30	13.10	13.35	13.75	14.10	18.40	25.15
45	11.70	12.70	13.00	13.30	13.70	14.00	18.30	25.00
46	11.65	12.60	12.90	13.20	13.60	13.90	18.20	24.80
47	11.60	12.55	12.85	13.10	13.50	13.80	18.05	24.65
48	11.52	12.45	12.75	13.00	13.40	13.70	17.95	24.46
49	11.45	12.40	12.70	12.90	13.30	13.60	17.80	24.30
50	11.40	12.30	12.60	12.80	13.20	13.50	17.70	2410
51	11.35	12.25	12.55	12.75	13.15	13.45	17.65	24.05
52	11.30	12.20	12.50	12.70	13.10	13.40	17.60	24.00
53	11.30	12.10	12.40	12.70	13.00	13.40	17.60	24.00
54	11.25	12.05	12.35	12.65	12.95	13.35	17.55	23.95
55	11.20	12.00	12.30	12.60	12.90	13.30	17.50	23.90

Accident rates on the improved network must be predicted. Accident statistics indicate that the following rates are appropriate to high standard road sections:

two lane roads: 3.6 accidents per million vehicle miles
dual carriageways: 1.8 accidents per million vehicle miles.

Multiplication of these accident rates by the vehicle mileage associated with through traffic gives the total annual accidents per section which is attributable to through traffic. This is set out in Column 13 of Worksheet 1.

Accident costs per section per annum may be derived by applying the appropriate cost per accident. These are:

	Inside Built-up Areas	Outside Built-up Areas
	£	£
1977	725	1,390
1981	820	1,595
1982	849	1,651
1983	879	1,709
1984	910	1,768
1985	942	1,830
1995	1,328	2,582
2005	1,873	3,642

The accident costs are in terms of 1977 prices. Values for other years are calculated on the assumption of a 3.5 per cent per annum growth in real accident costs.

Column 15 shows the annual accident costs per section obtained by multiplying Column 13 by Column 14 of Worksheet 1.

Maintenance costs

The provision of a bypass will normally add to maintenance costs, because road mileage will increase. The increase in maintenance costs may, therefore, be estimated by multiplying the maintenance costs per mile by the number of additional road miles. This assumes that the diversion of traffic to the bypass will not reduce maintenance costs on the existing road network.

The following maintenance costs per mile may be used:

	£
two-lane roads	1,900
dual carriageways	2,800

Calculation of project benefits and costs

The project benefits (B) for the years 1983, 1985, 1995 and 2005 may be obtained by subtracting the sum of T + O +A + M costs for the improved network from the corresponding costs for the do-nothing network. Benefits for intervening years are obtained through interpolation. The results are set out in Column 1 of Worksheet 2 in the appendix to this article.

The full construction costs (K) of the project must be estimated in 1977 prices and allocated to individual years according as construction is expected to take place. These costs comprise land, labour, materials, machinery and other costs. As the project benefits (B) have been measured net of tax, the tax element in construction costs should, as far as is practicable, also be netted out. The construction costs (K) appear in Column 2 of Worksheet 2.

Comparing costs and benefits

It is generally accepted that costs and benefits which occur in the future should be given less weight than current costs and benefits. To correct for this, all future costs and benefits are revalued in present-day terms by means of discounting procedures. For example, the present value B_o of annual benefits in any future year t is given by

$$\text{Bo} = \frac{\text{Bt}}{(1 + r)t} \qquad (4)$$

where r is the rate of discount.

The discount factor $\frac{1}{(1 + r)t}$ varies with the rate of discount adopted and the time period in question. Table 13.2 presents twenty-five year discount factors for discount rates of 5, 10 and 15 per cent. Multiplication of the costs and benefits by these factors yields the present value of future costs and benefits. The results of discounting future costs and benefits to 1980 values at a 5 per cent discount rate are set out in Columns 3 and 4 of Worksheet 2.

Having established the present value of benefits for each of the twenty-five future years of the evaluation period, these may be summed to give the gross present value of benefits (B):

$$\text{B}^1 = \sum_{t=0}^{t=24} = \frac{\text{Bt}}{(1 + t)} \qquad (5)$$

Similarly, the gross present value of all project costs (K^1) may also be calculated.

Table 13.2: Twenty-five year discount factors for discount rates of 5, 10 and 15 per cent

	Discount Rate		
Year	5	10	15
1	0.9524	0.9091	0.8696
2	0.9070	0.8264	0.7561
3	0.8638	0.7513	06575
4	0.8227	0.6830	0.5718
5	0.7835	0.6209	0.4972
6	0.7462	0.5645	0.4323
7	0.7107	0.5132	0.3759
8	0.6768	0.4665	0.3269
9	0.6446	0.4241	0.2843
10	0.6139	0.3855	0.2472
11	0.5847	0.3505	0.2149
12	0.5568	0.3186	0.1869
13	0.5303	0.2897	0.1625
14	0.4810	0.2633	0.1413
15	0.4581	0.2394	0.1229
16	0.4363	0.2176	0.1069
17	0.4155	0.1978	0.0929
18	0.3957	0.1799	0.0808
19	0.3769	0.1635	0.0703
20	0.3589	0.1486	0.0611
21	0.3419	0.1351	0.0531
22	0.3256	0.1228	0.0462
23	0.3101	0.1117	0.0402
24	0.2953	0.1015	0.0349
25	0.2812	0.0923	0.0304

For the improved network to be deemed acceptable, there must be an excess of benefits over costs, i.e. the net present value $(B^1 - K^1)$ must be greater than zero. It may be seen from Worksheet 2 that at a discount rate of 10 per cent, the net present value amounts to £1,693,009, so that the bypass project may be deemed worthwhile.

However, the particular bypass scheme depicted in Figure 13.1 may be only one of many possible designs. Alternative designs may be compared by estimating the net present value of each and expressing it as a proportion of K^1. This is the cost-benefit ratio:

$$\text{Cost-benefit ratio} = \frac{B^1 - K^1}{K^1} \qquad (6)$$

Finally, it must be remembered that in choosing between alternative designs or schemes, there may be a number of relevant costs and benefits which cannot be valued but are nevertheless worthy of consideration. These should be taken into account before a final decision is reached.

*

This article was first produced as a paper for An Foras Forbartha in 1984.

NOTES

1   1977 estimates are given in 'National Roads and Traffic Flows 1977', RT.200, 1978.
2   Factors for Expanding Short Term Counts to AADT, RT.200, Appendix 1, 1978.
3   'A Roads Needs Study – The National Primary Routes', An Foras Forbartha, RT. 126.
4   G.R. Wells, *High Planning Techniques – The Balance of Cost and Benefit*. Griffin & Co., 1971.

Appendix

Worksheet 1

(1) Year	(2) Network	(3) Section Length (Miles)	(4) Traffic Volume (AADT) (No.)	(5) Annual Vehicle Mileage (AVM) (Millions)	(6) Annual Vehicle Mileage of Through Traffic (Millions)	(7) Typical Hourly Volume (THV) (pcu)	(8) Section Capacity (pcu)	(9) Average Speed (mph)	(10) Time & Operating Costs per Vehicle Mile (pence)	(11) Time & Operating Costs per Section (£)	(12) Accident Rate per Million Vehicle Miles (No.)	(13) Annual Accs. per Section (No.)	(14) Cost per Acc. (£)	(15) Annual Acc. Cost per Section (£)	(16) Annual Mtce. Costs per Section (£)	(17) Total Costs (£)	(18) Annual Benefits (£)
1978	A	0.40	4,357														
	B	0.59	5,056														
	C	0.39	5,056														
	Do Nothing																
	A	0.40	5,600	0.818	0.613	457	1,000	37	14.30	116,974	6.7	4.1	1,709	7,007			
	B	0.59	6,500	1.400	0.905	530	900	26	17.50	145,000	13.0	11.8	879	10,372			
	C	0.30	6,500	0.925	0.598	530	900	35	14.70	135,975	7.0	4.2	1,709	7,178			
										397,949				24,557		522,404	
1983	Improved																
	A	0.40	1,400	0.204	—	114	1,000	47	13.10	26,724							
	B	0.59	2,300	0.495	—	188	900	26	17.50	86,624							
	C	0.39	2,300	0.327	—	188	900	43	13.45	43,982							
	D	0.98	4,200	0.1502	1,502	343	900	47	13.10	196,762	3.6	5.4	1,709	9,229	1,862		157,220
										354,092				9,229	1,862	365,184	

Worksheet 1 (contd)

(1)	(2)	(3)	(4)	(5)	(6)	(7)	(8)	(9)	(10)	(11)	(12)	(13)	(14)	(15)	(16)	(17)	(18)
1985	**Do Nothing**																
	A	0.40	6,100	0.891	0.668	498	1,000	37	15.00	133,650	6.7	4.5	1,830	8,235			
	B	0.59	7,078	1.524	0.985	578	900	26	18.45	281,178	13.0	12.9	942	12,058			
	C	0.39	7,978	1.008	0.651	578	900	35	15.40	155,232	7.0	4.6	1,830	8,418			
										570,060				28,711		598,771	
	Improved																
	A	0.40	1,525	0.223	–	124	1,000	46	13.90	30,997							
	B	0.59	2,503	0.539	–	204	900	26	18.45	99,446							
	C	0.39	2,503	0.356	–	204	900	43	14.15	50,374							
	D	0.98	4,575	1.636	1.636	373		46	13.90	227,404	3.6	5.9	1,830	10,797	1,862		
										408,221				10,797	1,862	420,880	177,891
1995	**Do Nothing**																
	A	0.40	8,714	1.272	0.954	711	1,000	33	21.05	267,756	6.7	6.3	2,582	16,267			
	B	0.59	10,112	2.178	1.407	825	900	26	24.65	536,877	13.0	18.3	1,328	24,302			
	C	0.39	10,112	1.439	0.939	825	900	29	22.65	325,934	7.0	6.5	2,482	16,783			
										1,130,567				57,352		1,187,919	
	Improved																
	A	0.40	2,178	0.319	–	178	1,000	44	18.55	58,989							
	B	0.59	3,576	0.770	–	292	900	26	24.65	189,805							
	C	0.39	3,576	0.509	–	292	900	40	18.09	96,201							
	D	0.98	6,536	2.338	2.338	533		45	18.30	427,854	3.6	8.4	2,582	21,689	1,862		
										772,849				21,689	1,862	796,400	391,519

Worksheet 1 (contd)

(1)	(2)	(3)	(4)	(5)	(6)	(7)	(8)	(9)	(10)	(11)	(12)	(13)	(14)	(15)	(16)	(17)	(18)
	Do Nothing																
	A	0.40	11,328	2.654	1,240	924	1,000	20	30.95	511,913	6.7	8.3	3,642	30,211			
	B	0.59	13,146	2.831	1,830	1,073	900	20	40.60	1,149,386	13.0	23.8	1,873	44,577			
	C	0.39	13,146	1.971	1,209	1,073	900	20	40.60	759,626	7.0	8.5	3,642	30,975			
										2,420,925				105,763		2,526,698	
2005	Improved																
	A	0.40	2,812	0.413		231	1,000	42	25.40	104,902							
	B	0.59	4,650	1.001		379	900	26	33.95	338,839							
	C	0.39	4,650	0.662		379	900	38	26.50	175,430							
	D	0.08	8,106	8.010	3,010	693		44	25.15	764,309	3.6	10.9	3,642	33,608	1,863	1,425,040	
										1,383,480				33,608	1,863		1,101,648

Appendix

Worksheet 2

Year	Benefits	Costs	Benefits Discounted at 5% £	Costs Discounted at 5% £	Benefits Discounted at 10% £	Costs Discounted at 10% £	Benefits Discounted at 15% £	Costs Discounted at 15% £
1978	–	–	–	–	–	–	–	–
1979	–	–	–	–	–	–	–	–
1980	–	–	–	–	–	–	–	–
1981	–	250,000	–	238,100	–	227,275	–	217,400
1982	–	500,000	–	453,500	–	413,200	–	312,421
1983	157,220	–	135,807	–	118,119	–	103,372	–
1984	167,238	–	137,587	–	114,223	–	95,627	–
1985	177,891	–	139,377	–	110,453	–	88,447	–
1986	192,493	–	143,638	–	108,720	–	83,215	–
1987	208,293	–	148,029	–	106,895	–	78,297	–
1988	225,389	–	152,543	–	105,144	–	73,680	–
1989	243,890	–	157,211	–	103,433	–	69,338	–
1990	263,910	–	162,014	–	101,737	–	65,239	–
1991	285,570	–	166,973	–	100,089	–	61,369	–
1992	309,010	–	172,057	–	98,451	–	57,754	–
1993	334,374	–	177,319	–	96,868	–	54,336	–
1994	361,820	–	182,755	–	95,267	–	51,125	–
1995	391,519	–	188,321	–	93,729	–	48,118	–
1996	434,192	–	198,903	–	94,480	–	46,415	–
1997	481,516	–	210,085	–	95,244	–	44,733	–
1998	533,998	–	221,876	–	96,066	–	43,147	–
1999	592,200	–	234,333	–	96,825	–	41,632	–
2000	651,441	–	245,528	–	97,593	–	40,127	–
2001	728,327	–	261,397	–	98,397	–	38,674	–
2002	807,946	–	276,156	–	99,187	–	37,316	–
2003	895,746	–	291,654	–	100,055	–	36,009	–
2004	993,376	–	308,046	–	100,827	–	34,669	–
2005	1,101,648	–	325,317	–	101,682	–	33,490	–
TOTAL	–	–	4,636,926	691,600	2,333,484	640,475	1,326,129	529,821
NET PRESENT VALUE			3,945,326		1,693,009		796,308	
COST-BENEFIT RATIO			5.70		2.64		1.50	

14

The Naas Motorway Bypass – A Cost-Benefit Analysis*

SEÁN D. BARRETT and DAVID MOONEY[1]

Introduction

This chapter examines the Naas Motorway Bypass which cost £16m at 1983 prices. Twelve thousand vehicles a day using the bypass save 10 minutes between 8 am and 8 pm and 6 minutes at other times. Five thousand vehicles a day using the present route through Naas also benefit by saving 4 minutes due to reduced congestion in the town. In addition to time savings, the bypass reduces accidents and fuel costs. Ninety-one per cent of the benefits accrue in time savings. The internal rate of return on the project is estimated at 20.51 per cent, assuming 2 per cent annual traffic and income growth. The sensitivity tests of the results show that even with zero growth in incomes and traffic for twenty years, a high proportion of leisure time savings with zero value and no increase in the value of fuel savings, the project would have an internal rate of return which meets the test discount rate used by the Department of Finance.

The environmental aspects of the bypass are positive in terms of noise and smoke and lead pollution reduction. The impact on farm severance and natural amenities on the motorway route has been mitigated by several design features of the bypass.

The Road Development Plan for the 1980s proposed the expenditure of £1,072m (at 1978 prices) on the Irish road system over this decade. In 1983, major improvements to roads cost £48m. The total cost of improvements in respect of works in progress in 1983 was £268m according to the Department of Finance report on Comprehensive Public Expenditure Programmes.

The low rate of return on investment in the Public Capital Programme has been adversely commented upon by economists. In this chapter we apply cost-benefit analysis to a major project in an important area of public investment.

266

The project

The Naas Motorway Bypass cost £16m at 1983 prices. This includes the construction of the motorway, four public road bridges and approach roads, two interchanges, an accommodation bridge for farmers, an underpass and a bridge over the town branch of the Grand Canal.

Naas is the junction point of the national primary routes N7 (Cork/Limerick) and N9 (Waterford). The Naas Motorway Bypass will remove from the town through traffic on the N7. The bypass route lies to the west of the town.

The benefits from highway investments

Studies of highway investments have quantified three main benefits: time savings, accident reduction, and vehicle cost savings. Shadow prices are imputed for these and projections are made of their values over the life of the project. The internal rate of return on the project is the rate which equates the present values of the streams of benefits and costs. This can then be compared with the test discount rate set by the government for public sector projects.

In Britain, the computer programme COBA is used in the above way to evaluate trunk road investments. Following criticisms from environmental groups the Advisory Committee on Trunk Road Assessment was established in 1976 to comment on COBA 'taking account both of economic and environmental factors'. The committee's report, known as the Leitch Report, proposed the addition of environmental impact statements to give a wider view of a project in addition to the items quantified in COBA. Several environmental studies of the Naas Bypass were prepared. These are reviewed later in this chapter.

Valuing time and accident cost savings

Time savings allow further activities to be engaged in. When working time is saved, more goods and services can be produced with the labour released. These savings are valued at the cost to the employer of hiring labour. Employers are assumed to hire labour until it is known the cost of doing so equals the marginal revenue product of the employee.

The wage cost as an indicator of the value of working time has been shown by Harrison and Quarmby (1969) to be subject to a number of qualifications. It ignores labour market imperfections, the possibility that road-using enterprises may not be able to convert time savings into resource savings, that resources may not have alternative uses, and that in some cases travel time may be used productively.

The haulage market is, however, competitive since firms may substitute own vehicles for hired haulage. Fleischer (1962) and Hanning and McFarland (1963) found that firms were able, after adjustments to schedules, to attain the full benefits from highway improvements by economising on fleet and labour costs.

Monopolistic power in labour markets is limited for the groups which account for the bulk of working time travel. These groups include professional drivers, salesmen, commercial travellers, travelling sales engineers and mechanics. While some travel time on other modes may be used for productive purposes this is unlikely to apply to road travel.

The case for valuing leisure and work time at the same rate applies if the traveller is indifferent between work and leisure. Where the disutility attached to work is greater than to travel, leisure time savings are valued at less than the wage rate. If, for example, the disutility attached to travel is half that attached to work, leisure time savings would be valued at half work time savings.

Empirical studies in Britain indicate that the value of non-working time is approximately 25 per cent of working time values. These values are based on modal choices where the respondents choose between faster expensive modes thus trading off time against other costs. Barrett (1982) contains a summary of some of these studies.

In this chapter we follow the British practice in regard to both work and leisure time savings. However, we test the impact of changing these shadow prices on the rate of return on the project in a number of sensitivity tests.

Accident costs

The cost of injuries is estimated from hospital and other medical data and from the loss of output while the patient is undergoing treatment. In the case of fatalities we cannot establish the accident cost to the victim. This is the loss of utility from being alive. The four measures of loss which have been used are, therefore, imperfect.

The gross output approach measures the discounted value of the expected future earnings of the victim. The net output approach deducts from this consumption. The shadow price approach derives an implicit value of life where deaths are increased or decreased by public policy. The insurance method seeks to measure the value a person sets on his life from the sum for which he is insured and the probability of his being killed in a particular activity.

The output measures are based on Gross National Product as the sole criterion for economic performance. It does not include factors such as grief, suffering, and loss of utility from being alive. The shadow price approach may yield vastly differing estimates of the value of life derived from different programmes. The insurance method measures the victim's concern for his family and dependants.

The fatal accident costs used in the paper are taken from COBA. They are based on the loss of output of the victim with consumption included as part of the loss of utility from loss of life for the victim. An allowance is also made to cover the costs of pain, grief, and suffering. Society devotes resources to the saving of life and the avoidance of injury, even though such expenditure cannot be justified on the basis of lost output from the victims.

In this paper we estimate that the bypass will reduce accidents but the accident savings will be relatively small in relation to the total benefits from the project.

Two earlier studies evaluated road investments in the area of the Naas bypass. O'Keefe (1962) estimated that the time savings, accident cost reductions, and vehicle cost reductions for the Naas dual carriageway yielded a benefit-cost ratio of 1.02 with an annual average daily traffic of 6,000 vehicles. Traffic now exceeds 26,000 vehicles. Feeney (1976) estimated that either a roundabout or a flyover at the junction of the Naas bypass and the north access road to the town would return benefits in excess of costs.

The present pattern of traffic through Naas

Table 14.1 shows the 1982 traffic pattern on the national primary routes through Naas. Seventy-one per cent of traffic moves between 08.00 and 20.00 hours. The busiest hour is from 18.00 but traffic is heavy from 10.00 to 20.00 hours.

Table 14.1: Estimated traffic pattern at Naas in 1982

Hour from:	Share of flow (%)
08.00	2.7
09.00	4.2
10.00	5.5
11.00	6.8
12.00	6.1
13.00	5.5
14.00	5.1
15.00	7.1
16.00	6.2
17.00	6.8
18.00	8.0
19.00	6.9
Total of above	71.0
20.00 – 08.00	29.0
	100.0

Source: McCarthy and Partners; Naas Traffic Study for 10.00 hours to 19.00 hours. Kildare County Council for other hours.

Table 14.2: Estimated traffic times by hour of day without bypass

Hour	Journey Time (minutes)	Share of daily traffic
10.00 – 11.00	11.00	5.5
11.00 – 11.30	12.75	6.8
14.00 – 15.00	14.75	5.1
16.00 – 16.30	13.50	3.1
16.30 – 17.00	17.00	3.1
17.00 – 17.30	24.50	6.8
17.30 – 18.00	15.00	8.0
18.30 – 19.00	11.50	6.0
Weighted average	15.08	45.30

Source: McCarthy and Partners, Naas Traffic Study, 1971. (Based on 41 observations.)

In estimating the average speed of traffic during the period 08.00 to 20.00 hours we have 41 estimates of journey times from Monread, at the Dublin end of the bypass, to Ladytown which is one mile from the southern end of the bypass. We assume that the latter section is travelled at 40 mph. The times shown in Table 14.2 for travel on the route to be bypassed are the sum of observed times for the town section and 1.5 minutes for the remaining mile to the motorway.

The weighted average of the journey times in Table 14.2 is 15.08 minutes. We assume that this time is representative of all travel between 08.00 and 20.00 and use this in calculating the time savings in Table 14.3. We refer to this as peak traffic and to the remainder as off-peak traffic.

On the N7 route it is estimated that off-peak journey times are 10.90 minutes. This comprises 40 mph on the southern mile, 30 mph on the 2 miles at the Dublin side of Naas and 20 mph on the 1.8 miles at the centre of Naas.

The average speed assumed on the motorway is 60 mph. This may be conservative as the maximum permitted speed on motorways is 70 mph and there have been pressures to raise this to as high as 85 mph. The bypass design provides stopping sight distance of 75 mph for its entire length.

Times savings

Nineteen thousand vehicles used the N7 and N9 routes through Naas daily and carried almost 31,000 people. Twelve thousand vehicles use the bypass on the N7 while 5,000 on the N9 benefit from reduced traffic congestion in the centre of Naas, between 08.00 and 20.00.

Traffic through Naas between 08.00 and 20.00 accounts for 71 per cent of the daily total. Table 14.3 shows that this category has savings of 10.28 minutes on the N7 while the 29 per cent travelling between 20.00 and 08.00 enjoy time savings of 6.1 minutes. In the case of N9 traffic the savings are 4.18

minutes between 8 am and 8 pm. At the off-peak periods, no time savings are assumed for this group.

Table 14.3: Journey times through Naas with and without Naas Bypass (minutes)

	With Bypass	Without Bypass	Saving	Vehicles
N7 08.00 to 20.00	4.80	15.08	10.28	8,520
N7 20.00 to 08.00	4.80	10.90	6.10	3,480
N9 08.00 to 20.00	10.90	15.08	4.18	4,970
N9 20.00 to 08.00	10.90	10.90	0.00	2,930
				19,000

Table 14.4: Estimated time savings from the Naas Bypass, 1983

Category	Number Per day	Time saved (hours) per day	Value of time £ per day	Annual savings from Bypass £000
Car driver at work	5,548	630.6	3.362	774.0
Car passenger at work	1,102	125.3	2.196	133.4
Car driver non-work	8,512	967.5	0.725	256.0
Car passenger non-work	7,410	842.3	0.725	223.0
Goods vehicle occupants	6,251	710.5	2.464	639.0
Bus passengers	1,995	226.8	0.725	60.0
Bus driver	133	15.1	2.699	14.9
	30,951	3,518.1	12.896	2,100.3

In Table 14.4, we estimate the number of people travelling in the 19,000 vehicles by category of occcupant using the occupancy factors from COBA and the time savings for each group. Just under 31,000 people will save 3,518 hours per day due to the bypass.

We estimate also that the annual value of these time savings in 1983 would have been £2.0m. This is estimated by taking the British values of time savings and reducing them to 56 per cent of the British figure to take account of the income differential in sterling between the two countries. They are then stated in Irish currency at mid-1983 exchange rates.

There are a number of sources of possible understatement of the value of time savings in these estimates. The individual time savings are based on a 1971 traffic survey. The valuation of these time savings is based on the difference between Irish and British incomes per head for the population as a whole rather than income differences per vehicle occupant. Our estimates do not include any benefits for N9 traffic in the off-peak period and local traffic in Naas. Both can be expected to gain from the removal of through traffic by the bypass.

Accident cost savings

Accident data prepared by An Foras Forbartha show that in the thirteen years to 1980 there were seventeen deaths and 143 serious injuries in road accidents in Naas. The population of Naas in 1971 was 7,739 and the highest accident rate for towns of this size was Killarney (population 7,724) which had 20 fatalities and 201 serious injuries while the lowest was Mallow (population 6,609) with three fatalities and 99 serious injuries.

The contribution of the bypass to road safety is the reduction in traffic in the town centre and its transfer to the motorway. Accident rates are lower on motorways than on undivided highways because the central median and flyovers reduce head-on and junction accidents.

Motorway accidents

The probability of an accident on British motorways is 0.15 per million vehicle kilometres. There are 0.052 deaths per accident and 0.394 serious injuries per accident. The COBA motorway accident rates are thus 0.0078 deaths and 0.0591 serious injuries per million vehicle kilometres. The bypass is 8 kilometres and with an annual average daily traffic initially of 12,000 vehicles will generate 35.04 million vehicle kilometres of traffic per year with 0.273 deaths and 2,071 serious injuries.

We deduct from this accident figure the accident rate for 12,000 vehicles a day on the existing route. Daily traffic through the Naas section of the N7 grew from 9,165 to 18,918 between 1968 and 1981. The sum of the annual average daily traffic figures for the thirteen years was 165,523 vehicles. During this period there were seventeen fatal and 143 serious injury accidents. The same accident rates for an average annual daily traffic volume of 12,000 imply 1.23 fatal and 10.37 serious accidents per year.

Table 14.5: Estimated costs per accident, Ireland, 1983 (£IR)

Accident	Urban	Rural	Motorway
Fatal	127,977	142,942	150,017
Serious	6,594	12,290	12,897

Source: adapted from COBA.

In Naas at present rates, 12,000 vehicles a day would cause 1.23 fatal and 10.37 serious injury accidents a year. At the costs per urban accident in Table 14.5 above this is an annual cost of £225,791. On the motorway route there will be 0.273 fatal and 2.07 serious injury accidents. At the cost per motorway accident in the above table these accidents will cost £67,652. The annual saving from diverting the traffic from Naas to the motorway in lower accidents will therefore be £158,139. While Naas has a relatively good safety record compared to other towns of its size in Ireland, British motorway accident rates imply that the number of accidents will be further reduced on the bypass. The accident rate reduction will more than compensate for the higher average cost per accident on motorways than in urban areas. The higher cost per accident on motorways is due to the greater severity of impact.

Savings in fuel consumption

The third quantified benefit from highway investment in COBA is fuel saving. The bypass substitutes a section of motorway with an average speed of 60 mph at all times for a route comprising three sections which have lower peak and off-peak speeds.

Appendix V gives estimates of the average fuel consumption per vehicle for each section in peak and off-peak periods and shows the average fuel consumption for the pre-bypass route at 2,892 gallons of petrol and 1,596 gallons of diesel per day. The fuel consumption estimates are based on the speeds used in the section on time savings.

The 12,000 vehicles which use the motorway were assumed in the section on time savings to have an average speed of 60 mph. The consumption of these vehicles will be 1,904 gallons of petrol and 974 gallons of diesel per day.

The 7,000 vehicles remaining on the old route to reach the N9 will have average speeds throughout the day now attained only in the off-peak periods. The fuel consumption of the N9 traffic, based on estimates in Appendix V for off-peak consumption, is as follows, cars: 798 gallons, light goods: 118 gallons and diesel: 546 gallons.

Table 14.6: Total consumption per day in Naas with and without Bypass (gallons) and value of annual savings

	Petrol	Diesel
Without bypass	2,892	1,596
With bypass	2,820	1,520
Savings due to bypass	72	76
Resource cost per gallon(p)	118	131
Annual Saving (£)	31,010	36,339

We must now combine the fuel consumption data on the bypass and for traffic remaining on the N9 and compare this with the current fuel consumption by the through traffic at Naas. This is summarised in Table 14.6. Fuel savings are small compared to the total benefits from the bypass. The savings estimated in Table 14.6 are conservative since they do not take into account the extra consumption of fuel by vehicles accelerating and decelerating in the congested pre-bypass traffic conditions.

Summary of costs and benefits

Table 14.7 shows that the internal rate of return on the Naas bypass is 20.51 per cent assuming a 2 per cent annual growth in traffic and national income over a 20-year project life. Time savings account for 90.6 per cent of the benefits. Accidents cost savings and fuel savings account for 6.8 per cent and 2.6 per cent of the benefits respectively.

Table 14.7: Time stream of benefits and costs of Naas Bypass with 20.51 per cent discount rate (2% traffic growth and income growth assumed)

	Time (£'000)	Accident (£'000)	Fuel (£'000)	Total Benefit (£'000)	Costs (£'000)
1983	2100.3	158.1	67.3	2325.7	16012.0
1984	1813.3	136.5	57.0	2006.7	10.0
1985	1565.5	117.8	48.2	1731.6	8.3
1986	1351.6	101.7	40.8	1494.1	6.9
1987	1166.9	87.8	34.5	1289.2	5.7
1988	1007.4	75.8	29.2	1112.5	4.7
1989	869.7	65.5	24.7	960.0	3.9
1990	750.9	56.5	20.9	828.4	3.3
1991	648.3	48.8	17.7	714.8	2.7
1992	559.7	42.1	15.0	616.8	2.2
1993	483.2	36.4	12.7	532.3	1.9
1994	417.2	31.4	10.8	459.3	1.5
1995	360.2	27.1	9.1	396.1	2.6
1996	310.9	23.4	7.7	342.1	2.1
1997	268.5	20.2	6.5	295.2	1.8
1998	231.8	17.4	5.5	254.7	1.5
1999	200.1	15.1	4.7	219.8	1.2
2000	172.8	13.0	4.0	189.7	1.0
2001	149.1	11.2	3.3	163.7	0.8
2002	128.8	9.7	2.8	41.3	0.7
Totals	14556.0	1095.7	422.6	16074.3	16074.7

Note: Year begins October 1st. Values are at 1983 prices. Fuel prices are assumed fixed in real terms.

Table 14.8: Sensitivity test results on rate of return on Naas Bypass

Test	Title	Sensitivity Test Assumptions	Rate of Return (%)
1	Basic	2% traffic growth, 2% income growth, fixed fuel price	20.51
2	Basic + fuel price rise	2% traffic growth, 2% income growth, 2% fuel price growth	20.56
3	Zero value leisure	2% traffic growth, 2% income growth, fixed fuel price, zero value for leisure time	15.06
4	Zero growth 25 % leisure	Zero traffic and income growth, 25% rate applied to 83% of cars in valuing time savings	12.75
5	Zero growth Zero leisure	Zero growth in traffic and incomes Zero value for leisure time savings applied to 83% of cars	6.84
6	High Time	Basic assumptions with time savings increased 25%	25.16
7	Low Time	Basic assumptions with time savings decreased 25%	15.87
8	High Accident Value	Basic assumptions with accident costs increased 25%	20.86
9	Low Accident Value	Basic assumptions with accident costs decreased 25%	20.16

In Table 14.8 we show the sensitivity of the basic rate of return to changes in the benefits from the bypass. Since time accounts for an estimated 90.6 per cent of the benefits, the internal rate of return is most sensitive to changes in the time values used. The time sensitivity tests are tests 3 to 7 inclusive.

Test 3 attributes zero value to the non-work time savings due to the bypass. Table 14.4 shows that 58 per cent of those who benefit from the bypass save leisure rather than work time. The basic rate includes these savings at 25 per cent of the work rate. A zero value lowers the return to 15.06 per cent.

Tests 4 and 5 assume zero traffic and income growth. They increase the non-work share of car journeys on the bypass to 83 per cent, an increase of 25 percentage points over Tests 1 to 3 and 6 to 9 inclusive. Test 4 applies the 25 per cent value for leisure time savings while Test 5 uses the zero rate. Tests 6 and 7 increase and decrease the values of time in the basic test by 25 per cent. The rate of return is highly sensitive to these changes.

Tests 8 and 9 change the accident costs by 25 per cent but this makes minimal impact on the rate of return since these savings account for 6.8 per cent of the benefits from the bypass. Fuel savings account for only 2.6 per cent of the benefits. Test 2 shows that an annual rise of 2 per cent in real fuel prices makes minimal difference to the basic rate of return on the bypass.

Taken as a whole the tests show that the project is most sensitive to changes in the value of time. Even the most pessimistic scenario of zero traffic and income growth and zero value of leisure time applied to 83 per cent of cars leaves the project with a 6.84 per cent rate of return. The test discount rate used by the Department of Finance for public investment projects is 5 per cent.

Table 14.9: Naas Bypass rates of return (%) for various traffic and income growth rates

Traffic Growth(%)	Income Growth(%)					
	2	3	4	5	6	7
Case (a) Leisure Time Valued at 25% of Work Time						
2	20.51	21.70	22.88	24.06	25.25	26.44
3	21.66	22.87	24.06	25.25	26.46	27.66
4	22.83	24.04	25.24	26.45	27.66	28.87
5	23.98	25.21	26.43	27.65	28.87	30.08
6	25.16	26.39	27.62	28.85	30.08	31.31
7	26.32	27.56	28.80	30.04	31.29	32.52
Case (b) Zero value for Leisure						
2	15.06	16.19	17.32	18.46	19.59	20.72
3	16.16	17.30	18.45	19.59	20.73	21.87
4	17.27	18.42	19.57	20.72	21.87	23.03
5	18.37	19.53	20.70	21.87	23.03	24.19
6	19.47	20.64	21.83	23.00	24.18	26.35
7	20.59	21.77	22.95	24.14	25.32	26.51

In Table 14.9 we examine the effects of changing the assumptions for income and traffic growth on the rates of return for the basic model and the basic model with zero value of leisure time. These are Tests 1 and 3 of Table 14.8.

Implications for road investment policy

The positive rate of return on the Naas bypass suggests that similar projects might be examined for other congested towns on the national primary route network such as Newbridge, Athlone, Ballinasloe, Roscrea, Nenagh, and Arklow, including studies of less expensive inner relief roads such as that at Portlaoise.

The results indicate that in order to cover the annualised cost of the motorway, a toll of an average of 50p would have to be charged. Collection cost would absorb about 25 per cent of revenue according to the Road Research Laboratory estimates of the cost of converting the M1 to a tollway.

Table 14.3 shows that almost 5,000 vehicles using the N9 will benefit from the bypass through reduced traffic congestion in Naas. It will not be possible to recoup in toll revenue any of these benefits from the bypass or from traffic on the N7 which continued to go through Naas, or local Naas town traffic.

The average time saving for N7 traffic is low at 10.28 minutes from 8 am to 8 pm and 6.10 minutes for the rest of the day. Delays at the collection points would negative part of the savings. At off-peak times a toll might divert traffic to the centre of Naas when it is relatively uncongested. The toll might be more expensive to collect due to overtime working. Since over 70 per cent of traffic moves between 8 am and 8 pm there may be a case for having the bypass toll free after 8 pm in winter and somewhat later at other times.

The value of leisure time used in the study is 72.5p per hour. A 10.28 minute saving is worth only 12p per person and 22p including car passengers. With a toll of 22p, business travellers will enjoy a substantial consumer surplus from the bypass. Setting the toll high enough to recoup some of this consumer surplus would divert the leisure traffic back to Naas centre.

Road transport, on average, covers its road infrastructure costs. Feeney (1983) estimates that all classes of vehicles now cover their infrastructure costs. A case could be made, therefore, for setting any proposed toll on the bypass to cover only the marginal costs of the motorway over a normal dual-carriageway route. This is about 40 per cent of motorway costs and might divert traffic back to Naas centre. Some time savings would be lost in collection.

The environmental impact of the Naas Bypass

The COBA evaluation of highway investments in terms of time savings, accident cost reduction, and fuel savings was found by the Leitch Committee to be ' basically sound ... provided it is kept within the overall framework suggested' (p.87). The Leitch Committee examined 'the weights given to economic and environmental factors' and recommended that the COBA assessment be accompanied by a project impact matrix dealing with the amenity and environmental aspects of road investment. Table 10 shows the summary of this project impact matrix from Button (1982). In a ' first best' evaluation of the bypass these items would be shadow priced and included in the quantified internal rate of return. We are unable at present to give this breadth to the cost benefit analysis of road investment. These unquantifiable items are nonetheless important.

In the summaries of the environmental studies which follow, we see that Naas suffered from serious noise, lead and smoke pollution. However, the level of sulphur dioxide was only a third of the central Dublin level. The bypass will reduce the noise, lead and smoke pollution by removing 12,000 vehicles a day from Naas and increasing the speeds of those remaining. The other environmental impacts listed in the Leitch Report are small in the case of the Naas bypass. The impacts concerned are demolition of buildings, visual intrusion of the highway in the area of buildings, farm severance, and the effect on natural assets.

Table 14.10: The project impact matrix suggested by the Leitch Committee

Incidence Group	Nature of Effect	Number of Measure	
		Financial	Other
Road Users	Accident savings	1	3
	Comfort and convenience		1
	Time savings	6	
	Vehicle cost savings	5	
	Amenity		2
Non-road users	Demolition of property/disamenity		22
	Demolition/disamenity to users of schools, churches, public open space		25
	Land-take, severance, and disamenity to farmers		7
Those concerned with intrinsic value of area	Landscape, scientific and historic value	3*	
Those directly affected	Sterilisation of natural resources, land use planning effects, effects on other transport operators		6*
Financial authority	Cost and financial benefits	7	
		22	66

* plus verbal description   *Source*: K. Button, adapted from the Leitch Report.

Noise

Road traffic noise in Britain was found to be the most serious cause of noise nuisance by the Noise Advisory Council (1974). Noise nuisance is measured in weighted decibels or dB(A). The Wilson Committee (1963) recommended maximum daytime levels of 40 dB(A) in country districts, 45 dB(A) in suburban areas, and 50 dB(A) in urban areas and that these should not be exceeded for more than 10 per cent of the time.

Pryke and Dodgson (1975) estimate that in 1970, 21 million people in Britain lived in dwellings with an external noise level above 65 dB(A) for over 10 per cent of the time. Since closing windows reduces noise inside a dwelling by 16 dB(A) an acceptable level of noise inside the house is not possible where the external noise level exceeds 65 dB(A).

Noise levels in Naas exceeded the British target level of 65 dB(A) in two of the three locations examined by the Health Inspectorate of Dublin Corporation in 1978. The noise index values found were as follows:

Dublin Road	17 August 1978	79dB(A)
Naas centre	30 August 1978	82.5dB(A)
Newbridge Road	29 August 1978	64 dB(A)

The reduction in the number of vehicles using Naas from 19,000 to 9,000 per day will reduce the noise nuisance in the town centre. The new route has design features which minimise the impact of noise and confine it to a smaller number of people.

Atmospheric pollution

Lead pollution in Naas is reduced in two ways by the new road. Twelve thousand vehicles a day will be taken out of the town while those remaining move faster thus reducing their lead pollution. Mean air-lead concentration in Naas in the summer of 1979 was high and comparable with that in central Dublin.

Smoke pollution in Naas was also close to central Dublin levels. It is mostly due to traffic. Sulphur dioxide, on the other hand, was only a third of the central Dublin levels.

The transfer of vehicle pollution away from Naas disperses it over a wider area with a smaller population. Table 14.11 shows the pollution in Naas before the bypass.

Table 14.11: Pollution in Naas and Dublin, Summer 1979

	May	June	July	Mean
(a) Air Lead Concentration in Micrograms per Cubic Metre				
Naas Centre	2.65	2.06	1.42	2.04
O'Connell Street	2.30	2.30	2.30	2.30
Dame Street	4.5	2.7	2.3	3.5

(b) Sulphur and Smoke in Micrograms per Cubic Metre		
	Sulphur	Smoke
Naas Centre	19.8	36.3
Dame Street	61.8	32.5
Clontarf	20.5	9.3

Source: Kildare County Council and Dublin Corporation.

The impact on the physical environment

The Leitch Report proposed the inclusion of the following effects in the assessment of highway investments: (a) the number of buildings to be demolished, (b) the number of buildings exposed to visual intrusion, (c) the land of each grade required by the scheme, (d) the impact on farm severance and (e) the impact on natural assets.

Only one cottage was demolished in the construction of the Naas bypass. The main areas of housing close to the bypass are at Monread and Osberstown. Here the motorway is in a cutting and trees will be planted to reduce noise and visual intrusion. The land used in the bypass was of high grade. However, the use of material from two gravel pits in the vicinity of the bypass has exhausted the pits and the area can now be restored to agricultural use.

Two new bridges reduce the impact of farm severance and a new accommodation road has been built. Four farms severed have access through existing public roads. One has an accommodation bridge and six are served by a new bridge and accommodation road. Three small parcels of land (1.4, 1.5 and 5 acres) which were isolated from their main farms have been acquired by Kildare Council.

The bypass leaves adequate headroom over the Naas branch of the Grand Canal. This preserves the option that the branch might be restored as an amenity in the future.

The environmental costs of a motorway in a previously rural area are a relatively new area of research. The design of the Naas bypass incorporates several attempts to reduce these costs. They should, however, be kept under review but are probably much less than the environmental costs caused by the same traffic in the centre of Naas.

Improving road investment evaluation

Time, accident costs savings, and fuel savings are the quantified benefits from road investment. Time savings dominate the benefits from the Naas Bypass and should be carefully evaluated in the assessment of road investments.

Project surveys should ascertain the wage costs of those likely to benefit from the investment, the division of users between work and non-work trips, and the spread of traffic over 24 hours. Actual incomes of beneficiaries should be used rather than those imputed from COBA. A time savings study might also examine whether the 25 per cent value for leisure time savings is correct in Ireland.

Current British research seeks to establish accident costs from the compensation which people trade off against risks. It is likely that the COBA estimates of accident costs will be raised, thus increasing the rate of return from road investment.

A standard form of assessment, or Irish COBA, even if imperfect, would ensure comparability of highway investment appraisal between different projects. This would include both the quantified benefits and the environmental impact assessments recommended in the Leitch Report.

The development of wider cost-benefit analysis could permit comparison of transport and other investments including those in the private sector, with market prices 'corrected' for social spillovers and market imperfections. Finally, in the difficult circumstances of the Irish public finances it is important that the appraisal should not exclude low cost solutions such as inner relief roads.

This article was first published in *Quarterly Economic Commentary*, Dublin: Economic and Social Research Institute, pp 21-34, January, 1984

NOTES

1. The authors are indebted to Mr. J. Carrick, County Engineer, Mr. R.J. Burke, Chief Assistant Engineer, Kildare County Council and Mr. P. McGuinness and Mr. B. Feeney, Roads Division, An Foras Forbartha. The project was supported by the College research funds. The authors are also indebted to Mr. J. Sullivan, Department of the Environment, Highway Economics and Modelling Analysis Division, London. Michael Keane, Dermot McAleese, Bernard Feeney, Tim Callan, Jack Short and Susan Scott supplied helpful comments on earlier drafts. The usual disclaimer applies.

REFERENCES

Barrett, S.D. (1975). 'The Economic Evaluation of Road Investment in the Republic of Ireland,' *Journal of the Statistical and Social Inquiry Society of Ireland*, pp 1-36

Barrett, S.D. (1982). *Transport Policy in Ireland*, Dublin: Irish Management Institute, Chaps. 3 and 8

Button, K. (1982). *Transport Economics*, London: Heinemann, Chaps. 5,7 and 8

Feeney, B. (1976). *An Economic Analysis of Alternative Designs for Monread Junction*, Dublin: An Foras Forbartha, paper RT. 171

Feeney, B. (1983). 'Paying for Road Damage', in J. Blackwell and F. Convery (eds) *Promise and Performance; Irish Environmental Policies Analysed*, University College Dublin

Fleischer, G.A. (1962). *The Economic Utilisation of Commercial Vehicle Time Saved as a Result of Road Improvements*, Stanford University

An Foras Forbartha Road Accident Facts (annual)

An Foras Forbartha (1974). *A Road Needs Study*, Dublin: AFT Report RT. 126

Hanning, C.R., and W.F. McFarland (1963). 'The Value of Time Saved to Commercial Vehicles through Use of Improved Highways', *Texas Transportation Institute Bulletin*, September

Harrison, A.J., and D.A. Quarmby (1969). 'The Value of Time in Transport Planning', *Report of the Sixth Round Table on Transport Economics*, Paris, European Conference of Ministers of Transport

Kildare County Council (1978). *Naas Bypass Design Report*

Kildare County Council (1978). *Naas Bypass Noise Prediction Report*

Kildare County Council (1980). *Naas Bypass Environmental Study* (with Dublin Corporation Health Inspectorate)

Leitch, Sir G. (1977). *Report of the Advisory Committee on Trunk Road Assessment* (Chairman Sir G. Leitch), London: HMSO

McCarthy and Partners (1971). *Naas Traffic Study*, Dublin

Noise Advisory Council (1974). *Noise in the Next Ten Years*, London: HMSO

O'Keefe, P. (1962). 'Economic Aspects of Road Improvements in Ireland', *Administration*, Summer

Pryke, R., and J. Dodgson (1975). *The Rail Problem*, London: Robertson

Serle, G. (1972). *COBA: A Computer Programme for the Economic Assessment of Road Schemes;* Traffic Engineering and Control, December

Wilson, A., (1963). *Final Report of the Committee on the Problem of Noise*, London: HMSO, Cmnd. 2056

APPENDIX

Fuel Consumption on N7 through Naas (gallons)

	Section 1	2	3	Total per vehicle	Number of vehicles	Total fuel consumption
08.00 to 20.00						
Cars	0.056	0.103	0.031	0.19	9983	1897
Light goods	0.080	0.122	0.390	0.241	1139	274
Diesel	0.180	0.223	0.089	0.492	2369	1166
20.00 to 08.00						
Cars	0.056	0.067	0.031	0.154	4077	628
Light goods	0.080	0.081	0.039	0.200	465	93
Diesel	0.180	0.175	0.089	0.444	968	430

These estimates are based on COBA.

15

Traps in Appraising Public Projects*

PATRICK HONOHAN[1]

Introduction

In applying cost-benefit analysis to public projects, it is as important to avoid underestimating costs so as to take account of all benefits. This chapter reviews three traps for the unwary cost-benefit analyst which can lead to neglect of hidden costs.

Governments are frequently presented with proposals for new expenditures and for new tax-breaks, bolstered by claims for significant economic benefits. For assessing such proposals, there is a well established methodology in cost-benefit analysis.

Cost-benefit analysis is the method which economists apply to measure the net social advantage or disadvantage of a certain project or course of action. As its name implies, it involves evaluating all the costs, direct or indirect, of the project, and comparing their sum with the sum of all the benefits. The costs and benefits taken into account should include those which have no immediate monetary equivalent – such as the effects of air pollution, as in the case of an industrial process, or reduction in travel time or in accidents, as in the case of road improvements. Furthermore the value placed even on items which have a market price, as with costs like the wage bill in an industrial project, or benefits such as the receipts from passenger fares in a public transport undertaking, may differ from market value in the cost-benefit calculation to the extent that market prices do not reflect social values. There is likely to be a discrepancy between market price and social value in conditions of less than full employment or, for example, where there are monopolistic practices.

However, cost-benefit analysis is not as easy as it looks. Despite the existence of users' manuals – in themselves complex and detailed – there are areas of doubt and potential traps for the analyst.

This chapter reviews three such traps which are important in the Irish economy and which could lead to undesirable projects being approved. The

283

emphasis here is deliberately one-sided and concentrates on hidden costs; proponents of new subsidies and tax concessions are well-versed in the disclosure of concealed benefits.

Since cost-benefit analysis essentially consists of adding up all the benefits of a proposal (discounted back to the present) and subtracting the costs (also discounted), the only difference between cost-benefit analysis and a normal profitability calculation lies in the choice of prices and discount rates. In a cost-benefit analysis the prices are social or 'shadow' valuations rather than the market prices used in assessing private profitability. The three traps discussed below are, therefore, all related to wrong choices of various types of shadow price.

Trap 1: Underestimating the opportunity cost of labour and other inputs

In calculating private profitability, cash costs incurred may be readily identifiable. But in cost-benefit analysis the social cost of resources is often neglected or underestimated. The relevant cost concept is that of 'opportunity cost', which is the value of the resource in its next alternative use. An adequate cost-benefit analysis requires a rigorous search for hidden opportunity costs. The cumulative effect of neglecting such costs can be extremely important in the assessment of a venture. Some examples follow.

(a) Labour

In most projects, the difference between the product of direct and indirect labour and its estimated social opportunity cost, or shadow price, is by far the greatest element of measured benefit.[2]

Given the high rate of unemployment it is not surprising therefore that the shadow price of labour has been a central focus of attention in discussions of cost-benefit analysis in Ireland. Yet there is still no agreed value for this cost. It is worth recalling the major elements of the debate.

When evaluating the net benefit of a project it is important to count in only the extra output that is generated over and above what is required to produce that output. If the extra output is produced by, and attributable to, someone who would otherwise be unemployed in Ireland, then it is certainly a gain.[3] But we must also be conscious of the possibility that this new output displaces output and employment elsewhere in the economy. And if the new employee is someone who would otherwise be employed elsewhere in the economy, there is a loss of output elsewhere, unless his old position is filled.[4] Bearing in mind that the demand for labour from the new project being appraised may increase wage rates and lead other firms to consider lay-offs, there is no guarantee that overall employment will increase by as much as direct employment in the project. Nor can there be any assessment that unemployment will fall in line with increases in employment.

What empirical evidence there is suggests that the opportunity cost of labour is not close to zero. Econometric research suggests that it takes about two new jobs to reduce the level of unemployment by one, even in the short run. Even if it could be said that the particular project under assessment was not displacing other potential new jobs, this would imply an opportunity cost at least half the wage rate. To the extent that jobs might be created even if the project does not go ahead, the opportunity cost is higher still. Furthermore, the initial impact of job creation on unemployment levels tends to overstate the long-run effect, which is thought by some economists to be nil or negligible.

If the econometric evidence is to be taken at all seriously, the true shadow price of labour is therefore much higher than commonly believed. It is a matter of urgency that a consensus be arrived at on this issue. For the moment, it would be prudent to assume that the shadow price of labour lies between 50 per cent and 75 per cent of the wage rate – or three to four times what is often used.[5]

(b) Raw materials

Domestically produced raw materials must often have a ready world market at, or close to, the price at which they would be sold to the new project in question. Otherwise it would be hard to explain why the project is paying so much for them. This is especially so for agricultural produce and other items covered by EU price supports. The element of 'value added' coming from such commodities is equal only to the difference between the price paid for the commodities and the world price – a difference which will normally be a small fraction of the price paid. The opportunity cost of these raw materials is therefore close to the sale price.

Where a manufacturing operation involves a modest transformation on a high volume of materials, such as natural gas or metal ores, the calculation of value-added in the project will be very sensitive to whether the opportunity cost of the materials is put at, say, 95, 99 or 100 per cent of the purchase price. But it has been the practice to use shadow prices as low as 85 per cent of the market price even for commodity raw materials. For some ventures this would not matter. But where the processing of commodity raw materials is concerned the large throughput which is often involved makes this a crucial issue. In such cases the presumption should be that the opportunity cost equals the market price.

(c) Profits of Irish companies

There is a temptation to include profits of Irish companies as a pure benefit. This is certainly wrong: the equity injection must be entered as an offsetting cost. (There is also the consideration that, to the extent that the projected profit gives a windfall gain to the capitalist, an excessive level of grant assistance may be involved.)

(d) Service and manufactured materials bought in

The arguments applied above to direct factor use also apply to indirect factor use through the purchase of Irish produced services and materials. The very much higher opportunity costs which are advocated in this article must also be applied to these. The result will be much lower net benefits attributable here also.

Trap 2: Neglecting risk

(a) Evaluate projects at the best estimate – not the optimistic target

Projects are typically evaluated on the basis of targets, rather than expected outcome. Naturally, the targets tend to be pitched at a relatively optimistic level. Any project appraisal can only be as good as the forecasts underlying it, and a first rule of appraisal is to substitute sober mean values for optimistic targets. This will typically involve both higher (and more realistic) estimates of costs and, especially, a substantial scaling down of target benefits. Past experience would be a useful guide in this regard, and could be used to quantify the appropriate reduction of net benefits to take account of over-optimism.

(b) And then include a risk factor when discounting

Even the true mean expectation of outcomes would be too high a value to enter in view of the risk associated with most industrial projects: a bird in the hand is worth more than a fifty-fifty chance of two birds. For the state, the costs are incurred early on, the benefits received later. Discounting the future streams at a risk-free gilt yield would be inappropriate if these future streams are entered at their mean expected value. A further reduction should be made for the normal risk regarding the outcome of any project. In assessing the appropriate discount rate,[6] it should be recalled that in the postwar quarter-century in the US the *mean* real return on equities was 8 per cent.

Trap 3: Neglecting the cost of government and the external burden of raising public funds

(a) Proposals should 'normally' be valued at tax-inclusive prices

Not every economic undertaking in the country can be subvented up to the point where the marginal costs equal marginal benefits. This is because private economic activity must, on average, contribute to the expenses of government.

The best analogy is with a public utility or other monopoly with heavy fixed costs and a constant variable cost. In order to be viable, the utility must recover its fixed costs from the customers. If there is an extra customer willing to pay just a little more than variable cost, then it will sell to the new customer only if it can do so without fear of damaging its relations with the remaining customers who are contributing to fixed costs.

The analogy arises like this: government has many expenses – education, health, administration, infrastructure. These are analogous to the utility's fixed costs. They must be recovered by a tax charge. But tax is distorting, and will discourage 'customers' – that is, economic activity that should otherwise take place. Even if the government can deal separately with some 'customers' who would 'not be prepared to pay the average contribution to fixed costs',[7] it should do so only if this will not cause irresistible pressure for comparable treatment by some of those who are at present contributing their share of the fixed costs.

The most obvious candidates for such special concessions are companies on the brink of collapse. But it should not be assumed that freeing even these from tax will be possible without precedents being set and incentives being weakened. This must be the touch-stone: can the company be rescued without implying rescue also for other companies? The economic evaluation of a rescue must take such external factors into account. It is not enough to say that the loss of tax and of PRSI, and the increase in unemployment payments, would cost more than the price of rescue. If that means virtually no net revenue from a sizeable segment of economic activity, and if that creates irresistible political pressures for a corresponding relief to other related segments of economic activity, then the residual burden on remaining sectors would grow in an unacceptable spiral. In that event the rescue should not proceed.

More generally, this brief account of some difficult considerations explains why one cannot always say that a project should proceed if its 'benefit-cost ratio' exceeds one. This is especially true for sectors of the economy which are expected not just to pay their way but also to be an 'engine of growth'.[8]

(b) The shadow price of public funds is higher than that of private funds

An additional but related point arises out of the excess burden of funding government spending. Financing grants and other concessions raises taxes to other sectors of the economy, damaging their competitiveness and distorting economic decision-making. The cost of these distortions is likely to be considerable in Ireland when the tax base is so narrow, marginal tax rates high and international mobility of factors of production, as well as goods, is well established.

These external dis-economies need to be taken into account in any proper cost-benefit study.

It is characteristic of applications of cost-benefit analysis in Ireland that these considerations are neglected, and that public and private funds are treated as comparable. Thus €1000 of additional private consumption achieved by the imposition of €999 of additional tax is regarded as a net gain. However, it should be well-known that such a practice can lead to an overexpansion of grant assistance, or at least to a misallocation of grants.

There are various ways of developing this argument. One way relies on the assumption of an absolute constraint on government resources and concludes that this constraint generates a scarcity value for government funds. Even if the constraint on government resources is not a rigid one, the relevance of this argument for Ireland today is nevertheless clear.

If additional grant-aid must be financed by extra taxation, the impact of that extra taxation on the taxpayer's behaviour must be considered. High taxation rates already distort economic behaviour and induce under-utilisation of many economic resources. Because of these existing distortions, extra taxation will have an even greater cost over and above the resources it makes available to the public sector. Therefore, the use of public funds must yield comparably greater benefits in order to be justified.

Another way of putting this is that if all possible projects were evaluated on a cost-benefit basis, neglecting the point about limited public resources, then the level of taxation required to pay for the projects that passed the test could easily exceed GNP.

Brought down to basics, it would follow from this way of thinking that the existing jobs displaced by the higher taxation could exceed the new jobs created.

To take account of this consideration, private funds generated by a project should, in cost-benefit calculations, be reduced by a factor to make them commensurate with the social cost of public funds. The correct factor will result in just enough projects passing the test as will absorb the funds available to government for assisting projects. The marginal social benefit of expenditure will then not fall short of the marginal social cost of taxation.[9]

Conclusion

Now that the pressure on the public finances is so severe, arguments in favour of expanded spending are being evaluated more critically. It is important that the main tool which economic methodology provides for this purpose be applied rigorously.

The arguments presented here would imply a dramatic change in cost-benefit calculations, and are not just refinements involving only small modifications in practice.

Cost-benefit analysis is not an idle academic exercise. Getting it right matters.

*

This article was first published in The Irish Banking Review, pp 28-35, Spring, 1986

NOTES

1   Earlier versions of this article were read to the Industrial Studies Association and to the Dublin Economic Workshop Conference. I am indebted to Michael Cuddy, Brendan Dowling, John McMahon, Jim O'Leary, Mike Redmond, Frances Ruane, John Travers and Paul Turpin for helpful comments. Full blown cost-benefit analysis is not often carried out in Ireland. The only place where it is used extensively is in the Industrial Development Authority (IDA). But even informal analyses will be subject to the same sort of trap, so the points made below have more general application.

2   For instance, in the usual calculations, the cost of factory construction – a major up-front element of the cash-flow – is entered with a shadow net-benefit rate which is based on the labour employed.

3   Though at a theoretical level one would want to take account of such factors as the value of lost leisure on the one hand the satisfaction of having a job, as opposed to the misery of involuntary unemployment, on the other. Some projects include a lot of shift-work and overtime. The overtime or shift premiums on the basic wage rate should not be included as a net benefit. This is because they are probably close to reflecting the extra effort and inconvenience involved in unsocial hours worked. That cost must be taken into account, and it will be largely offset by the extra wage payments.

4   Similar considerations apply to output produced by an immigrant, or would-be emigrant, though his presence in the economy and his employment *per se* are usually thought to have some social value.

5   Some readers of an earlier draft have objected to 75% as being too low while others have argued that 50% is too high. There is possibly no other major issue of economic policy on which opinions differ so widely.

6   The literature cautions against automatically selecting the discount rate as the place to apply risk adjustment. Often it will be better to adjust the stream of net benefits first to a certainty equivalent and then discount for time preference.

7   That is, if there are specific concessions which would restore economic activity discouraged by the tax rates.

8   This problem is an aspect of the general question of whether to value goods and factors at tax-inclusive or tax-exclusive prices in cost-benefit analysis. The

question is regarded in the literature as remaining open. A full analytical solution for the Irish case would seem to require a programming model of the economy as a whole. This complex issue clearly needs further examination but, for the time being, one suggested rule-of-thumb would be to disregard tax revenues (and social welfare savings) in arriving at the net Exchequer cost of a project. After all, resources drawn into, say, manufacturing from production in other sectors will tend to yield *less* by way of taxation due to the low tax rate.

9   Various approaches to assessing the appropriate factor have been suggested in the literature. Each requires analysis of the tax distortions in the economy or of the productivity of the best alternative use of public funds. No analysis of what the appropriate ratio might be has been carried out in Ireland. (The two examples in the well-known manual by I.M.D. Little and James Mirrlees reduce private funds by 33% and 89% respectively). Bearing in mind that in industrial projects many of the benefits are private and the costs public, even the smaller reduction would have a very substantial effect on the appraisal of projects.

Discount Tables

Table 1: Present value of €1

Years	1%	2%	3%	4%	5%	6%	7%	8%	9%	10%
1	0.9901	0.9804	0.9709	0.9615	0.9524	0.9434	0.9346	0.9259	0.9174	0.9091
2	0.9803	0.9612	0.9426	0.9426	0.9070	0.8900	0.8734	0.8573	0.8417	0.8264
3	0.9706	0.9423	0.9151	0.8890	0.8638	0.8396	0.8163	0.7938	0.7722	0.7513
4	0.9610	0.9238	0.8885	0.8548	0.8227	0.7921	0.7629	0.7350	0.7084	0.6830
5	0.9515	0.9057	0.8626	0.8219	0.7835	0.7473	0.7130	0.6806	0.6499	0.6209
6	0.9420	0.8880	0.8375	0.7903	0.7462	0.7050	0.6663	0.6302	0.5963	0.5645
7	0.9327	0.8706	0.8131	0.7599	0.7107	0.6651	0.6227	0.5835	0.5470	0.5132
8	0.9235	0.8535	0.7894	0.7307	0.6768	0.6274	0.5820	0.5403	0.5019	0.4665
9	0.9143	0.8368	0.7664	0.7026	0.6446	0.5919	0.5439	0.5002	0.4604	0.4241
10	0.9053	0.8203	0.7441	0.6756	0.6139	0.5584	0.5083	0.4632	0.4224	0.3855
11	0.8963	0.8043	0.7224	0.6496	0.5847	0.5268	0.4751	0.4289	0.3875	0.3505
12	0.8874	0.7885	0.7014	0.6246	0.5568	0.4970	0.4440	0.3971	0.3555	0.3186
13	0.8787	0.7730	0.6810	0.6006	0.5303	0.4688	0.4150	0.3677	0.3262	0.2897
14	0.8700	0.7579	0.6611	0.5775	0.5051	0.4423	0.3878	0.3405	0.2992	0.2633
15	0.8613	0.7430	0.6419	0.5553	0.4810	0.4173	0.3624	0.3152	0.2745	0.2394
16	0.8528	0.7284	0.6232	0.5339	0.4581	0.3936	0.3387	0.2919	0.2519	0.2176
17	0.8444	0.7142	0.6050	0.5134	0.4363	0.3714	0.3166	0.2703	0.2311	0.1978
18	0.8360	0.7002	0.5874	0.4936	0.4155	0.3503	0.2959	0.2502	0.2120	0.1799
19	0.8277	0.6864	0.5703	0.4746	0.3957	0.3305	0.2765	0.2317	0.1945	0.1635
20	0.8195	0.6730	0.5537	0.4564	0.3769	0.3118	0.2584	0.2145	0.1784	0.1486
21	0.8114	0.6598	0.5375	0.4388	0.3589	0.2942	0.2415	0.1987	0.1637	0.1351
22	0.8034	0.6468	0.5219	0.4220	0.3418	0.2775	0.2257	0.1839	0.1502	0.1228
23	0.7954	0.6342	0.5067	0.4057	0.3256	0.2618	0.2109	0.1703	0.1378	0.1117
24	0.7876	0.6217	0.4919	0.3901	0.3101	0.2470	0.1971	0.1577	0.1264	0.1015
25	0.7798	0.6095	0.4776	0.3751	0.2953	0.2330	0.1842	0.1460	0.1160	0.0923

Table 1: Present value of €1 (continued)

Years	11%	12%	13%	14%	15%	16%	17%	18%	19%	20%
1	0.9009	0.8929	0.8850	0.8772	0.8696	0.8621	0.8547	0.8475	0.8403	0.8333
2	0.8116	0.7972	0.7831	0.7695	0.7561	0.7432	0.7305	0.7182	0.7062	0.6944
3	0.7312	0.7118	0.6931	0.6750	0.6575	0.6407	0.6244	0.6086	0.5934	0.5787
4	0.6587	0.6355	0.6133	0.5921	0.5718	0.5523	0.5337	0.5158	0.4987	0.4823
5	0.5935	0.5674	0.5428	0.5194	0.4972	0.4761	0.4561	0.4371	0.4190	0.4019
6	0.5346	0.5066	0.4803	0.4556	0.4323	0.4104	0.3898	0.3704	0.3521	0.3349
7	0.4817	0.4523	0.4251	0.3996	0.3759	0.3538	0.3332	0.3139	0.2959	0.2791
8	0.4339	0.4039	0.3762	0.3506	0.3269	0.3050	0.2848	0.2660	0.2487	0.2326
9	0.3909	0.3606	0.3329	0.3075	0.2843	0.2630	0.2434	0.2255	0.2090	0.1938
10	0.3522	0.3220	0.2946	0.2697	0.2472	0.2267	02080	0.1911	0.1756	0.1615
11	0.3173	0.2875	0.2607	0.2366	0.2149	0.1954	0.1778	0.1619	0.1476	0.1346
12	0.2858	0.2567	0.2307	0.2076	0.1869	0.1685	0.1520	0.1372	0.1240	0.1122
13	0.2575	0.2292	0.2042	0.1821	0.1625	0.1452	0.1299	0.1163	0.1042	0.0935
14	0.2320	0.2046	0.1807	0.1597	0.1413	0.1252	0.1110	0.0985	0.0876	0.0779
15	0.2090	0.1827	0.1599	0.1401	0.1229	0.1079	0.0949	0.0835	0.0736	0.0649
16	0.1883	0.1631	0.1415	0.1229	0.1069	0.0930	0.0811	0.0708	0.0618	0.0541
17	0.1696	0.1456	0.1252	0.1078	0.0929	0.0802	0.0693	0.0600	0.0520	0.0451
18	0.1528	0.1300	0.1108	0.0946	0.0808	0.0691	0.0592	0.0508	0.0437	0.0376
19	0.1377	0.1161	0.0981	0.0829	0.0703	0.0596	0.0506	0.0431	0.0367	0.0313
20	0.1240	0.1037	0.0868	0.0728	0.0611	0.0514	0.0433	0.0365	0.0308	0.0261
21	0.1117	0.0926	0.0768	0.0638	0.0531	0.0443	0.0370	0.0309	0.0259	0.0217
22	0.1007	0.0826	0.0680	0.0560	0.0462	0.0382	0.0316	0.0262	0.0218	0.0181
23	0.0907	0.0738	0.0601	0.0491	0.0402	0.0329	0.0270	0.0222	0.0183	0.0151
24	0.0817	0.0659	0.0532	0.0431	0.0349	0.0284	0.0231	0.0188	0.0154	0.0126
25	0.0736	0.0588	0.0471	0.0378	0.0304	0.0245	0.0197	0.0160	0.0129	0.0105

Table 1: Present value of €1 (continued)

Years	21%	22%	23%	24%	25%	26%	27%	28%	29%	30%
1	0.8264	0.8197	0.8130	0.8065	0.8000	0.7937	0.7874	0.7813	0.7752	0.7692
2	0.6830	0.6719	0.6610	0.6504	0.6400	0.6299	0.6200	0.6104	0.6009	0.5917
3	0.5645	0.5507	0.5374	0.5245	0.5120	0.4999	0.4882	0.4768	0.4658	0.4552
4	0.4665	0.4514	0.4369	0.4230	0.4096	0.3968	0.3844	0.3725	0.3611	0.3501
5	0.3855	0.3700	0.3552	0.3411	0.3277	0.3149	0.3027	0.2910	0.2799	0.2693
6	0.3186	0.3033	0.2888	0.2751	0.2621	0.2499	0.2383	0.2274	0.2170	0.2072
7	0.2633	0.2486	0.2348	0.2218	0.2097	0.1983	0.1877	0.1776	0.1682	0.1594
8	0.2176	0.2038	0.1909	0.1789	0.1678	0.1574	0.1478	0.1388	0.1304	0.1226
9	0.1799	0.1670	0.1552	0.1443	0.1342	0.1249	0.1164	0.1084	0.1011	0.0943
10	0.1486	0.1369	0.1262	0.1164	0.1074	0.0992	0.0916	0.0847	0.0784	0.0725
11	0.1228	0.1122	0.1026	0.0938	0.0859	0.0787	0.0721	0.0662	0.0607	0.0558
12	0.1015	0.0920	0.0834	0.0757	0.0687	0.0625	0.0568	0.0517	0.0471	0.0429
13	0.0839	0.0754	0.0678	0.0610	0.0550	0.0496	0.0447	0.0404	0.0365	0.0330
14	0.0693	0.0618	0.0551	0.0492	0.0440	0.0393	0.0352	0.0316	0.0283	0.0254
15	0.0573	0.0507	0.0448	0.0397	0.0352	0.0312	0.0277	0.0247	0.0219	0.0195
16	0.0474	0.0415	0.0364	0.0320	0.0281	0.0248	0.0218	0.0193	0.0170	0.0150
17	0.0391	0.0340	0.0296	0.0258	0.0225	0.0197	0.0172	0.0150	0.0132	0.0116
18	0.0323	0.0279	0.0241	0.0208	0.0180	0.0156	0.0135	0.0118	0.0102	0.0089
19	0.0267	0.0229	0.0196	0.0168	0.0144	0.0124	0.0107	0.0092	0.0079	0.0068
20	0.0221	0.0187	0.0159	0.0135	0.0115	0.0098	0.0084	0.0072	0.0061	0.0053
21	0.0183	0.0154	0.0129	0.0109	0.0092	0.0078	0.0066	0.0056	0.0048	0.0040
22	0.0151	0.0126	0.0105	0.0088	0.0074	0.0062	0.0052	0.0044	0.0037	0.0031
23	0.0125	0.0103	0.0086	0.0071	0.0059	0.0049	0.0041	0.0034	0.0029	0.0024
24	0.0103	0.0085	0.0070	0.0057	0.0047	0.0039	0.0032	0.0027	0.0022	0.0018
25	0.0085	0.0069	0.0057	0.0046	0.0038	0.0031	0.0025	0.0021	0.0017	0.0014

Table 1: Present value of €1 (continued)

Years	31%	32%	33%	34%	35%	36%	37%	38%	39%	40%
1	0.7634	0.7576	0.7519	0.7463	0.7407	0.7353	0.7299	0.7246	0.7194	0.7143
2	0.5827	0.5739	0.5653	0.5569	0.5487	0.5407	0.5328	0.5251	0.5176	0.5102
3	0.4448	0.4348	0.4251	0.4156	0.4064	0.3975	0.3889	0.3805	0.3724	0.3644
4	0.3396	0.3294	0.3196	0.3102	0.3011	0.2923	0.2839	0.2757	0.2679	0.2603
5	0.2592	0.2495	0.2403	0.2315	0.2230	0.2149	0.2072	0.1998	0.1927	0.1859
6	0.1979	0.1890	0.1807	0.1727	0.1652	0.1580	0.1512	0.1448	0.1386	0.1328
7	0.1510	0.1432	0.1358	0.1289	0.1224	0.1162	0.1104	0.1049	0.0997	0.0949
8	0.1153	0.1085	0.1021	0.0962	0.0906	0.0854	0.0806	0.0760	0.0718	0.0678
9	0.0880	0.0822	0.0768	0.0718	0.0671	0.0628	0.0588	0.0551	0.0516	0.0484
10	0.0672	0.0623	0.0577	0.0536	0.0497	0.0462	0.0429	0.0399	0.0371	0.0346
11	0.0513	0.0472	0.0434	0.0400	0.0368	0.0340	0.0313	0.0289	0.0267	0.0247
12	0.0392	0.0357	0.0326	0.0298	0.0273	0.0250	0.0229	0.0210	0.0192	0.0176
13	0.0299	0.0271	0.0245	0.0223	0.0202	0.0184	0.0167	0.0152	0.0138	0.0126
14	0.0228	0.0205	0.0185	0.0166	0.0150	0.0135	0.0122	0.0110	0.0099	0.0090
15	0.0174	0.0155	0.0139	0.0124	0.0111	0.0099	0.0089	0.0080	0.0072	0.0064
16	0.0133	0.0118	0.0104	0.0093	0.0082	0.0073	0.0065	0.0058	0.0051	0.0046
17	0.0101	0.0089	0.0078	0.0069	0.0061	0.0054	0.0047	0.0042	0.0037	0.0033
18	0.0077	0.0068	0.0059	0.0052	0.0045	0.0039	0.0035	0.0030	0.0027	0.0023
19	0.0059	0.0051	0.0044	0.0038	0.0033	0.0029	0.0025	0.0022	0.0019	0.0017
20	0.0045	0.0039	0.0033	0.0029	0.0025	0.0021	0.0018	0.0016	0.0014	0.0012
21	0.0034	0.0029	0.0025	0.0021	0.0018	0.0016	0.0013	0.0012	0.0010	0.0009
22	0.0026	0.0022	0.0019	0.0016	0.0014	0.0012	0.0010	0.0008	0.0007	0.0006
23	0.0020	0.0017	0.0014	0.0012	0.0010	0.0008	0.0007	0.0006	0.0005	0.0004
24	0.0015	0.0013	0.0011	0.0009	0.0007	0.0006	0.0005	0.0004	0.0004	0.0003
25	0.0012	0.0010	0.0008	0.0007	0.0006	0.0005	0.0004	0.0003	0.0003	0.0002

Table 2: Present value of €1 received annually

Years	1%	2%	3%	4%	5%	6%	7%	8%	9%	10%
1	0.990	0.980	0.971	0.962	0.952	0.943	0.935	0.926	0.917	0.909
2	1.970	1.942	1.913	1.886	1.859	1.833	1.808	1.783	1.759	1.736
3	2.941	2.884	2.829	2.775	2.723	2.673	2.624	2.577	2.531	2.487
4	3.902	3.808	3.717	3.630	3.546	3.465	3.387	3.312	3.240	3.170
5	4.853	4.713	4.580	4.452	4.329	4.212	4.100	3.993	3.890	3.791
6	5.795	5.601	5.417	5.242	5.076	4.917	4.767	4.623	4.486	4.355
7	6.728	6.472	6.230	6.002	5.786	5.582	5.389	5.206	5.033	4.868
8	7.652	7.325	7.020	6.733	6.463	6.210	5.971	5.747	5.535	5.335
9	8.566	8.162	7.786	7.435	7.108	6.802	6.515	6.247	5.995	5.759
10	9.471	8.983	8.530	8.111	7.722	7.360	7.024	6.710	6.418	6.145
11	10.368	9.787	9.253	8.760	8.306	7.887	7.499	7.139	6.805	6.495
12	11.255	10.575	9.954	9.385	8.863	8.384	7.943	7.536	7.161	6.814
13	12.134	11.348	10.635	9.986	9.394	8.853	8.358	7.904	7.487	7.103
14	13.004	12.106	11.296	10.563	9.899	9.295	8.745	8.244	7.786	7.367
15	13.865	12.849	11.938	11.118	10.380	9.712	9.108	8.559	8.061	7.606
16	14.718	13.578	12.561	11.652	10.838	10.106	9.447	8.851	8.313	7.824
17	15.562	14.292	13.166	12.166	11.274	10.477	9.763	9.122	8.544	8.022
18	16.398	14.992	13.754	12.659	11.690	10.828	10.059	9.372	8.756	8.201
19	17.226	15.678	14.324	13.134	12.085	11.185	10.336	9.604	8.950	8.365
20	18.046	16.351	14.877	13.590	12.462	11.470	10.594	9.818	9.129	8.514
21	18.857	17.011	15.415	14.029	12.821	11.764	10.836	10.017	9.292	8.649
22	19.660	17.658	15.937	14.451	13.163	12.042	11.061	10.201	9.442	8.772
23	20.456	18.292	16.444	14.857	13.489	12.303	11.272	10.371	9.580	8.883
24	21.243	18.914	16.939	15.247	13.799	12.550	11.469	10.529	9.707	8.985
25	22.023	19.523	17.413	15.622	14.094	12.783	11.654	10.675	9.823	9.077

Table 2: (continued)

Years	11%	12%	13%	14%	15%	16%	17%	18%	19%	20%
1	0.901	0.893	0.885	0.877	0.870	0.862	0.855	0.847	0.840	0.833
2	1.713	1.690	1.668	1.647	1.626	1.605	1.585	1.566	1.547	1.528
3	2.444	2.402	2.361	2.322	2.283	2.246	2.210	2.174	2.140	2.106
4	3.102	3.037	2.974	2.914	2.855	2.798	2.743	2.690	2.639	2.589
5	3.696	3.605	3.517	3.433	3.352	3.274	3.199	3.127	3.058	2.991
6	4.231	4.111	3.998	3.889	3.784	3.685	3.589	3.498	3.410	3.326
7	4.712	4.564	4.423	4.288	4.160	4.039	3.922	3.812	3.706	3.605
8	5.146	4.968	4.799	4.639	4.487	4.344	4.207	4.078	3.954	3.837
9	5.537	5.328	5.132	4.946	4.772	4.607	4.451	4.303	4.163	4.031
10	5.889	5.650	5.426	5.216	5.019	4.833	4.659	4.494	4.339	4.192
11	6.207	5.938	5.687	5.453	5.234	5.029	4.836	4.656	4.486	4.327
12	6.492	6.194	5.918	5.660	5.421	5.197	4.988	4.793	4.611	4.439
13	6.750	6.424	6.122	5.842	5.583	5.342	5.118	4.910	4.715	4.533
14	6.982	6.628	6.302	6.002	5.724	5.468	5.229	5.008	4.802	4.611
15	7.191	6.811	6.462	6.142	5.847	5.575	5.324	5.092	4.876	4.675
16	7.379	6.974	6.604	6.265	5.954	5.668	5.405	5.162	4.938	4.730
17	7.549	7.120	6.729	6.373	6.047	5.749	5.475	5.222	4.990	4.775
18	7.702	7.250	6.840	6.467	6.128	5.818	5.534	5.273	5.033	4.812
19	7.839	7.366	6.938	6.550	6.198	5.877	5.584	5.316	5.070	4.843
20	7.963	7.469	7.025	6.623	6.259	5.929	5.628	5.353	5.101	4.870
21	8.075	7.562	7.102	6.687	6.312	5.973	5.665	5.384	5.127	4.891
22	8.176	7.645	7.170	6.743	6.359	6.011	5.696	5.410	5.149	4.909
23	8.266	7.718	7.230	6.792	6.399	6.044	5.723	5.432	5.167	4.925
24	8.348	7.784	7.283	6.835	6.434	6.073	5.746	5.451	5.182	4.937
25	8.422	7.843	7.330	6.873	6.464	6.097	5.766	5.467	5.195	4.948

Table 2: *(continued)*

Years	21%	22%	23%	24%	25%	26%	27%	28%	29%	30%
1	0.826	0.820	0.813	0.806	0.800	0.794	0.787	0.781	0.775	0.769
2	1.509	1.492	1.474	1.457	1.440	1.424	1.407	1.392	1.376	1.361
3	2.074	2.042	2.011	1.981	1.952	1.923	1.896	1.868	1.842	1.816
4	2.540	2.494	2.448	2.404	2.362	2.320	2.280	2.241	2.203	2.166
5	2.926	2.864	2.803	2.745	2.689	2.635	2.583	2.532	2.483	2.436
6	3.245	3.167	3.092	3.020	2.951	2.885	2.821	2.759	2.700	2.643
7	3.508	3.416	3.327	3.242	3.161	3.083	3.009	2.937	2.868	2.802
8	3.726	3.619	3.518	3.421	3.329	3.241	3.156	3.076	2.999	2.925
9	3.905	3.786	3.673	3.566	3.463	3.366	3.273	3.184	3.100	3.019
10	4.054	3.923	3.799	3.682	3.571	3.465	3.364	3.269	3.178	3.092
11	4.177	4.035	3.902	3.776	3.656	3.543	3.437	3.335	3.239	3.147
12	5.278	4.127	3.985	3.851	3.725	3.606	3.493	3.387	3.286	3.190
13	4.362	4.203	4.053	3.912	3.780	3.656	3.538	3.427	3.322	3.223
14	4.432	4.265	4.108	3.962	3.824	3.695	3.573	3.459	3.351	3.249
15	4.489	4.315	4.153	4.001	3.859	3.726	3.601	3.483	3.373	3.268
16	4.536	4.357	4.189	4.033	3.887	3.751	3.623	3.503	3.390	3.283
17	4.576	4.391	4.219	4.059	3.910	3.771	3.640	3.518	3.403	3.295
18	4.608	4.419	4.243	4.080	3.928	3.786	3.654	3.529	3.413	3.304
19	4.635	4.442	4.263	4.097	3.942	3.799	3.664	3.539	3.421	3.311
20	4.657	4.460	4.279	4.110	3.954	3.808	3.673	3.546	3.427	3.316
21	4.675	4.476	3.292	4.121	3.963	3.816	3.679	3.551	3.432	3.320
22	4.690	4.488	4.302	4.130	3.970	3.822	3.684	3.556	3.436	3.323
23	4.703	4.499	4.311	4.137	3.976	3.827	3.689	3.559	3.438	3.325
24	4.713	4.507	4.318	4.143	3.981	3.831	3.692	3.562	3.441	3.327
25	4.721	4.514	4.323	4.147	3.985	3.834	3.694	3.564	3.442	3.329

Table 2: (continued)

Years	31%	32%	33%	34%	35%	36%	37%	38%	39%	40%
1	0.763	0.758	0.752	0.746	0.741	0.735	0.730	0.725	0.719	0.714
2	1.346	1.331	1.317	1.303	1.289	1.276	1.263	1.250	1.237	1.224
3	1.791	1.766	1.742	1.719	1.696	1.673	1.652	1.630	1.609	1.589
4	2.130	2.096	2.062	2.029	1.997	1.966	1.935	1.906	1.877	1.849
5	2.390	2.345	2.302	2.260	2.220	2.181	2.143	2.106	2.070	2.035
6	2.588	2.534	2.483	2.433	2.385	2.339	2.294	2.251	2.209	2.168
7	2.739	2.677	2.619	2.562	2.508	2.455	2.404	2.355	2.308	2.263
8	2.854	2.786	2.721	2.658	2.598	2.540	2.485	2.432	2.380	2.331
9	2.942	2.868	2.798	2.730	2.665	2.603	2.544	2.487	2.432	2.379
10	3.009	2.930	2.855	2.784	2.715	2.649	2.587	2.527	2.469	2.414
11	3.060	2.978	2.899	2.824	2.752	2.683	2.618	2.555	2.496	2.438
12	3.100	3.013	2.931	2.853	2.779	2.708	2.641	2.576	2.515	2.456
13	3.129	3.040	2.956	2.876	2.799	2.727	2.658	2.592	2.529	2.469
14	3.152	3.061	2.974	2.982	2.814	2.740	2.670	2.603	2.539	2.478
15	3.170	3.076	2.988	2.905	2.825	2.750	2.679	2.611	2.546	2.484
16	3.183	3.088	2.999	2.914	2.834	2.757	2.685	2.616	2.551	2.489
17	3.193	3.097	3.007	2.921	2.840	2.763	2.690	2.621	2.555	2.492
18	3.201	3.104	3.012	2.926	2.844	2.767	2.693	2.624	2.557	2.494
19	3.207	3.109	3.017	2.930	2.848	2.770	2.696	2.626	2.559	2.496
20	3.211	3.113	3.020	2.933	2.850	2.772	2.698	2.627	2.561	2.497
21	3.215	3.116	3.023	2.935	2.852	2.773	2.699	2.629	2.562	2.498
22	3.217	3.118	3.025	2.936	2.853	2.775	2.700	2.629	2.562	2.498
23	3.219	3.120	3.026	2.938	2.854	2.775	2.701	2.630	2.563	2.499
24	3.221	3.121	3.027	2.939	2.855	2.776	2.701	2.630	2.563	2.499
25	3.222	3.122	3.028	2.939	2.856	2.777	2.702	2.631	2.563	2.499